BEFORE THE MUSIC STARTS
MAXIMILIAN BECKER

DISTANZ

POSTDIGITAL DANCE MUSIC?
TECHNO IM 21. JAHRHUNDERT

Techno ist historisch geworden. Kanonisierung und Musealisierung dieser Musik sind in vollem Gange. In den letzten Jahren ist ein regelrechter Techno-Memory-Boom zu beobachten, mit zahlreichen Filmen, Büchern und Ausstellungen zum Thema, und nicht selten begegnet man dabei gerade im deutschsprachigen Raum entlang griffiger Slogans wie dem vom „Soundtrack der Wende" einer auffälligen Verschränkung von Musik- und Zeitgeschichte. Aber Techno heißt nicht nur Erinnerung an heroische Zeiten einer der letzten großen popmusikalischen Jugendbewegungen des 20. Jahrhunderts. Als kulturelle Praxis ist Techno, verstanden als *Umbrella Term* für alle Spielarten elektronischer Club- und Tanzmusik, nach wie vor aktuell und kommerziell erfolgreicher denn je. Weltweit feiern jedes Wochenende Zehntausende in den einschlägigen Clubs, und ausgehend von den USA entwickelte sich mit Electronic Dance Music (EDM) in den letzten Jahren einmal mehr ein Techno-Subgenre zum veritablen Festival-Massenmarkt – mit Dimensionen, wie man sie zuletzt in der Ära von Großveranstaltungen der 1990er Jahre erlebt hatte.

Aber wofür steht Techno heute? Geht es inzwischen in erster Linie darum, eine gut geölte und vorwiegend nach wirtschaftlichen Interessen getaktete Unterhaltungs-Maschinerie am Laufen zu halten, aufgespannt entlang der Low-Cost-Fluglinien der Welt, expansiv und immer neue Gebiete kolonialisierend, wie zuletzt etwa Georgien oder Nicaragua? Oder ist da doch immer noch mehr? Ein subkulturelles Versprechen auf eine Gegenwelt, auf Gemeinschaft, eine bestimmte Art zu leben, zu denken und zu feiern? Eine ästhetische, vielleicht sogar politische Utopie? Techno als musikalische Abfahrt, als Abbild oder Kritik einer inzwischen nahezu ausweglos digitalisierten, vernetzten, ebenso radikal beweglich wie unverbindlich gewordenen Welt im 21. Jahrhundert?

In seinen Anfangsmomenten Ende der 1980er Jahre hatte Techno vor allem auch den Aufbruch aus der vielbeschworenen „Referenzhölle" Pop bedeutet, aus einem ins Labyrinthisch-Komplexe verfeinerten System der Verweise auf Texte, Klänge, Attitüden, Styles, Moden und Frisuren früherer Popmusiken, wobei gerade das virtuose Spiel mit diesen Verweisen Distinktionsgewinn und Welthaltung versprach. Techno war ganz und gar ein Kind dieses Systems und zugleich eine Gegenbewegung, und zwar im wörtlichen Sinne: In die Musik hineingehen, Rhythmus, Sound, Maschine werden, ein sich bewegender, tanzender Körper unter Körpern sein, das Erleben einer gesteigerten Intensität des Momenthaften, auf Dauer gestellt, für Stunden, Tage, ob mit oder ohne Drogen – und eben nicht sich ins Verhältnis setzen mit Stimmen, Performances, Star-Personae, Lyrics, Songstrukturen und -dramaturgien, mit nach Identifikation heischenden Bedeutungen, Erzählungen und deren vielfachen Brechungen und Spiegelungen. Hedonistisch, naiv, affirmativ, verdummend, eskapistisch: Derlei *Moral Panic*-Etiketten waren seinerzeit entsprechend schnell unter Techno-Kritikern aus ganz unterschiedlichen Lagern an der Hand, wie es sich gehört für eine Jugendbewegung von entsprechender Tragweite. Und ebenso rasch wurde die bewusst erzeugte Leerstelle im Bedeutungssystem Pop mit neuen Zuschreibungen und Bebilderungen überschrieben, Techno als Klang aus dem Inneren der Maschinen und Computer etwa oder als Musik der Netzkultur – und schließlich war natürlich schon die Rede von Techno als vermeintlicher „Stunde Null" der Popmusik selbst eine einzige große Projektion gewesen. Als Randnotiz und Beleg dafür, dass gerade die „sprachlose" Musik Techno einen steten Strom von Erzählungen erzeugt, kann gelten, dass diese Musik und vor allem ihre Großereignisse wie die Love-parade durch das Berlin der Nachwende-Zeit heute vielen in der historischen Rückschau als Geburtshelfer einer wiedergefundenen, positiv besetzten nationalen deutschen (Pop)Identität erscheinen, was auch immer sich dahinter konkret verbergen mag.

Für Techno selbst besteht wohl die eigentlich erstaunliche Volte darin, dass nach dem Ende der Bewegung und des Hypes, nach dem in den 2000er Jahren erfolgten weitgehenden Rückzug von der Straße und aus der Öffentlichkeit in die Clubs, Studios, Soft- und Hardwareschmieden, die Grundlagen für eine zweite, viel tiefergreifende Erfolgsgeschichte dieser Musikkultur gelegt wurden, die letztlich bis heute anhält. Die Clubs perfektionierten und professionalisierten nicht nur ihre Soundsysteme, sondern vor allem auch ihre Konzepte und Images – die Ausdehnung der After-Hour auf Tages- oder gar Wochendauer etwa, die Ausschlussmechanismen und deren Inszenierung, die „harte Tür" als Teil der Legendenbildung – und wurden auf diese Weise zu den eigentlichen Stars dieser Ära mit weltweiter, vor allem auch touristischer Strahlkraft. In technischer Hinsicht setzten sich – nach den performativ wenig befriedigenden Laptop-Setups der frühen 2000er Jahre – Controller-, Instrumenten- und vor allem Software-Standards durch, die weit über die elektronische Clubmusik hinaus Relevanz erlangten. Denn im Bereich der musikalischen Mittel ist Techno heute omnipräsent in sämtlicher zeitgenössischer Popmusik, von der Beat- und Soundgestaltung bis hin zur vielfach adaptierten *Build-up and Drop*-Ästhetik vieler EDM-Tracks. Und selbst die derzeit auffälligsten Praktiken des Musikhörens scheinen ohne die Prägung durch Techno kaum denkbar und sind insofern tatsächlich als postdigital zu verstehen: Sei es die gegenwärtige hipsteresk-biedermeierliche Vinyl-Renaissance (ein Medium, das ohne Techno vermutlich gar nicht bis heute überlebt hätte), seien es andererseits die großflächig expandierenden Streamingdienste, bei denen etwa auch Popmusik – aller ihrer vormals so wichtigen Kontexte entkleidet – sich als Strom niederschwellig kuratierter Musikdaten in Dauerschleife durch die Kopfhörer der User/innen schiebt.

Mit dem Blick auf das Kuratorische stellt sich abschließend die Frage nach der Figur der/des DJs. Nach wie vor ganz überwiegend männlich (hierin ist Techno immer noch ähnlich archaisch wie die restliche Rock- und Popwelt), hat sich an ihrer/seiner Rolle über die Jahrzehnte auf den ersten Blick scheinbar nur wenig geändert. Noch immer ist sie/er Dirigent/in, Kurator/in und Zeremonienmeister/in der Party – und geht zugleich doch ganz in ihr auf. In den 1990er Jahren zunächst in der Club- und Ausgehkultur ausdrücklich marginalisiert – die Partizipation aller Beteiligten stand im Vordergrund und nicht das Künstlerego von Einzelnen – brachten spätestens die Groß- und Straßen-Raves schließlich doch DJ-Superstars und Celebrities hervor, bei gleichzeitiger Stilisierung der/des DJs zur zentralen Figur eines grundlegenden mediengeschichtlichen Wandels hin zu einer Kultur aus Mixes, Cuts und Samples. Auch diese Diskurse haben sich in der Zwischenzeit abgekühlt. Eine ebenfalls hochprofessionalisierte Kaste weltweit tätiger DJs bespielt heute Clubs und Festivals, teilweise mit sechs und mehr Gigs an einem Wochenende, fürstlich entlohnt und dabei in Zeiten zunehmender Marginalisierung von Plattenverkäufen mit den Einnahmen aus den Live-Sets Labels und Vertriebsstrukturen querfinanzierend. Doch mit wenigen Ausnahmen bleiben die heutigen DJs als Personen weitgehend im Hintergrund, werden nicht mehr zu Popstars. Vielmehr prägt ein Selbstverständnis als Dienstleister an der Party die Szene, wie es Ricardo Villalobos jüngst im Film *Denk ich an Deutschland in der Nacht* (2017) von Romuald Karmakar ausdrückte: „Diese Musik […] schafft es, sehr viele Leute in diesen Zeiten von Atomisierung und Vereinzelung zusammenzubringen. Und das ist das, was so faszinierend an der ganzen Sache ist. Und wir kümmern uns um dieses Zusammenbringen. […] Aus dieser Einsamkeit heraus kommen die Leute und treffen sich auf Partys. Dieser Situation zu helfen, das ist das, was wir eigentlich alle machen und was uns alle so fasziniert. Das ist eigentlich das Tolle an der Sache."

Wofür steht Techno heute? Die eingangs gestellte Frage ist kaum eindeutig zu beantworten. Sicher, der rebellische Geist des Aufbruchs, das Selbstverständnis auch als politisch denkende Bewegung sind längst verloren gegangen, das Label „Underground" heute oft nur noch äußerliches Etikett. An die Stelle ist eine nicht weniger faszinierende weltumspannende Musikkultur getreten, wirtschaftsmächtig, hochprofessionell, in feinste stilistische Verästelungen ausdifferenziert, mit kommerziellen Auswüchsen ebenso wie mit noch immer innovativen Nischen, produktiv bis an die Grenzen der Überhitzung und attraktiv für einen steten Zustrom junger Nachwuchskünstlerinnen und -künstler. Techno is here to stay, so scheint es, und hat damit die mit der massenhaften Verbreitung von Tonträgern in den 1950ern beginnende Reihe aufeinanderfolgender, in immer wieder neuem pubertären Gestus von Vorherigem sich gewaltsam ablösender Jugendpopmusikbewegungen durchbrochen – und so offenbar eine neue Zeitrechnung populärer Musik eingeläutet. Ob die Bezeichnung postdigitale Tanz- oder Popmusik hierfür ein geeignetes Label ist, wird die Zeit zeigen. Vor allem aber liefert diese Musik wie kaum eine andere noch immer das Versprechen auf „the perfect night out", auf die persönliche „Party des Jahrhunderts", auf Intensität, Körperlichkeit, Unmittelbarkeit, sei es für ein paar Stunden, sei es für ein komplettes Wochenende. Und gerade darin dürfte der Grund für die nach wie vor ungebrochene Attraktion von Techno liegen.

Matthias Pasdzierny, Berlin

POST-DIGITAL DANCE MUSIC? TECHNO IN THE TWENTY-FIRST CENTURY

Techno has become historic. The canonization and museumization of this music are in full swing. In recent years there's been an observable Techno-memory boom in countless films, books, and exhibitions centered around the topic, and, especially in the German-speaking world, it's not infrequent to encounter a conspicuous entanglement of music and history alongside catchy slogans like that of the "soundtrack of the reunification." But Techno isn't merely a reminder of the heroic times of one of the last great Pop music youth movements of the twentieth century. As a cultural practice, Techno, understood as an umbrella term for all types of electronic club and dance music, still prevails and is commercially more successful than ever. Every weekend tens of thousands of people party in Techno-relevant clubs and in the USA, Electronic Dance Music (EDM) has developed out of a Techno subgenre into a verifiable festival mass market – and it's progressed with dimensions that were last experienced in the 1990s era of large-scale events.

But what does Techno stand for today? Is it primarily a question of maintaining the well-oiled machinery of the entertainment industry, driven by economic interests, spread along with the low-cost airlines of the world, expansive and increasingly colonizing new territories, such as Georgia or Nicaragua? Or is there still more? A subcultural promise of an alternative world, of community, a certain way of living, thinking, and celebrating? An aesthetic, maybe even a political utopia? Techno as a musical departure, an image, or critique of a now almost hopelessly digitized, networked, even radically mobile, and at the same time, noncommittal world of the twenty-first century?

In its early days in the late 1980s, more than anything Techno meant a departure from the much touted "reference hell" of Pop – the labyrinthine complex of references to the texts, sounds, attitudes, styles, fashions, and hairstyles of early Pop music, in which the virtuoso play with these references promised distinction and an attitude towards the world. Techno was very much a child of this system and at the same time, quite literally, a counter movement: to get into the music, to become rhythm, sound, machine, to be a moving, dancing body among bodies, the experience of a heightened intensity of the moment, in perpetuity, for seconds, days, with or without drugs – and without the connection to voices, performances, star personas, lyrics, song structures, and dramaturgical reflections, with the identification of demanding meanings, narratives, and their multiple refractions and reflections. Hedonistic, naïve, affirmative, dulling, escapist. Such morally panicking labels were, at the time, relatively quick among Techno critics from differing camps, as is necessary for a youth movement of corresponding consequence. And just as quickly, the empty space that was deliberately created within Pop's system of meaning was overwritten with new attributes and illustrations, such as Techno as a sound from inside the machine and computer, or as the music of the net culture – and finally, the discussion of Techno as a supposed "zero hour" of Pop music itself became a massive projection. As a side note and proof that the "speechless" music of Techno created a steady stream of tales, it would seem that this music, and above all its major events such as the Love Parade in Berlin, aided, in historical retrospect, in the re-established, positively-cast, national German (Pop)identity in the post-reunification era, whatever exactly may be hidden behind this.

Within Techno itself lies the incredible power that – after the end of the movement and hype, after the extensive retreat from the streets in the 2000s, and out of the public arena of the clubs, studios, and the soft and hardware forges – laid the foundation for a second, much deeper story of success of this musical culture, one which ultimately continues to this day. The clubs perfected and professionalized not only their sound systems, but also their concepts and images: the extension of the after-hour to days or even week-long periods, the mechanisms of exclusion and their staging, the "hard door" as a part of the formation of the legend, became the actual stars of this era, and their power was strong enough internationally to draw tourists. From a technical point of view – according to the disappointing performances of laptop setups of the early 2000s – controller, instrument, and above all software standards, attained relevance far beyond club music. Today, Techno is omnipresent in all contemporary Pop music, from the beat to the sound design to the much-adapted build-up and drop aesthetic of many EDM tracks. Even the most prominent methods of listening to music seem to be barely conceivable without the influence of Techno, and in this respect, they are actually understood as post-digital: be it the present-day hipster-conventionality of the vinyl Renaissance (a medium that likely would not have survived to today without Techno), or the large-scale expansion of streaming services, in which Pop music – stripped of all its previously vital contexts – pushes itself as a stream of low-threshold curated music data in a continuous loop through the headphones of users.

In light of the curatorial, the question arises concerning the personage of the DJ. Still predominantly male (in this respect, Techno is still as archaic as the rest of the Rock and Pop world), their role, at first glance, has barely changed over the decades. He or she is a conductor, a curator, and a master of ceremonies for the party – and at the same time, is completely absorbed by it. In the 1990s, DJs were initially marginalized within the club and nightlife culture – the participation of everyone was what was important, not the artist's individual ego. What ultimately brought the DJ superstars and celebrities to the fore were the big raves and street parties, which simultaneously stylized the DJ as a central figure of a fundamental media-historical transformation to a culture made up of mixes, cuts, and samples. In the meantime, these discourses too, have cooled. Today, a likewise highly professionalized cast of globally active DJs plays clubs and festivals, occasionally with six or more gigs over the course of a single weekend, earning princely sums, and, in times of the increasing marginalization of record sales, cross-finances labels and distribution structures with the revenues from live-sets. But, with a few exceptions, today's DJs usually remain in the background as individuals. They no longer become Pop stars. Rather, there is a sense of self-understanding as a party service-provider, as Ricardo Villalobos expresses in the recently released Romuald Karmakar film *If I Think of Germany at Night* (2017), "This music (…) manages to bring a lot of people together in these times of atomization and isolation. And that is what is so fascinating about the whole thing. And we take care of this act of bringing together. (…) The people come out of their seclusion and meet at parties. To assist this situation, that is actually what we all do and what fascinates us so much. That's what's amazing about the thing."

So what does Techno stand for today? There is hardly an explicit answer to the question posed at the beginning. Sure, the rebellious spirit of awakening and self-understanding as a politically-minded movement has long been lost. Today the label "underground" is usually only an external one. In its place now stands a culture of world-encompassing music that is no less fascinating. It is economically powerful, highly professional, differentiated into fine stylistic divisions, with commercial growth as well as innovative niches, productive to the limits, and attractive to a steady influx of young future artists. Techno is here to stay, so it seems. Techno has initiated a new chronology of popular music by breaking through a successive series of youth Pop music movements, which began in the 1950s with the massive spread of devices for listening and constantly provided new gestures of adolescence. Only time will tell if the label post-digital Dance or Pop music is the right one. Above all and like almost no other, this music still delivers the promise of the perfect night out, of a personal party of the century, of intensity, physicality, immediacy, whether for a few hours or a complete weekend. And that is precisely the reason for the still undefeated attraction of Techno.

Matthias Pasdzierny, Berlin

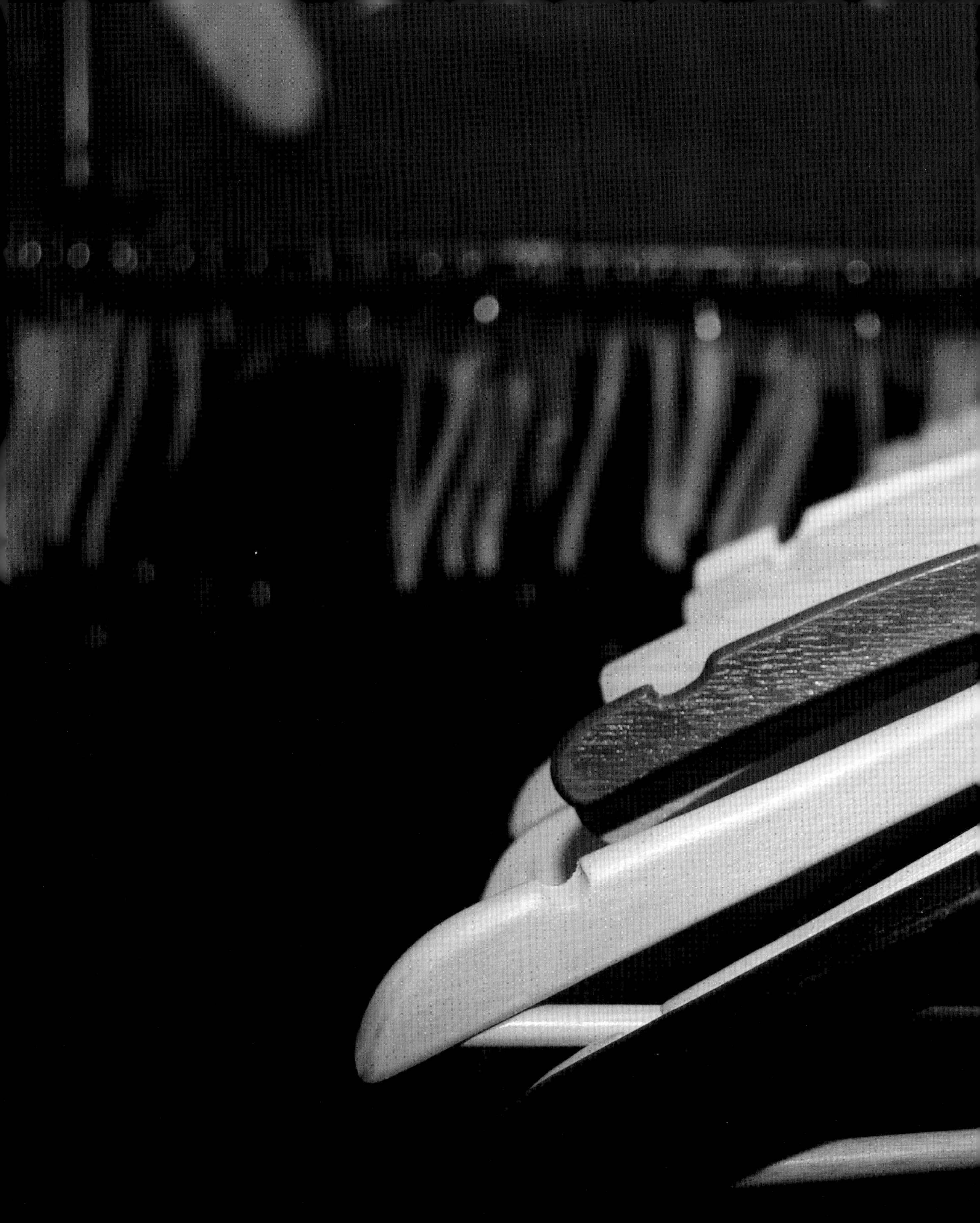

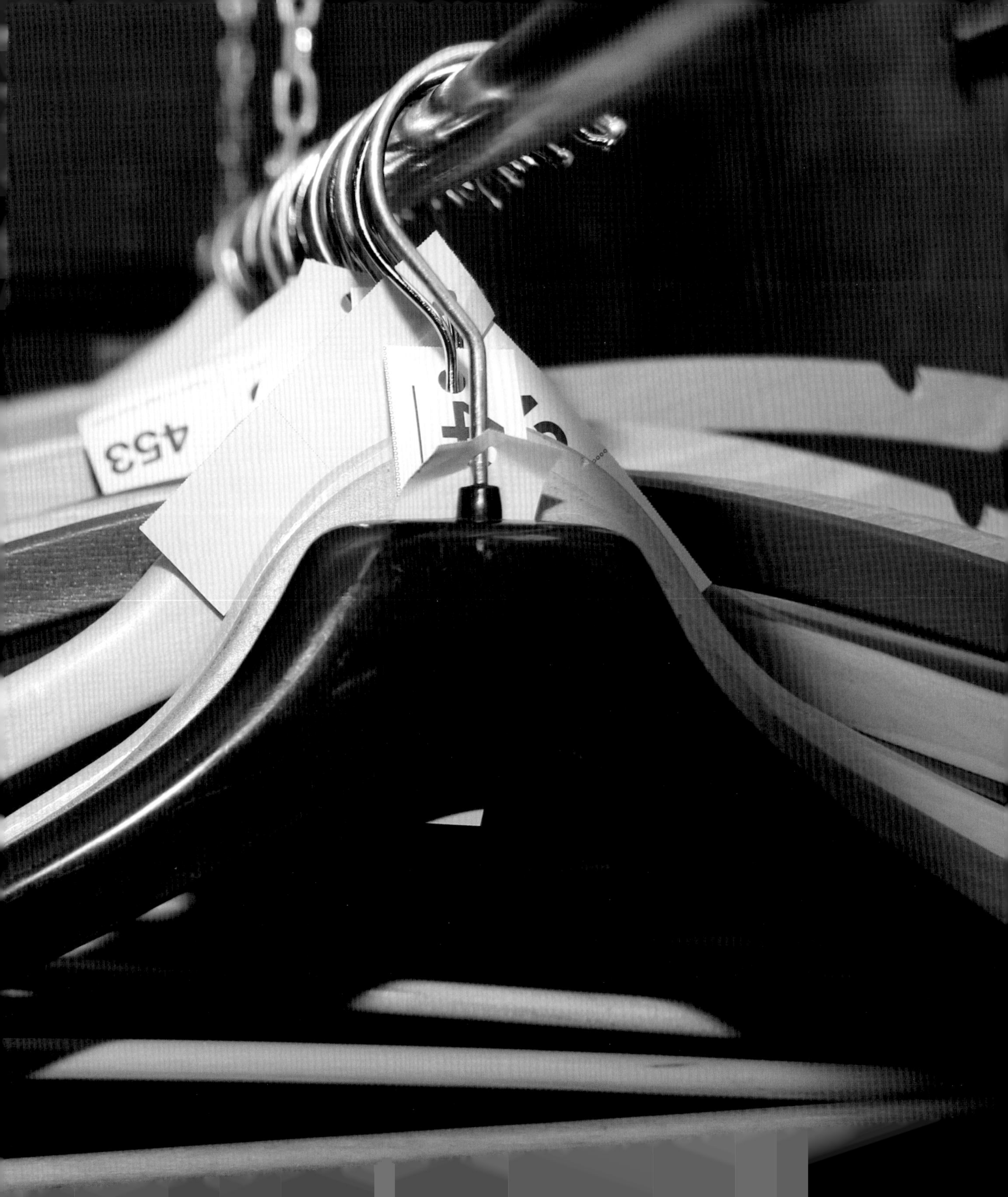

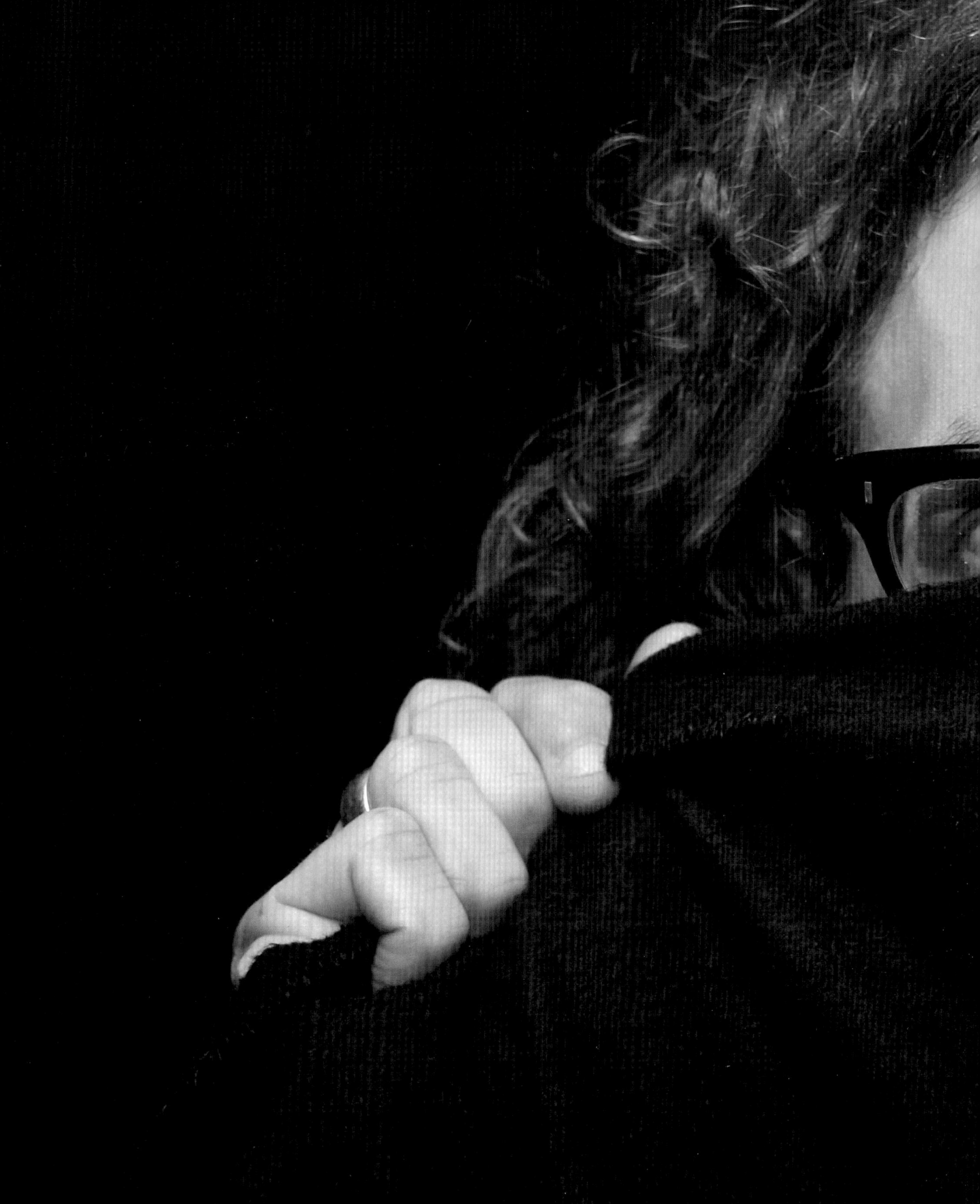

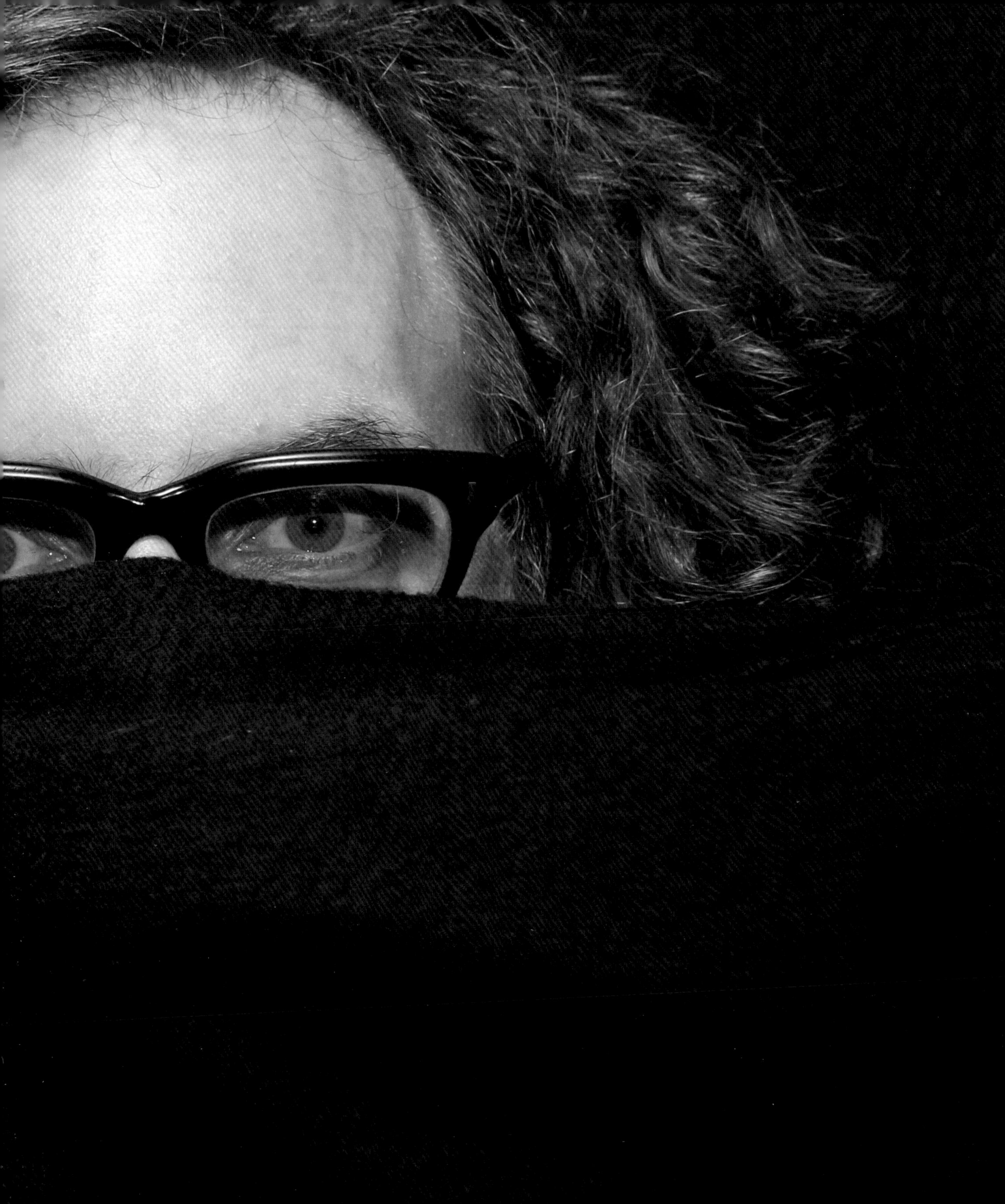

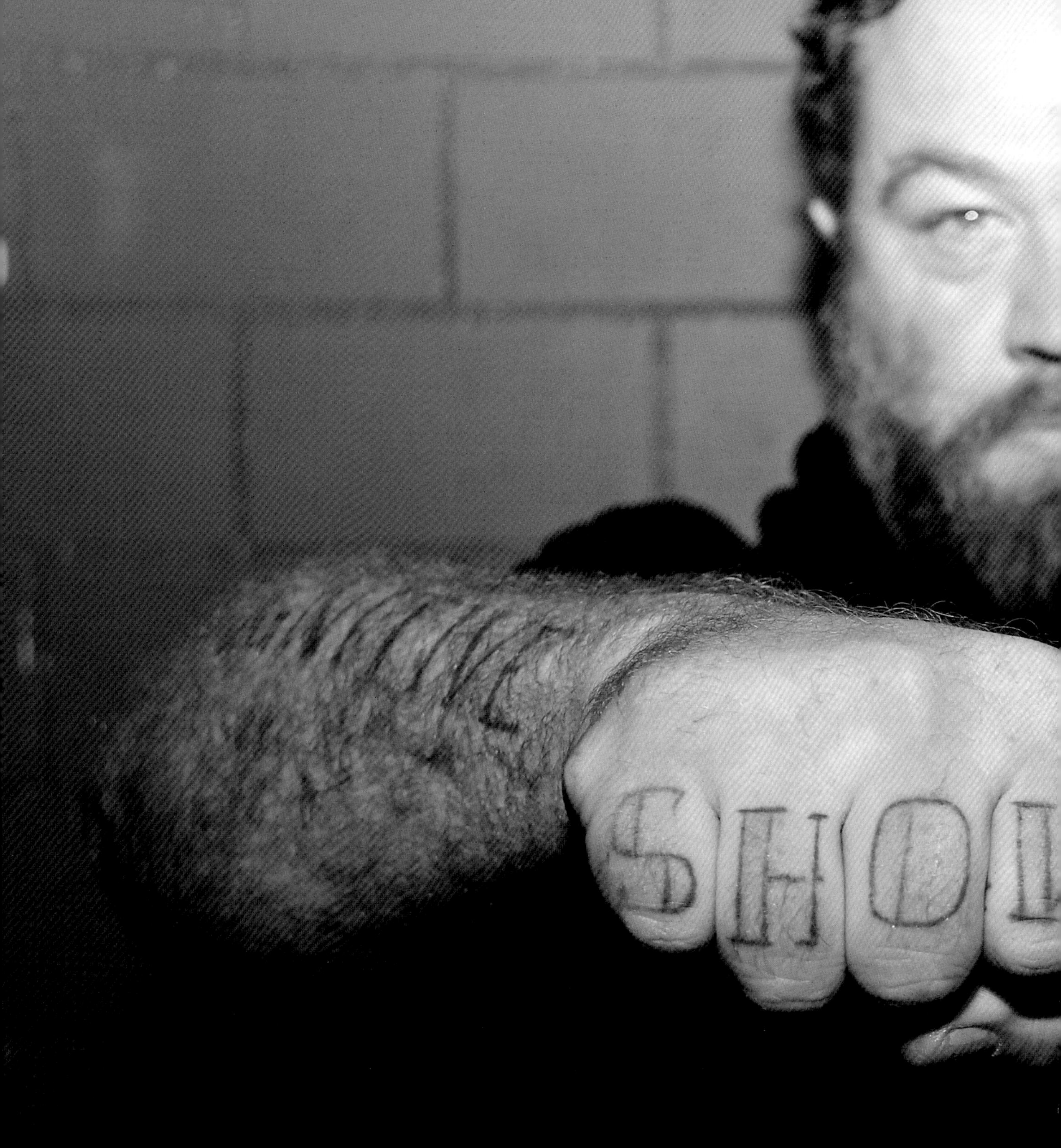
SHO

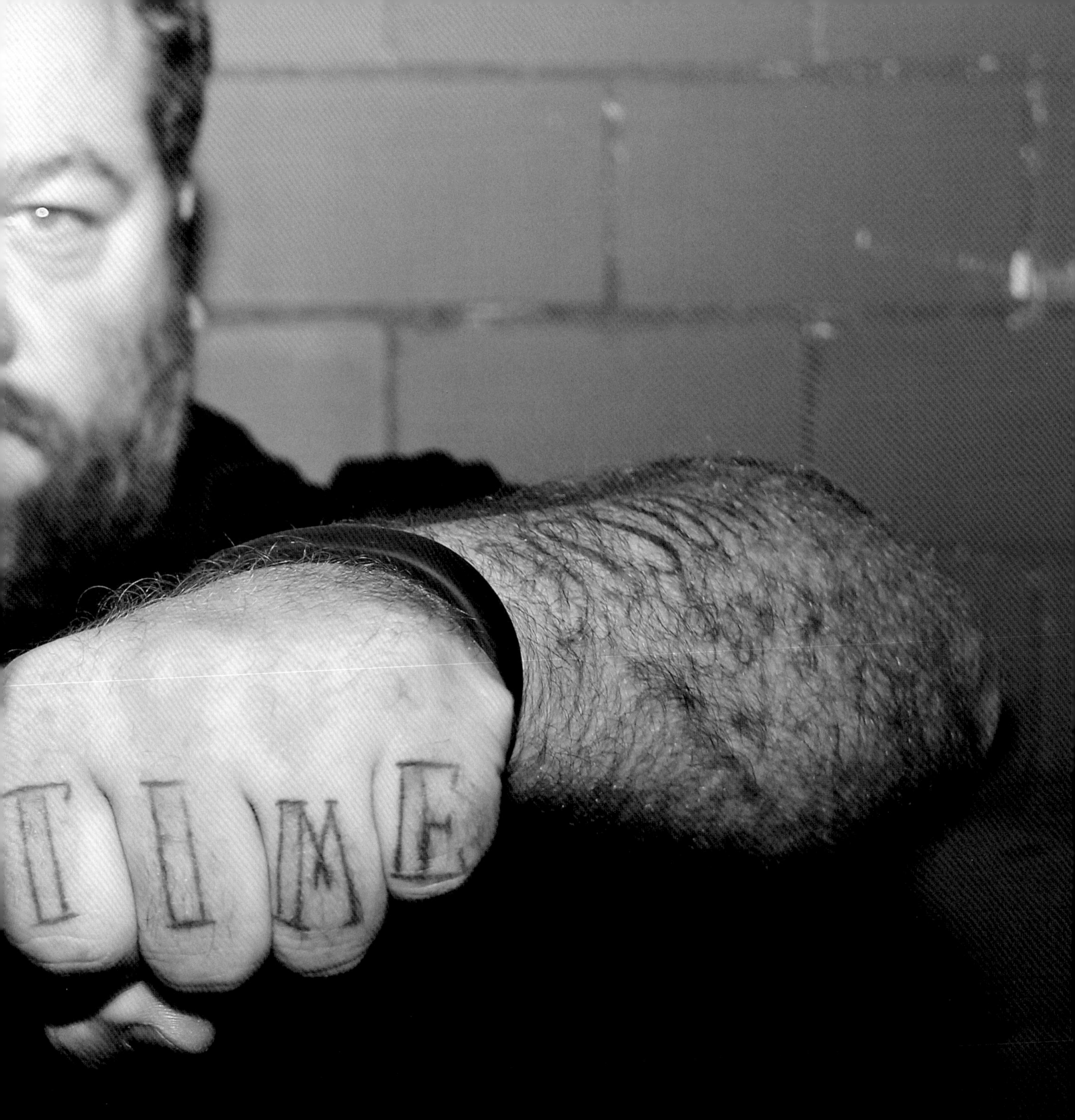
TIME

JESSE ROSE

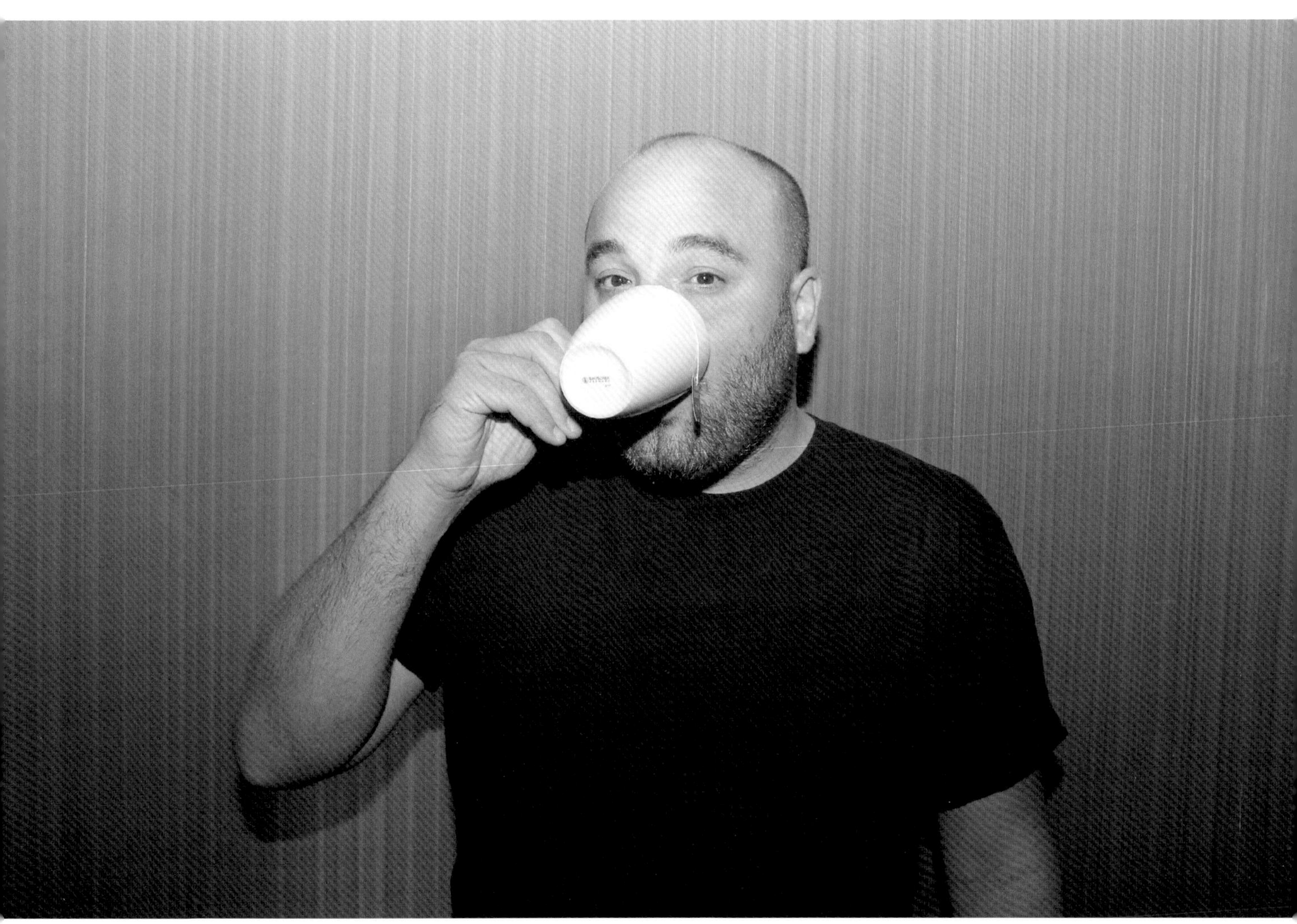

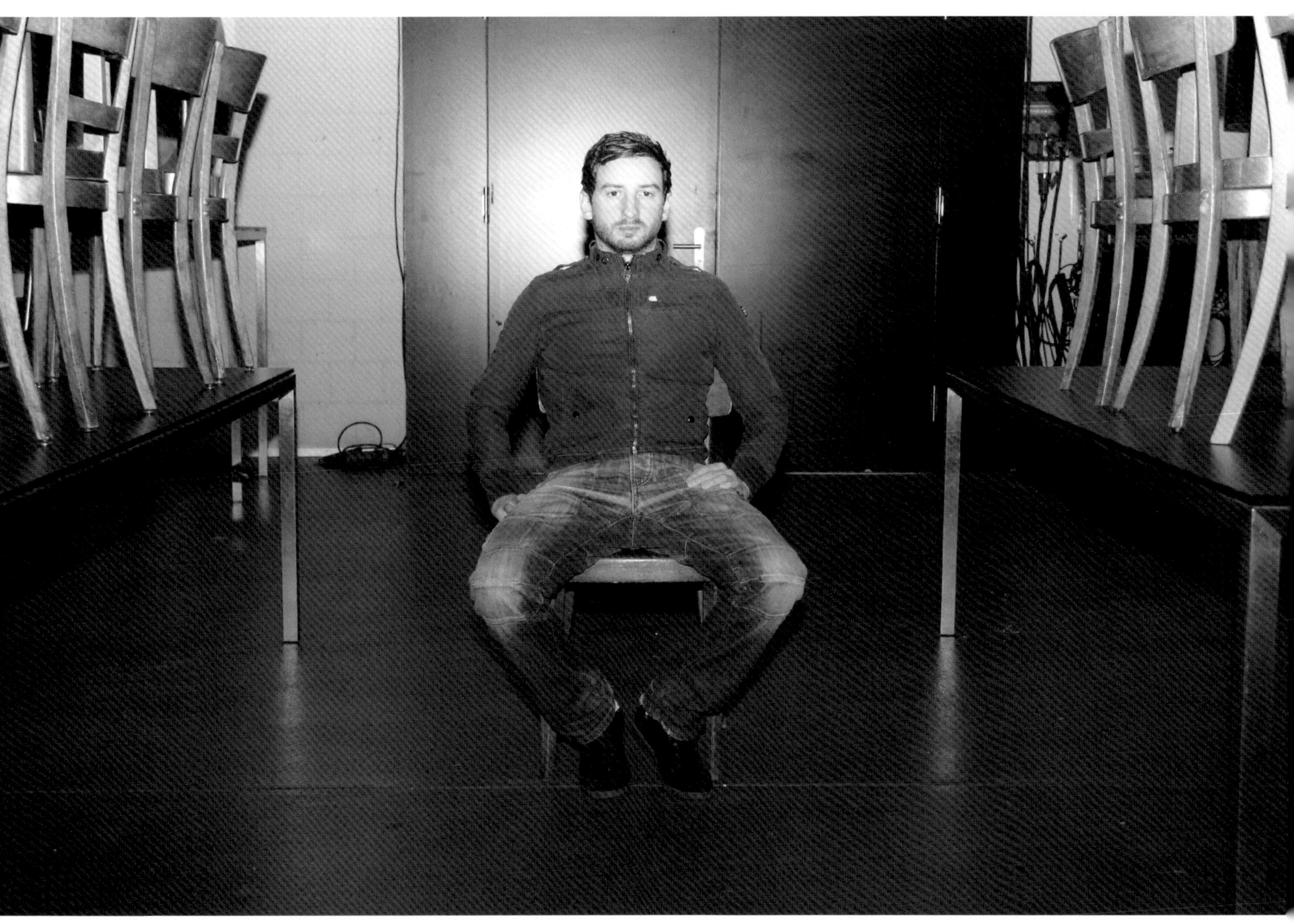

ANDY STOTT

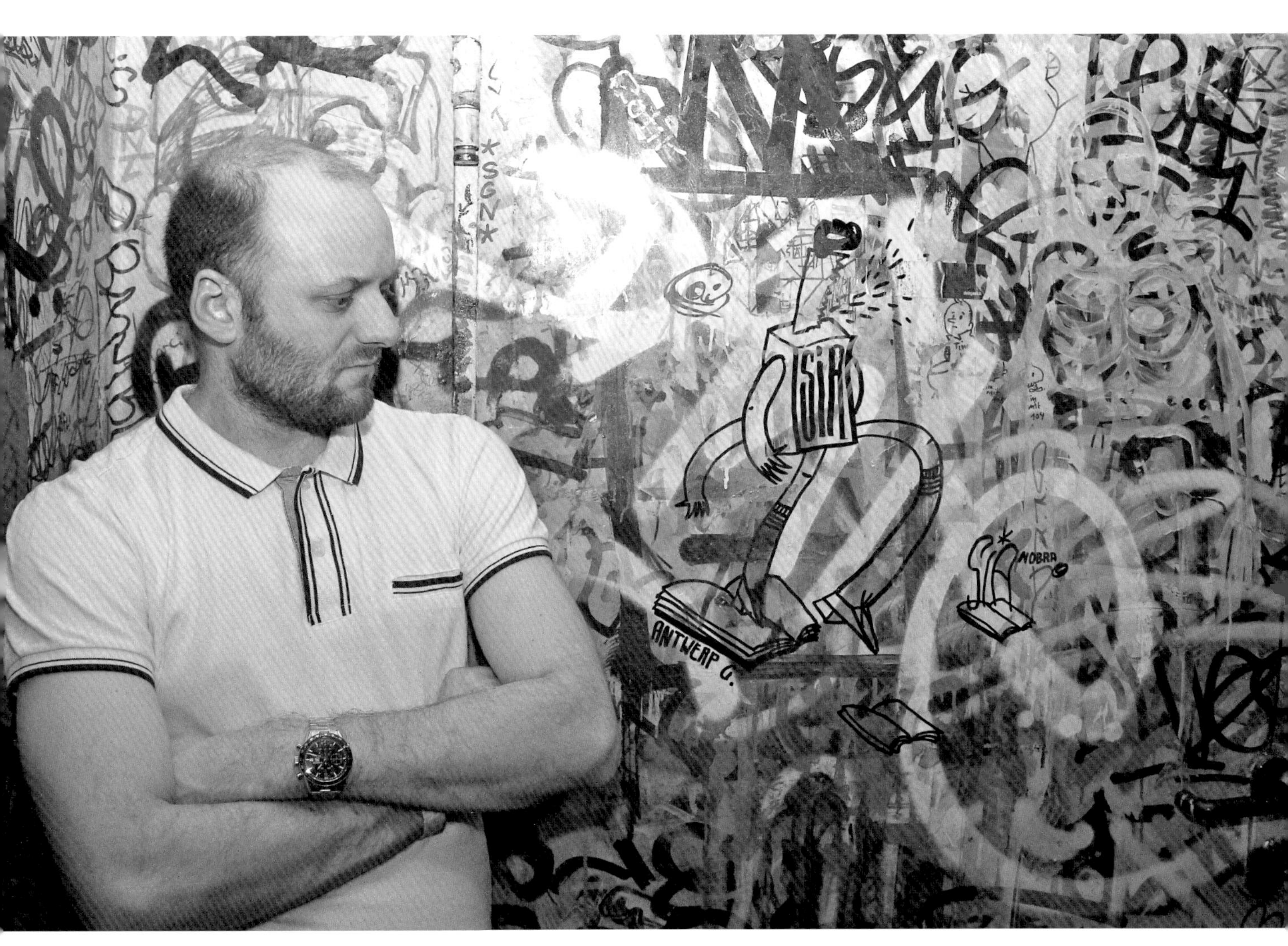

ANTWERP C.
NOBRA

LAURA JONES

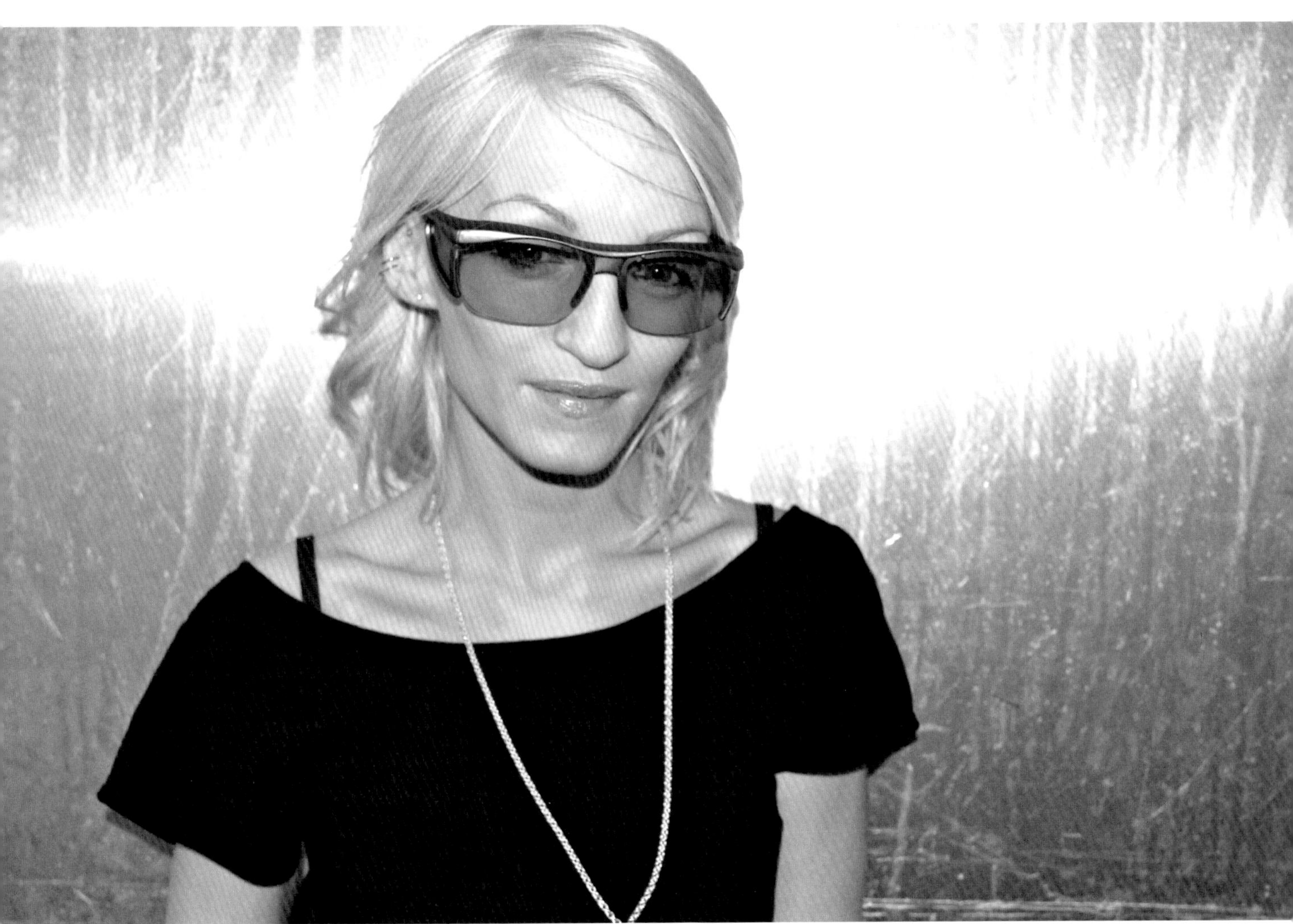

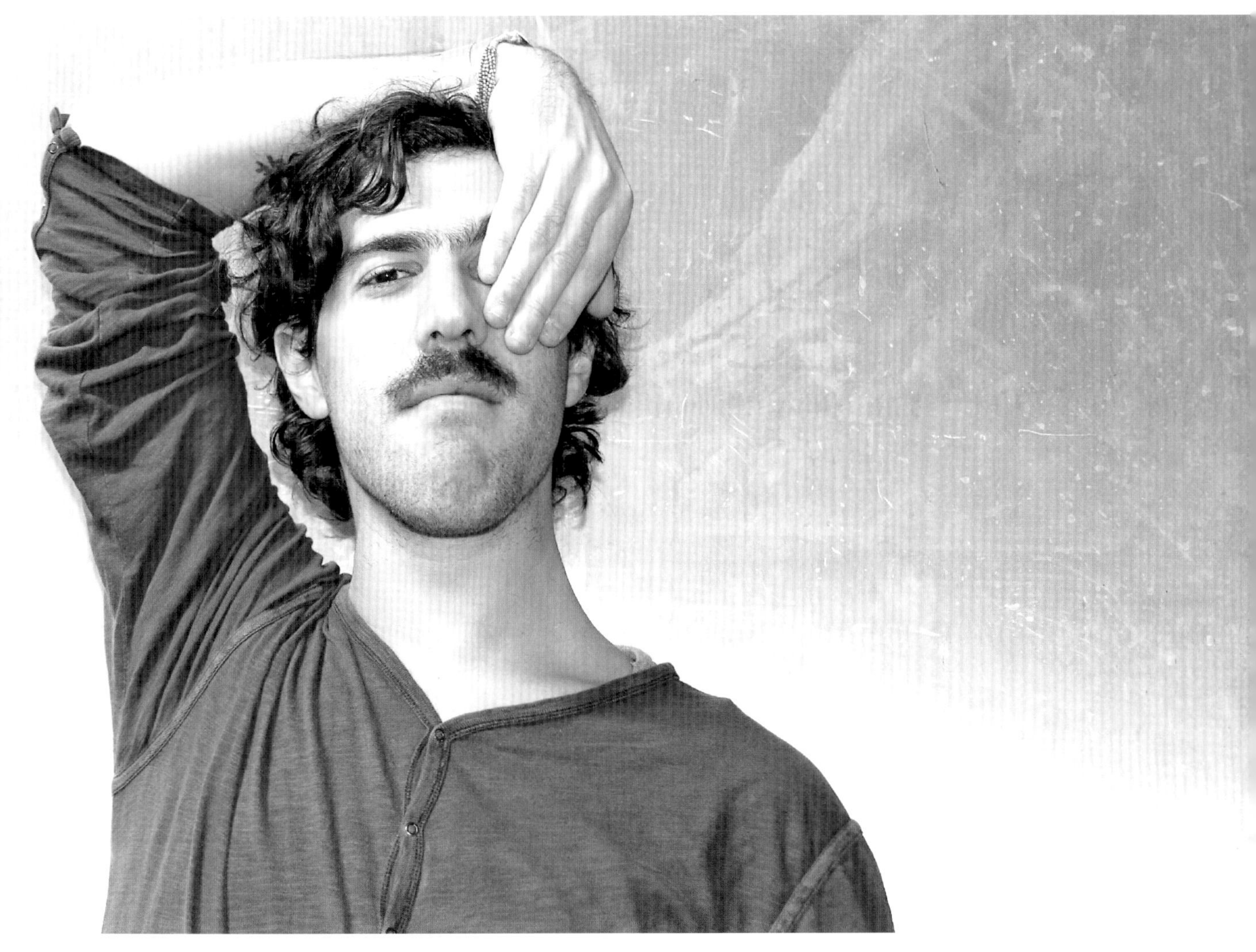

JUSTUS KÖHNKE

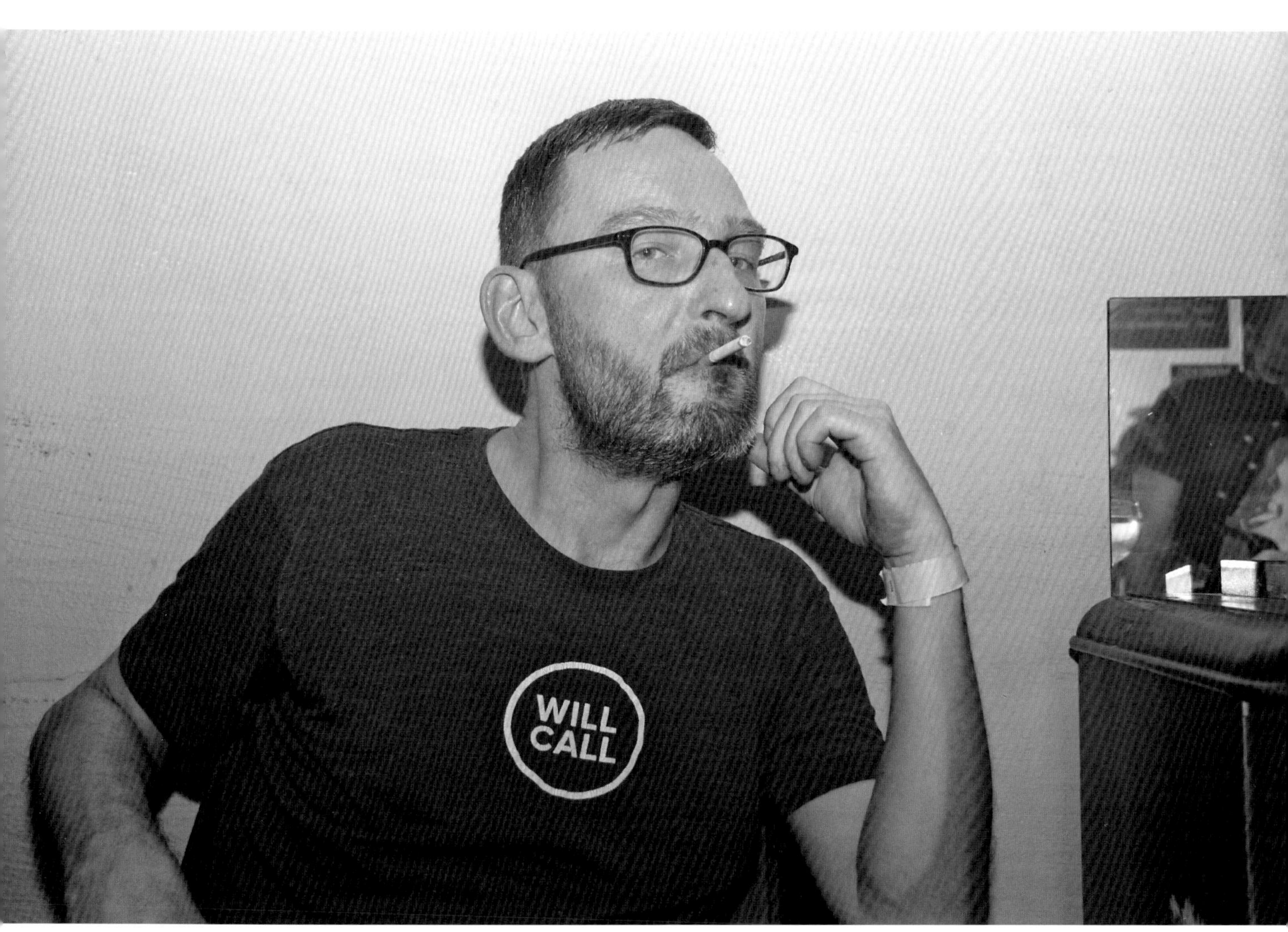
WILL
CALL

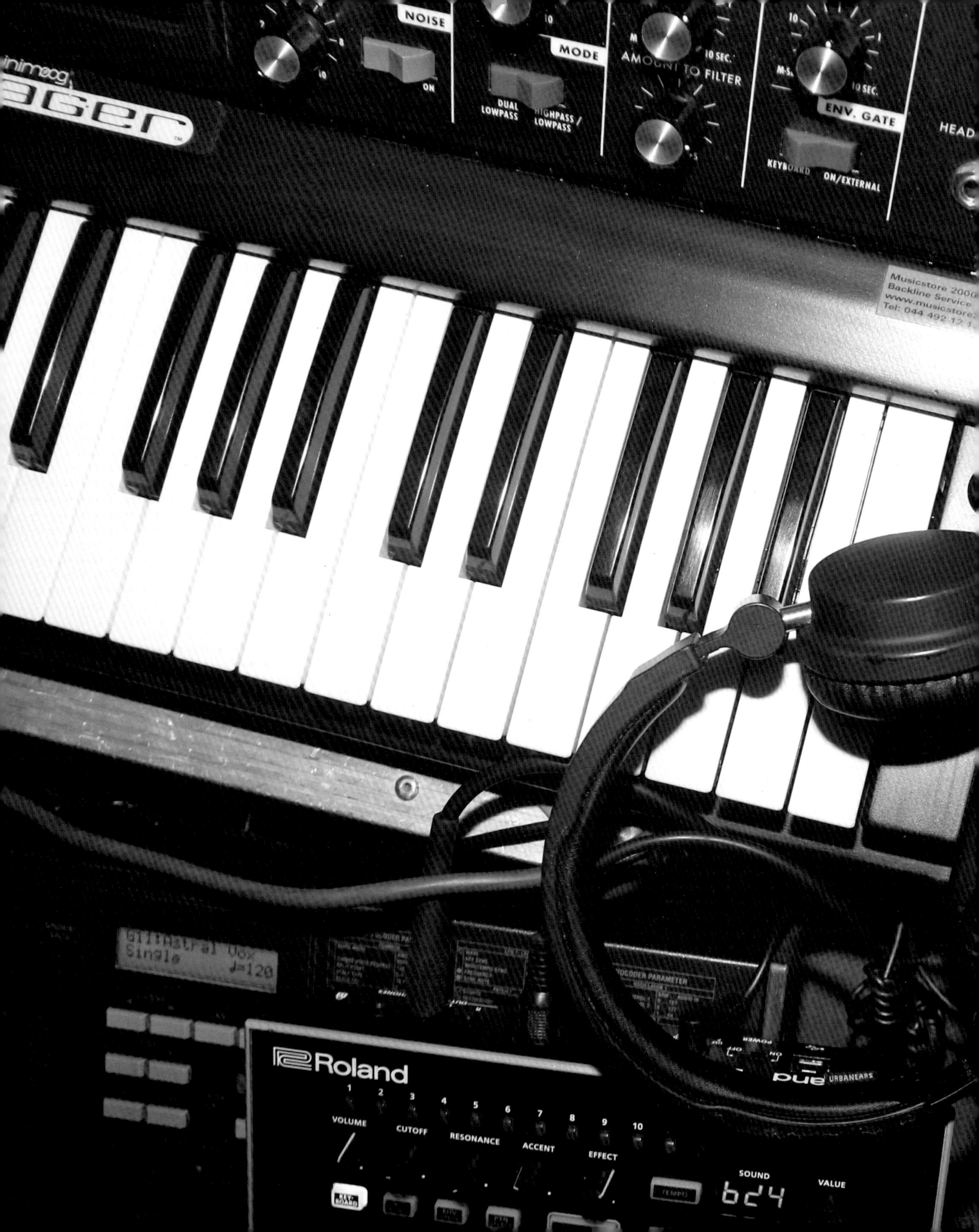
NOISE
ON
MODE
DUAL LOWPASS
HIGHPASS / LOWPASS
AMOUNT TO FILTER
10 SEC.
ENV. GATE
KEYBOARD
ON/EXTERNAL
Musicstore 2000
Backline Service
Single
Roland
VOLUME
CUTOFF
RESONANCE
ACCENT
EFFECT
TEMPO
SOUND
VALUE
URBANEARS

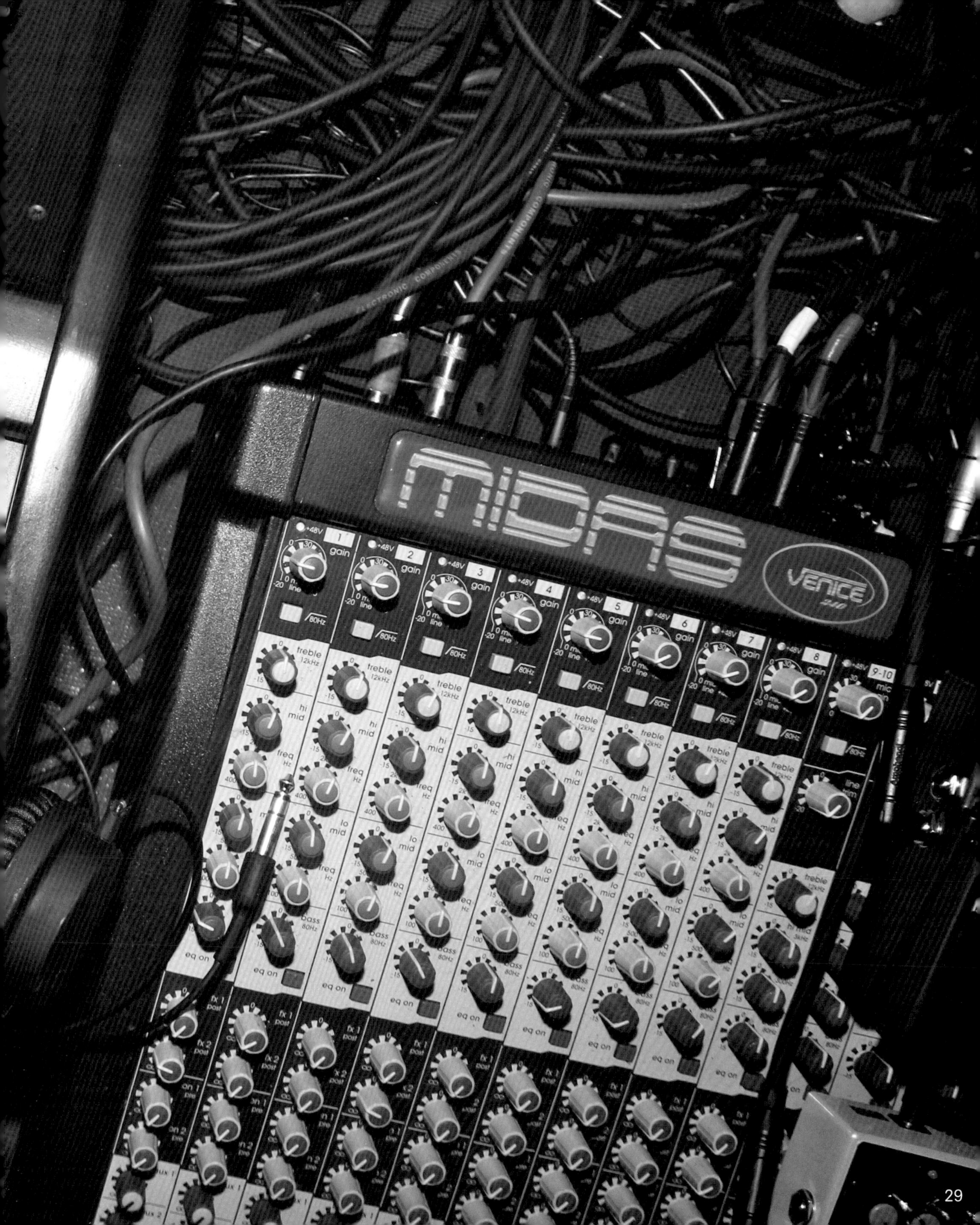
MIDAS
VENICE

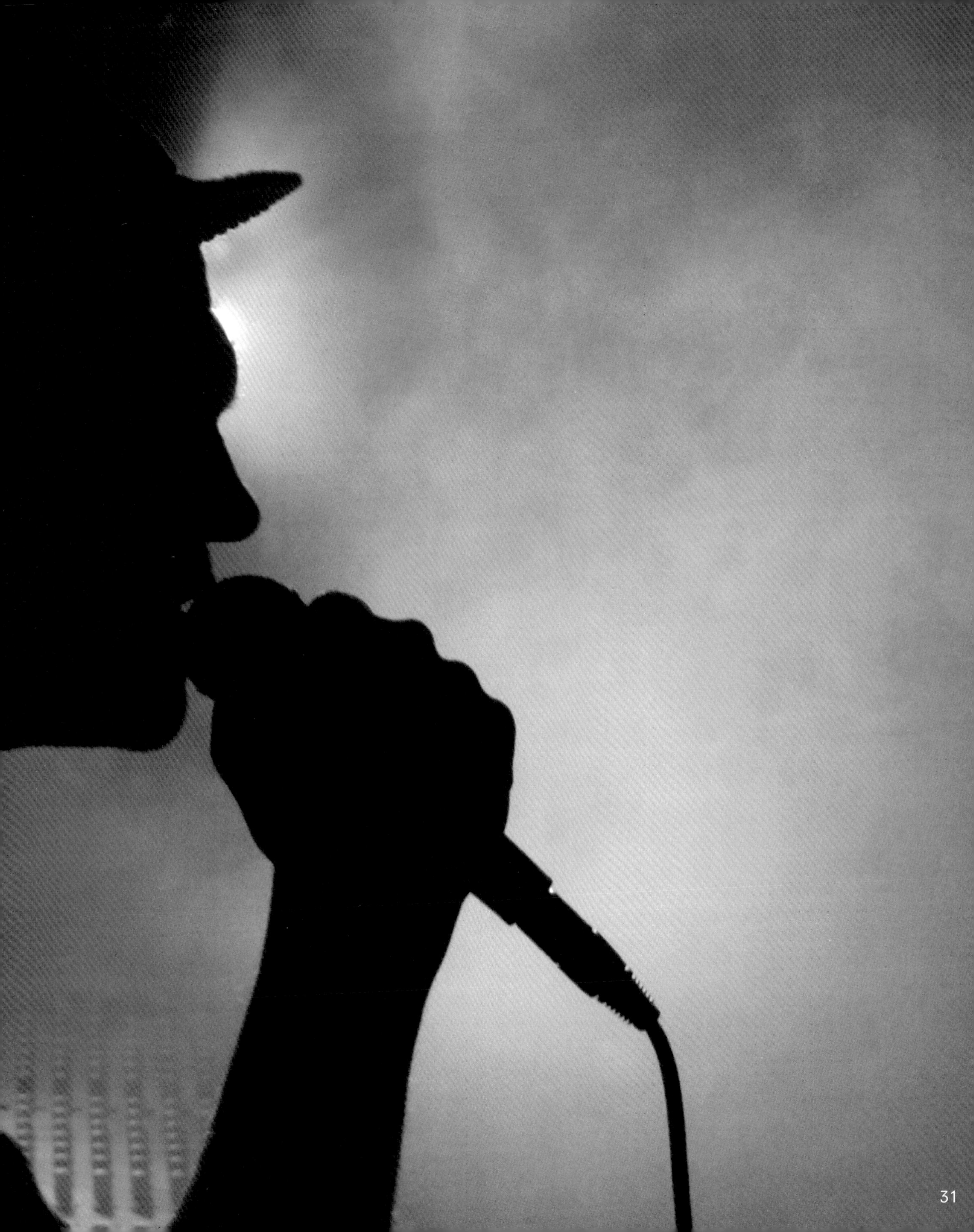

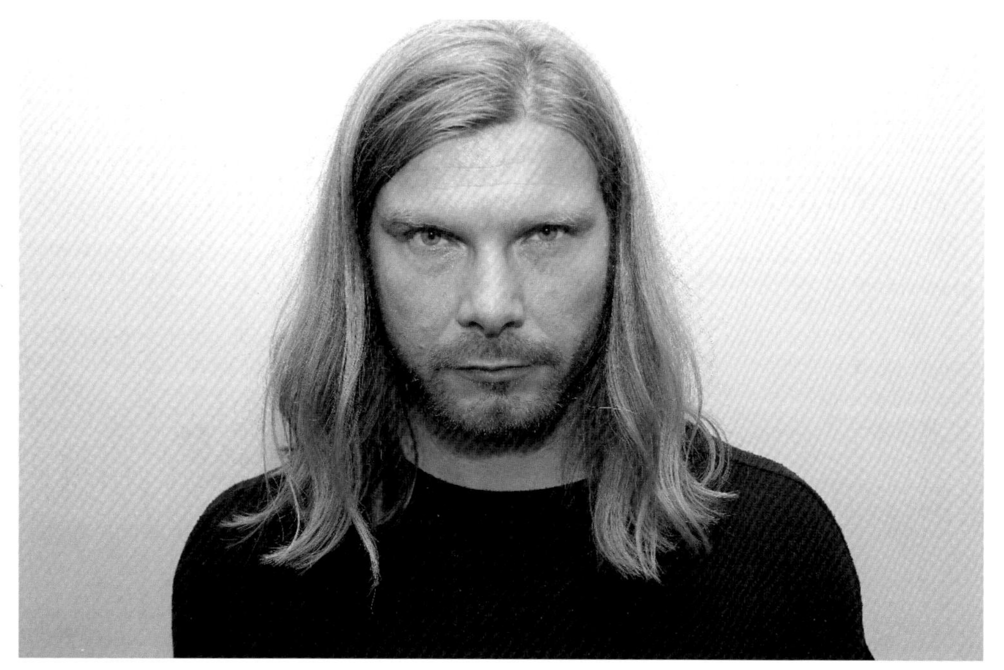

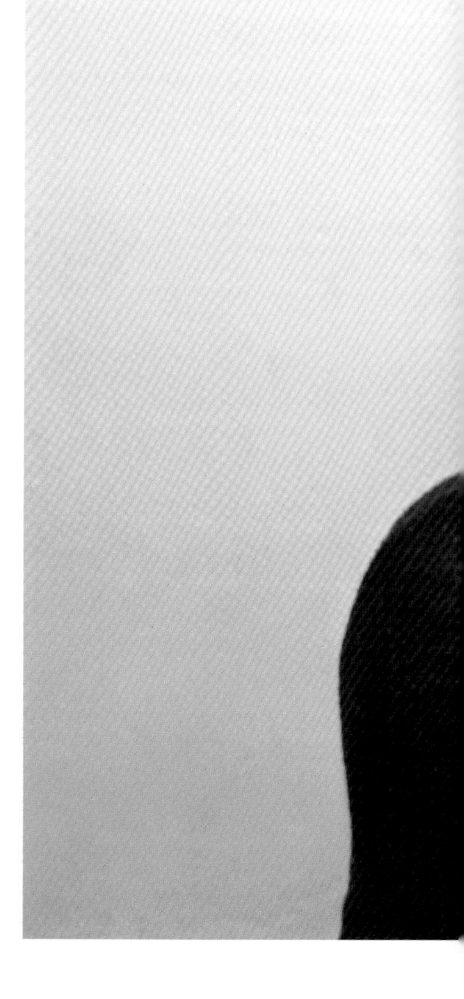

MARCEL DETTMANN

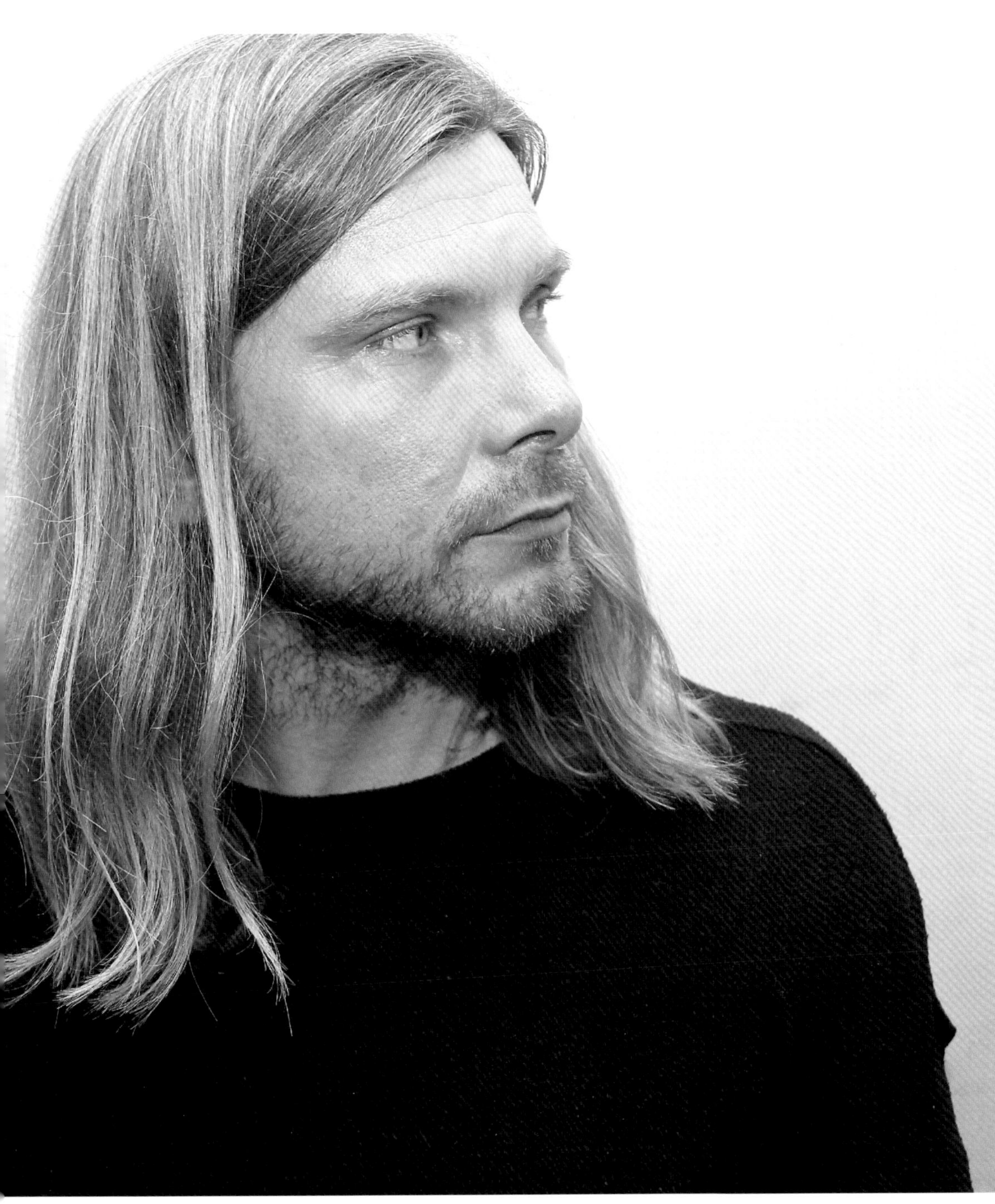

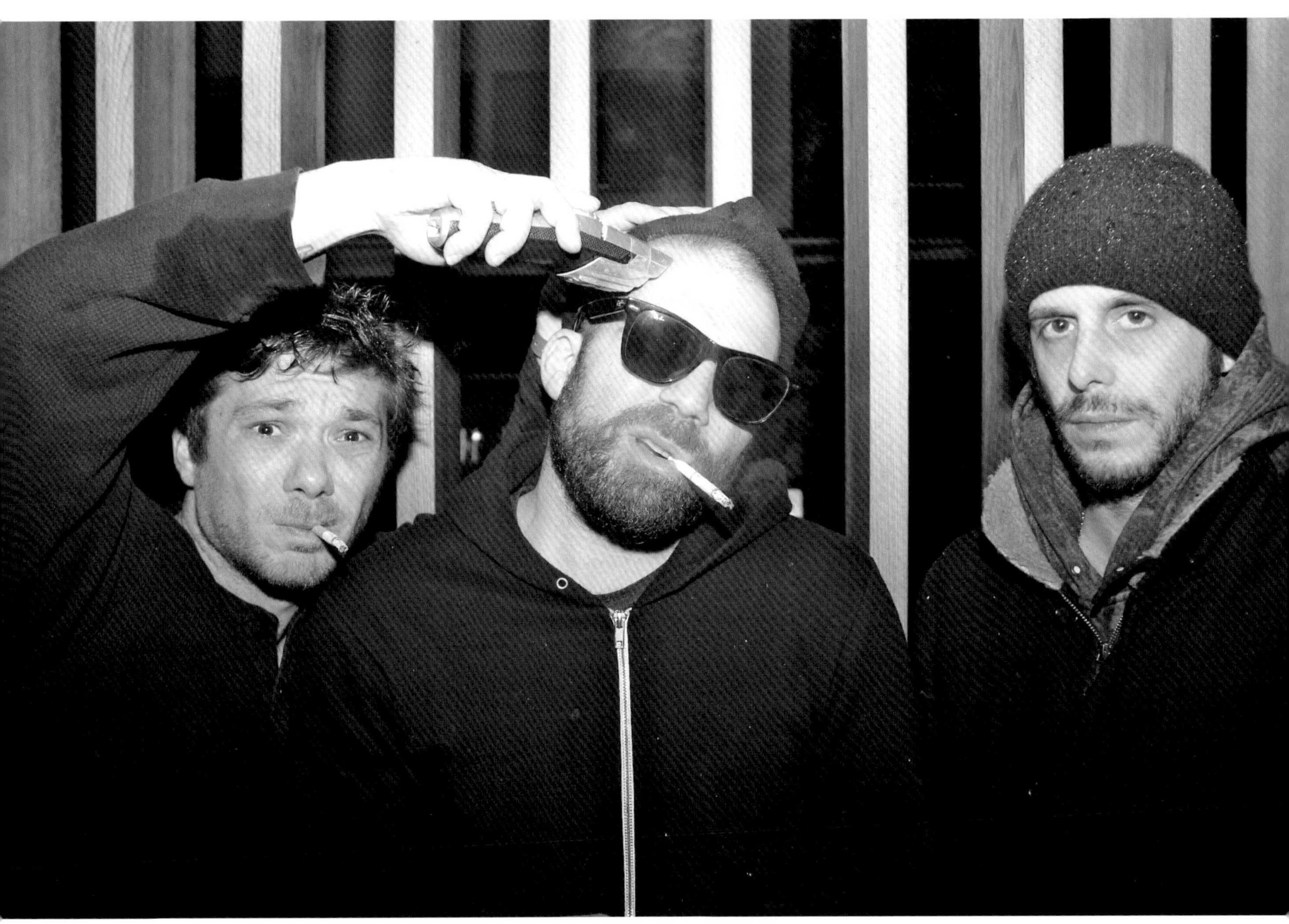

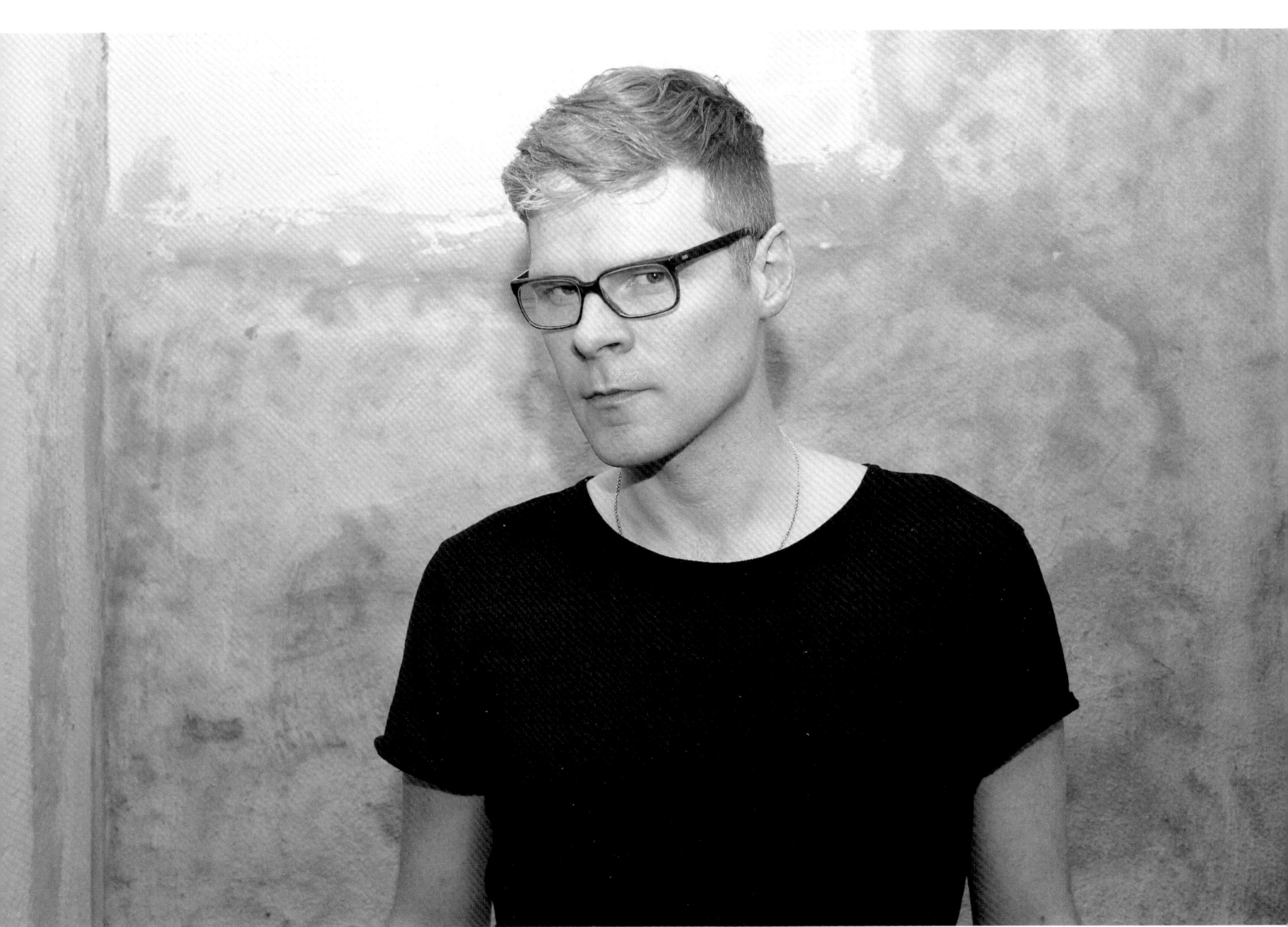

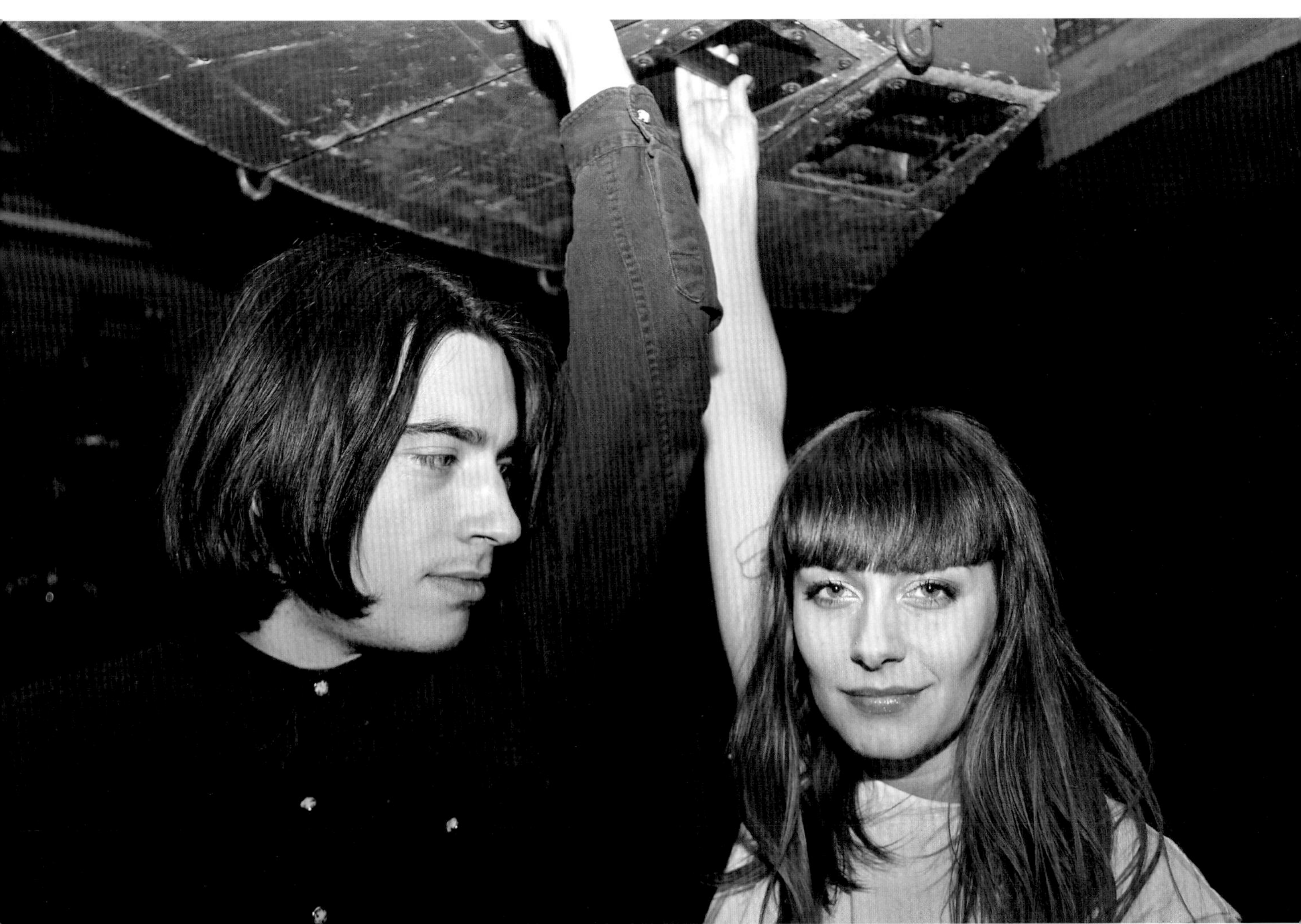

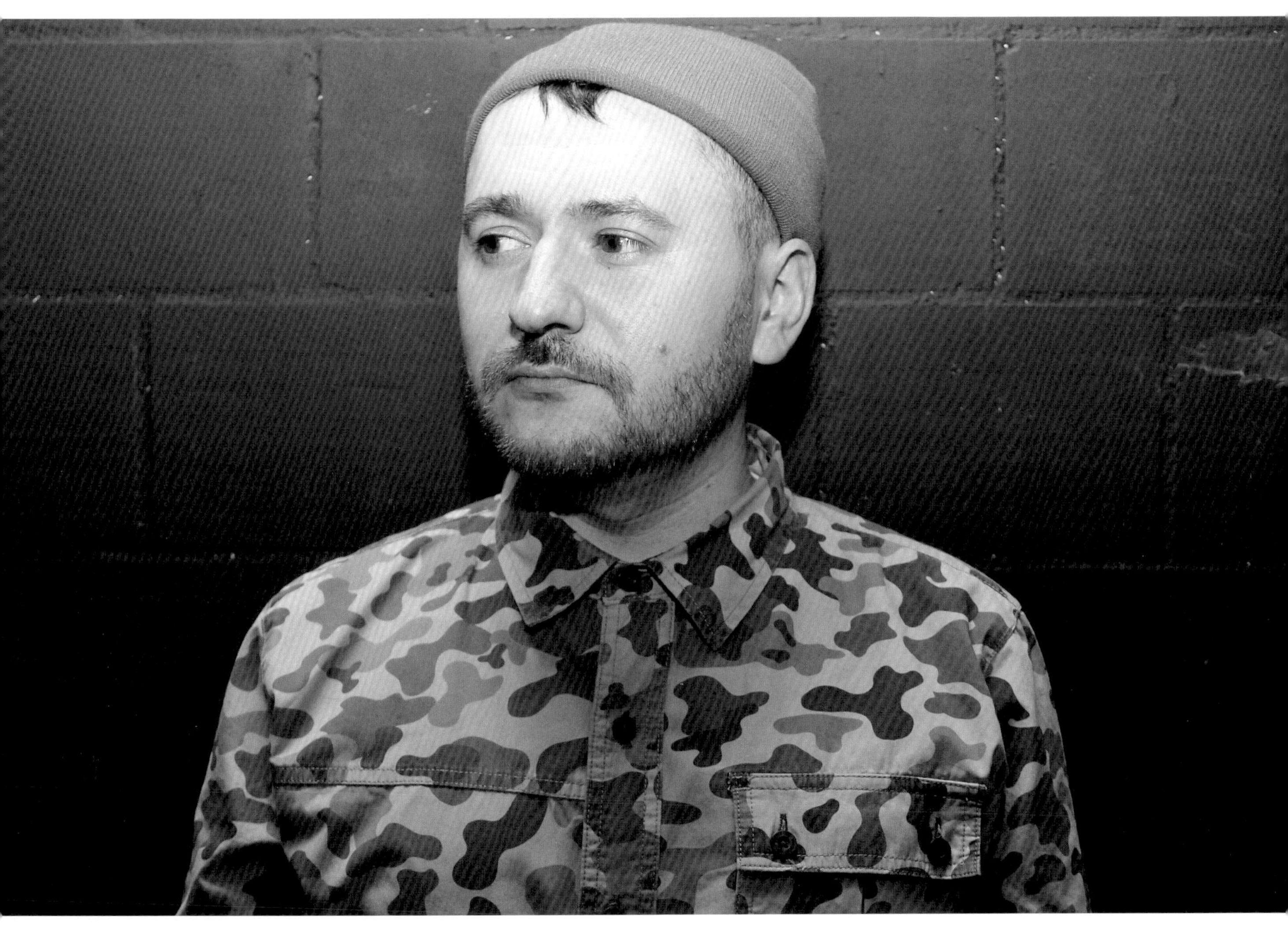

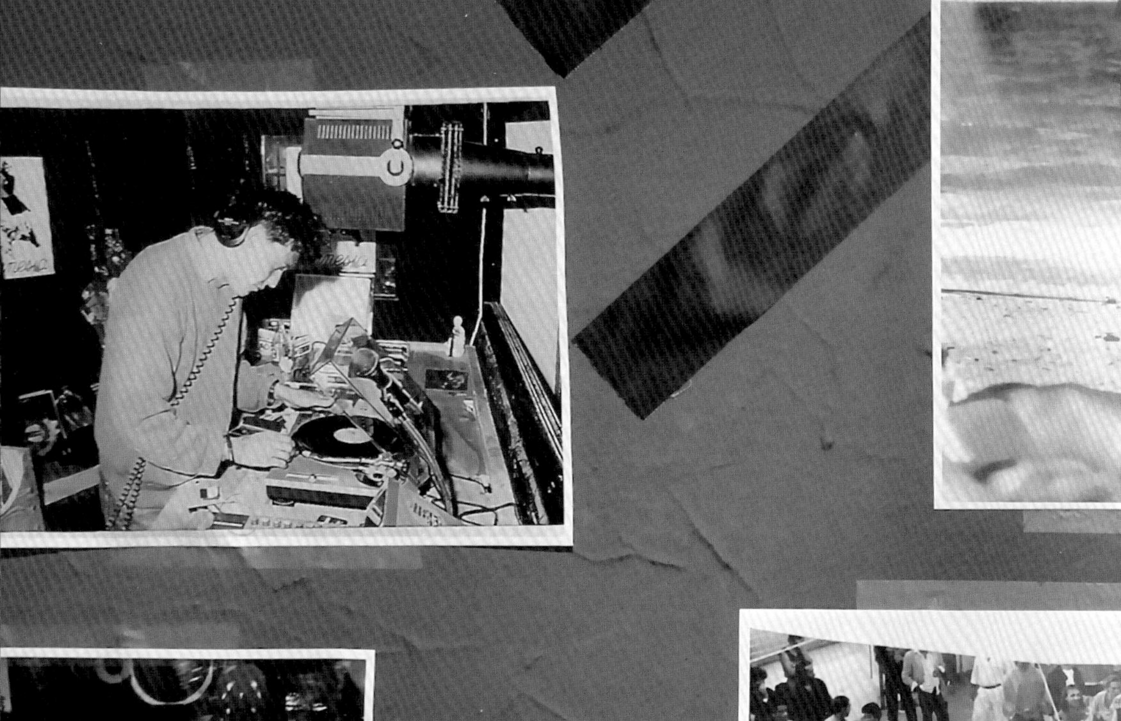

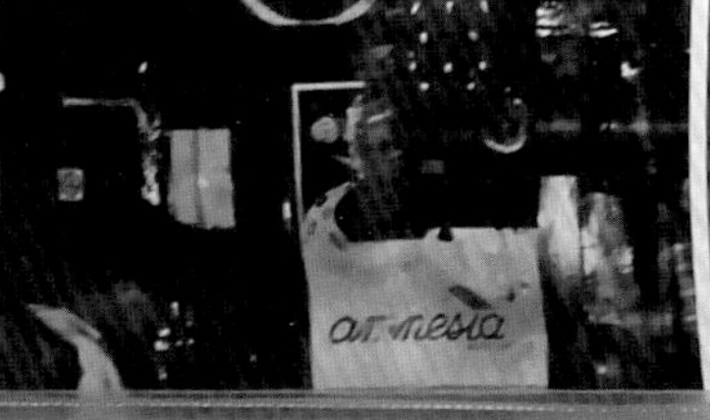
amnesia

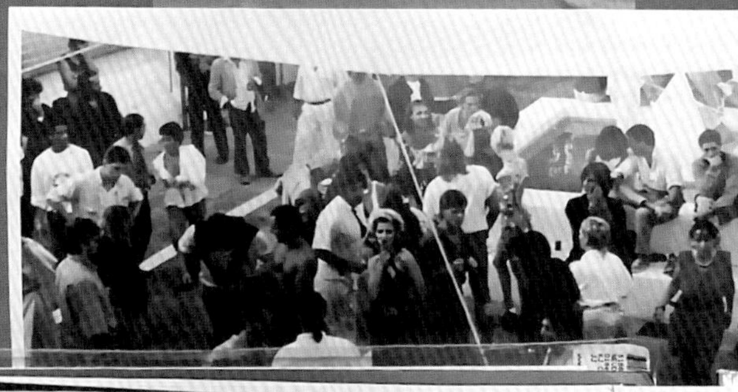

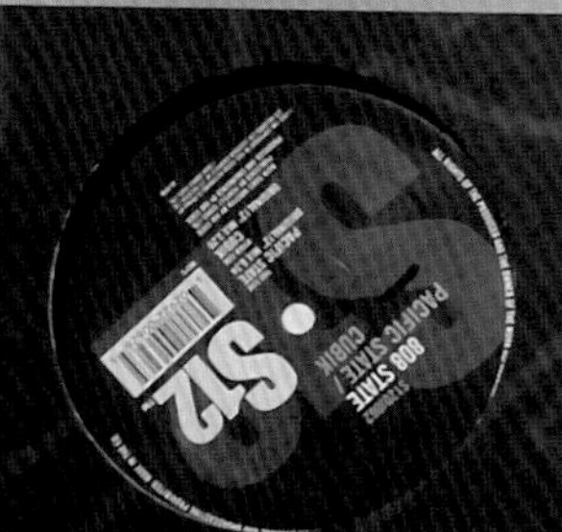
S12
808 STATE
PACIFIC STATE / CUBIK

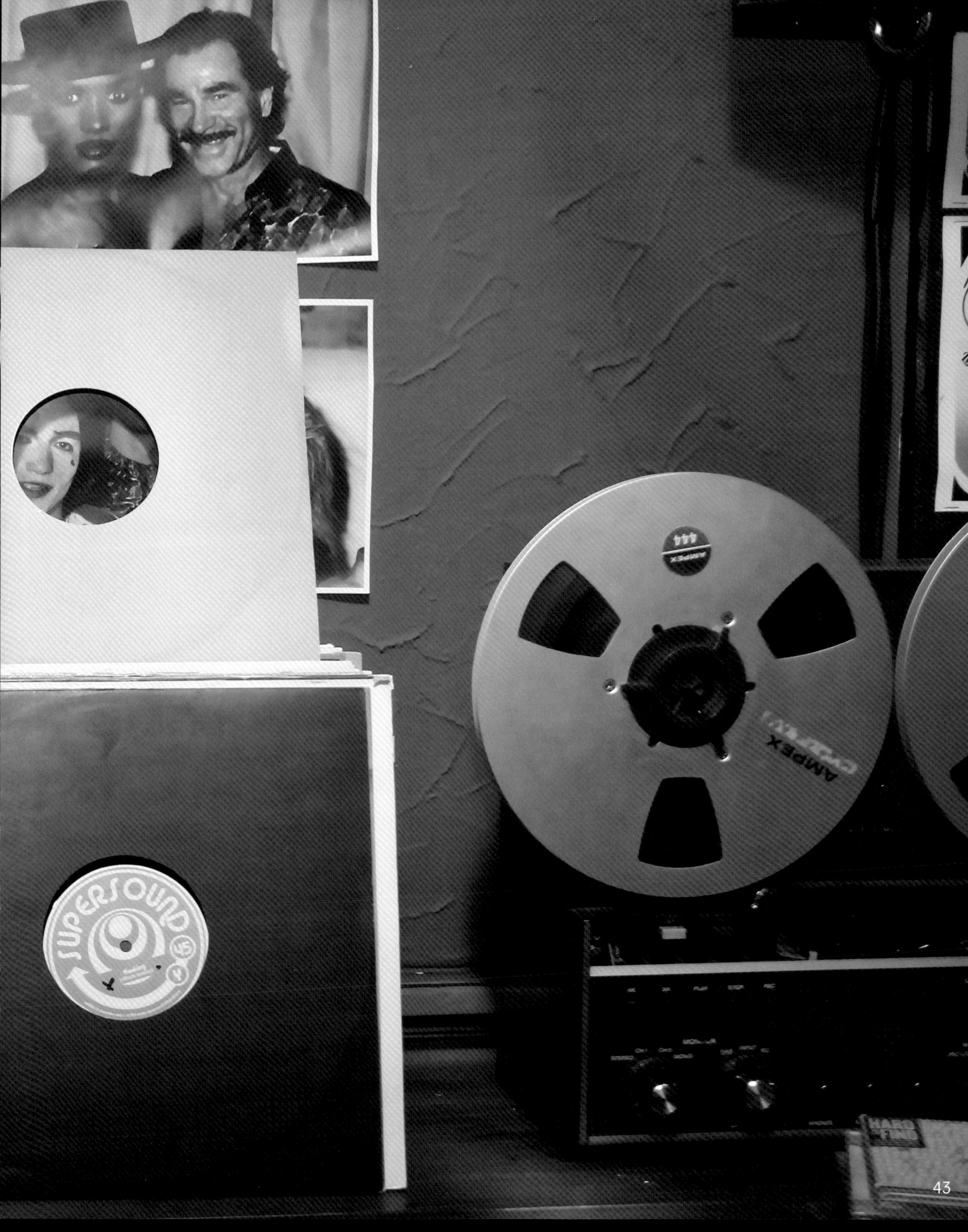
SUPERSOUND
45
AMPEX
444

LOS SURUBA

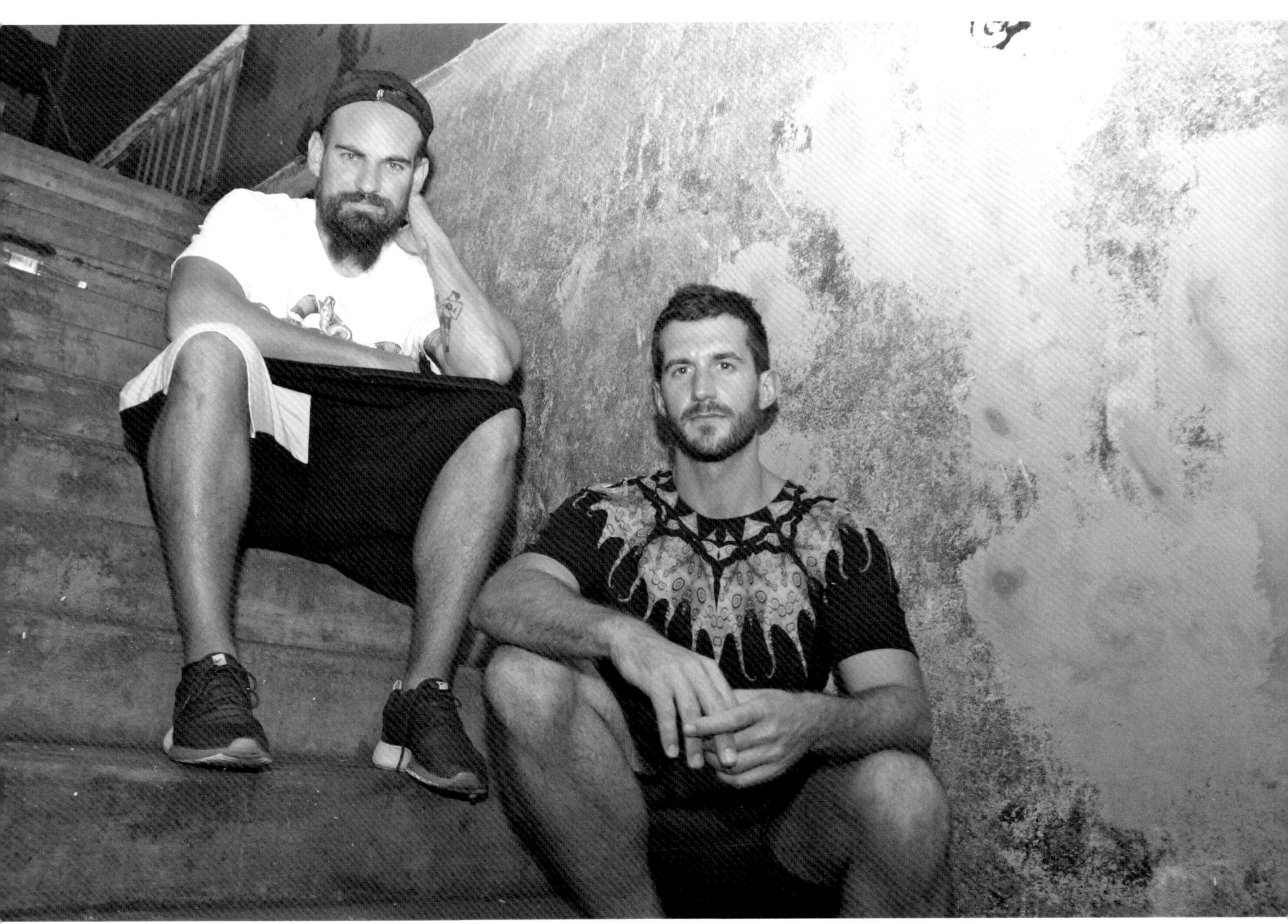

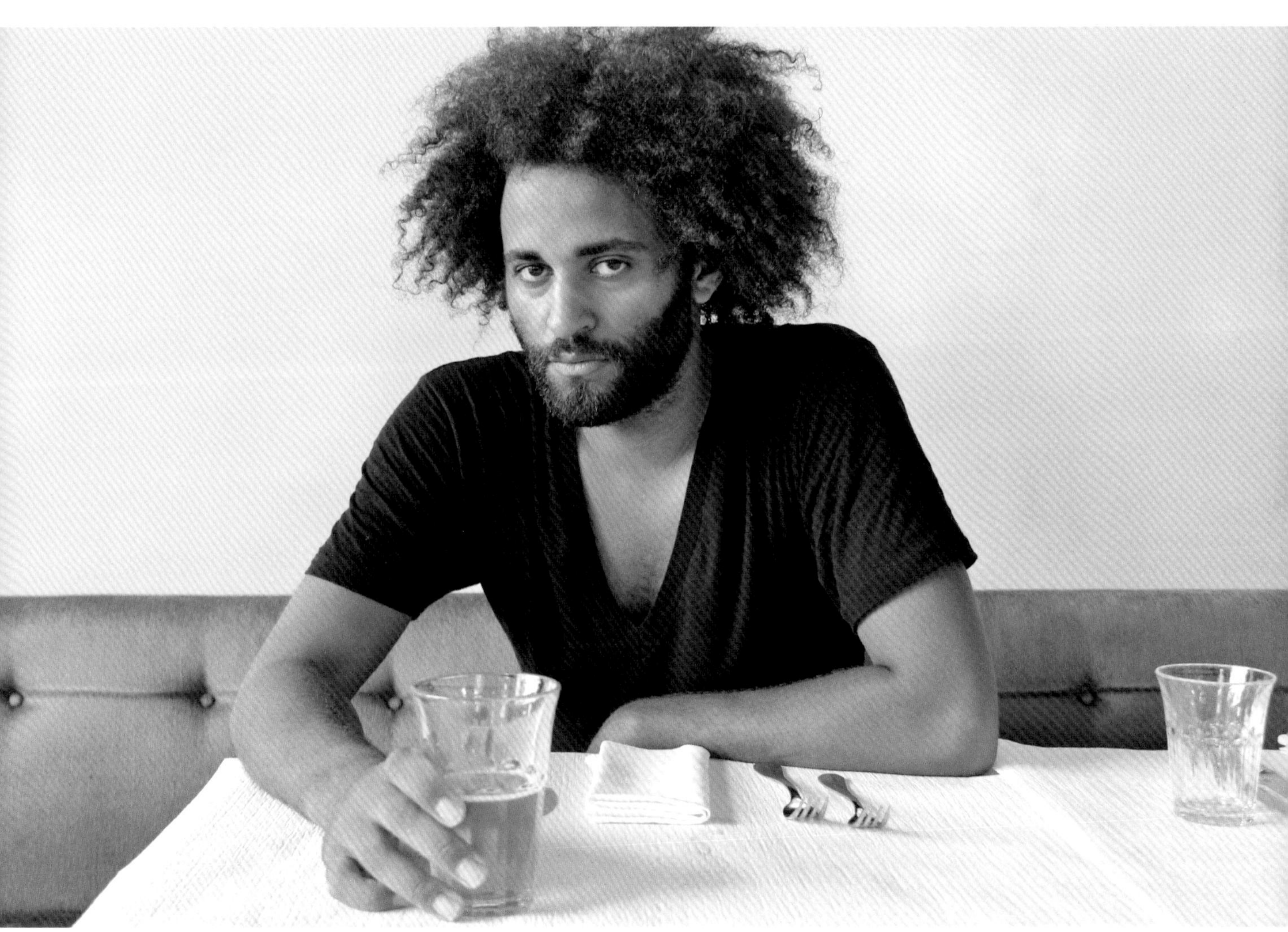

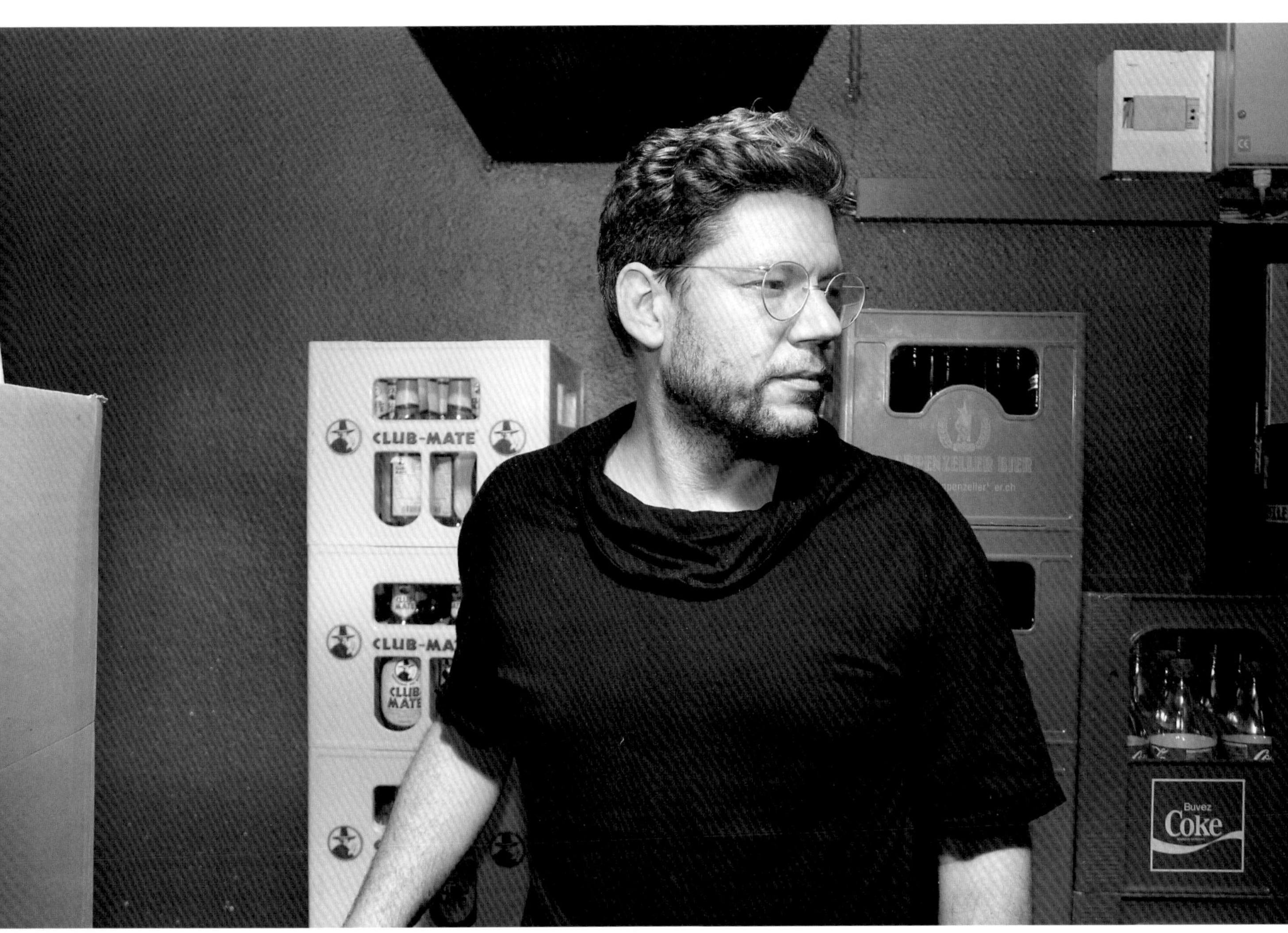
CLUB-MATE
Buvez
Coke

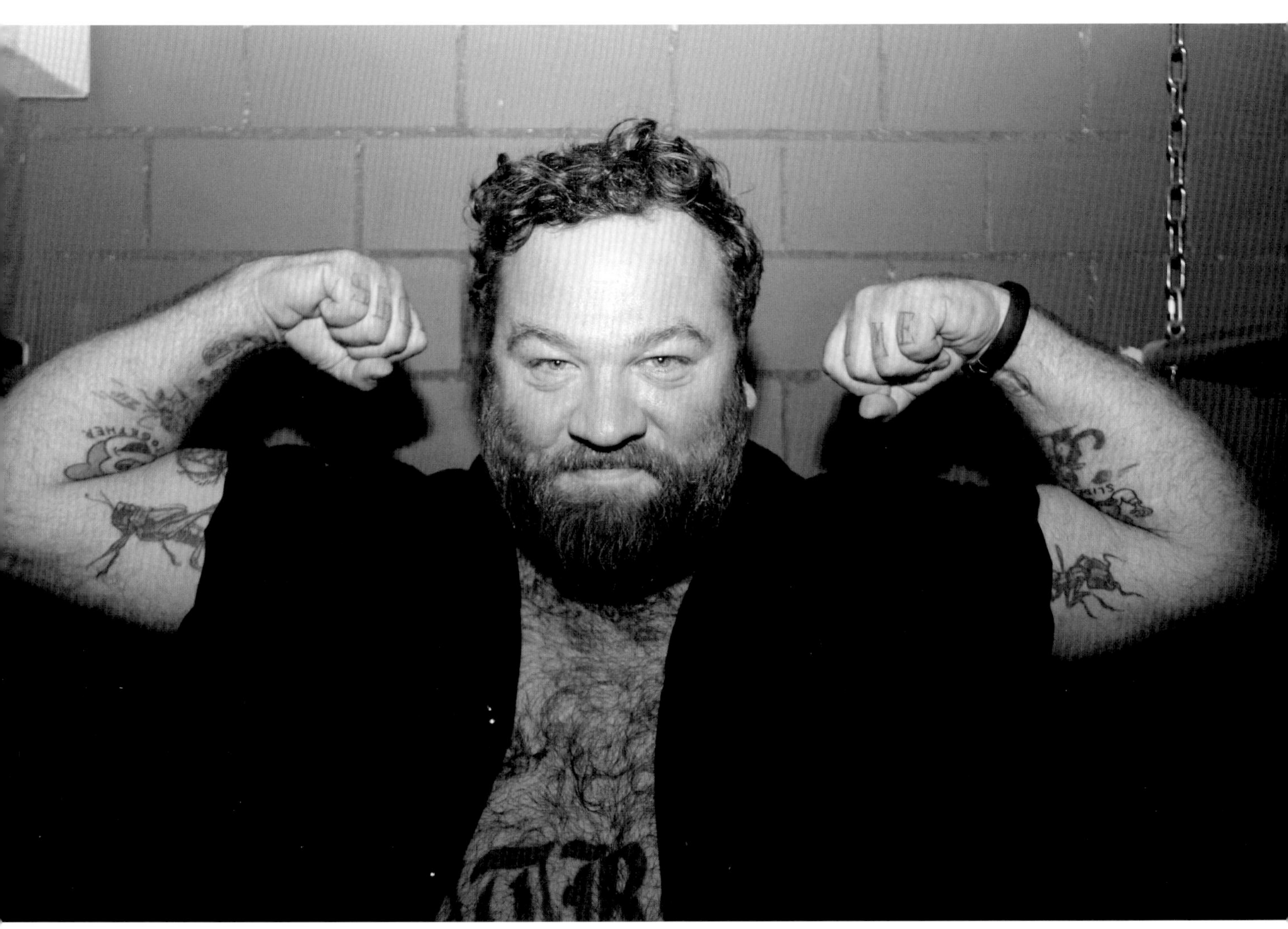

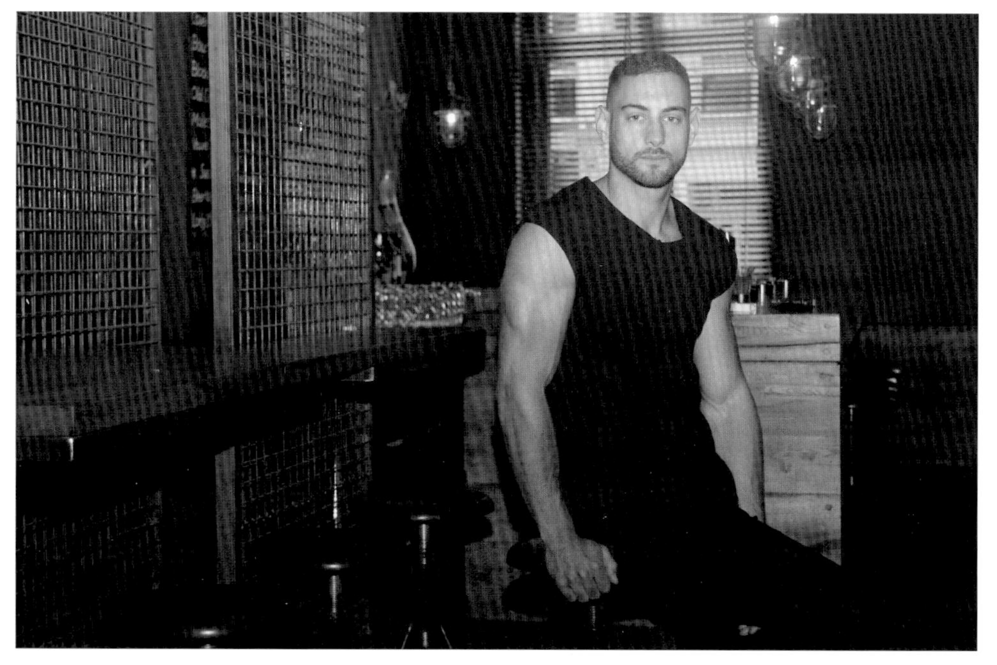

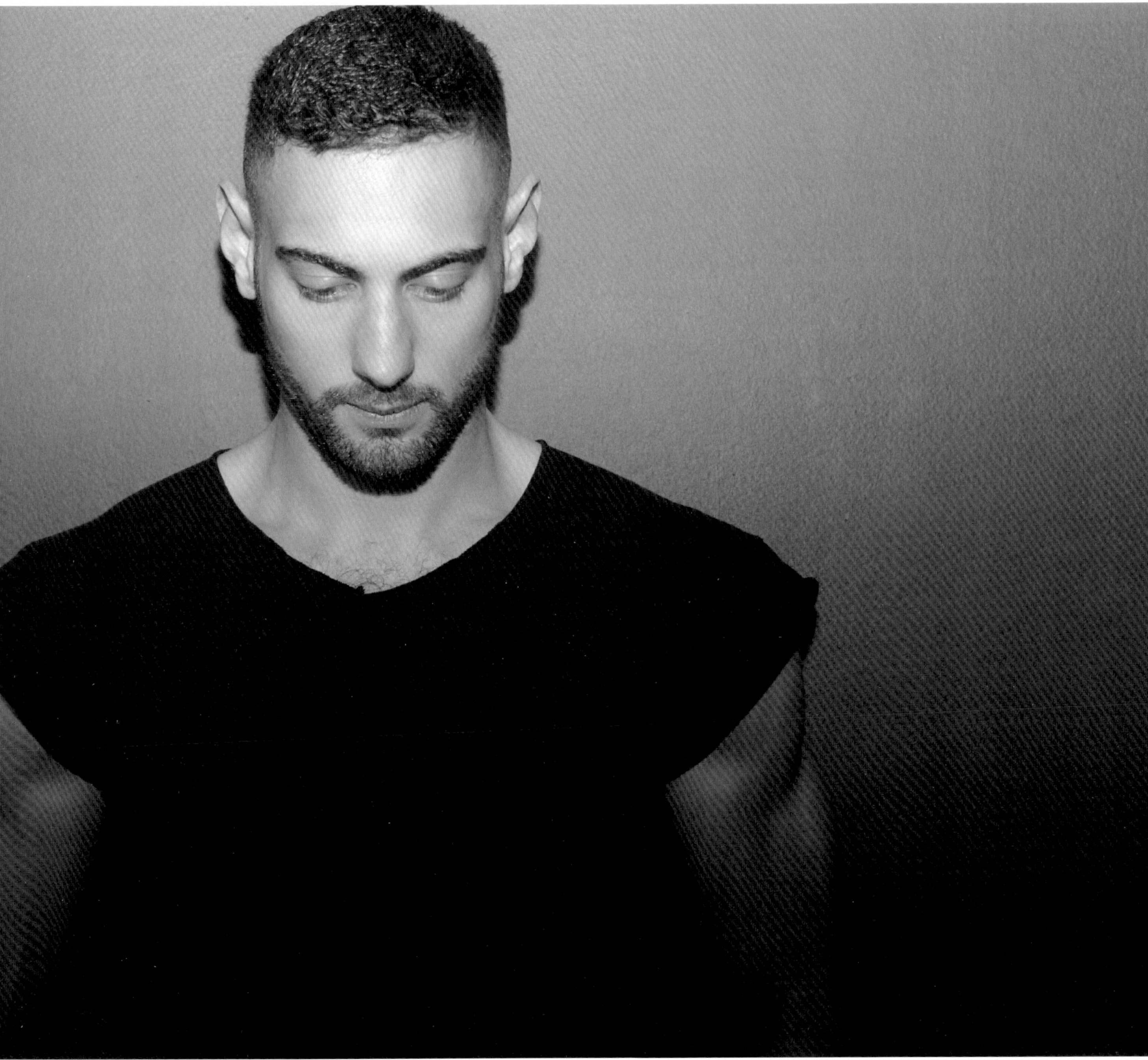

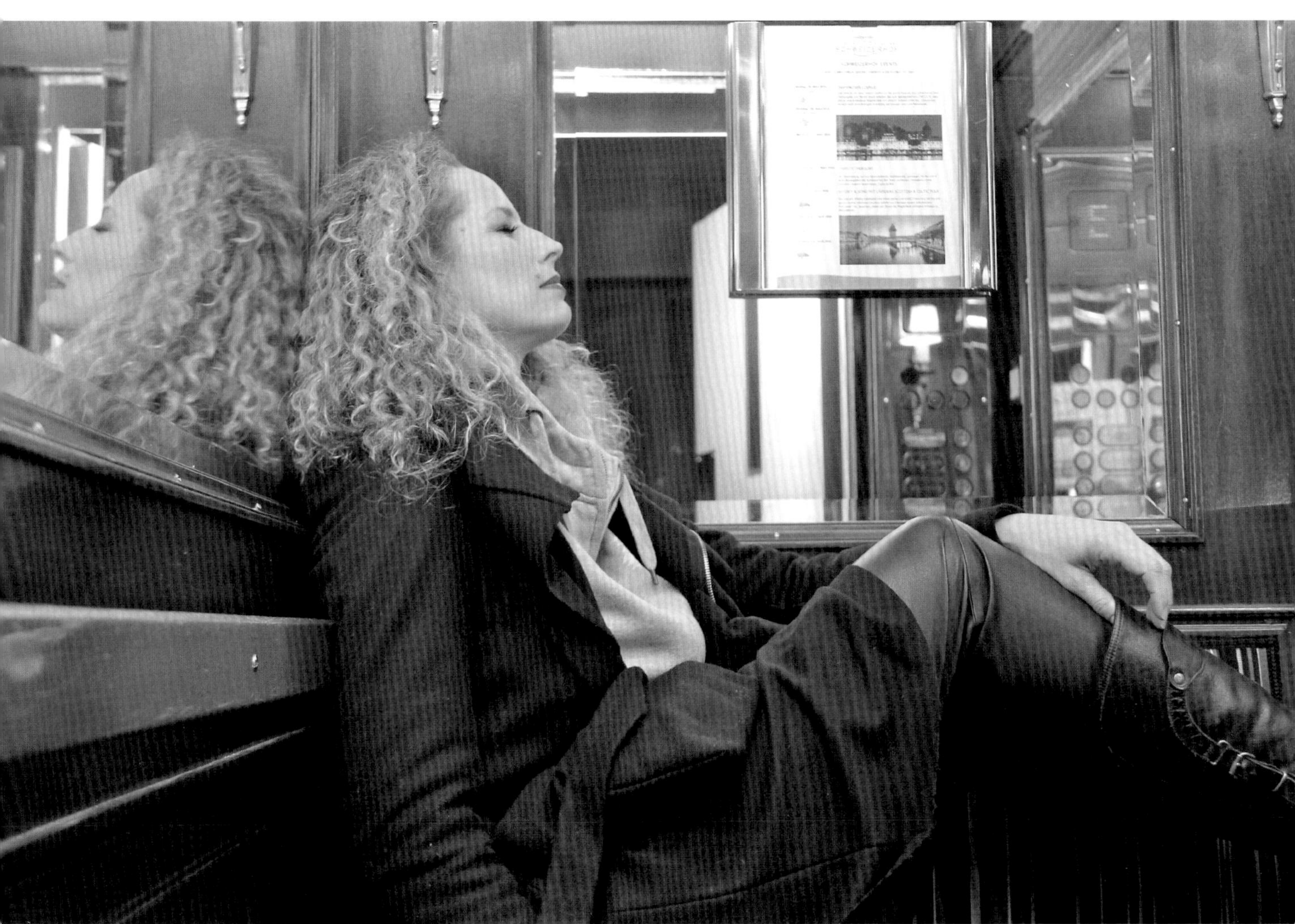

STEVE BUG

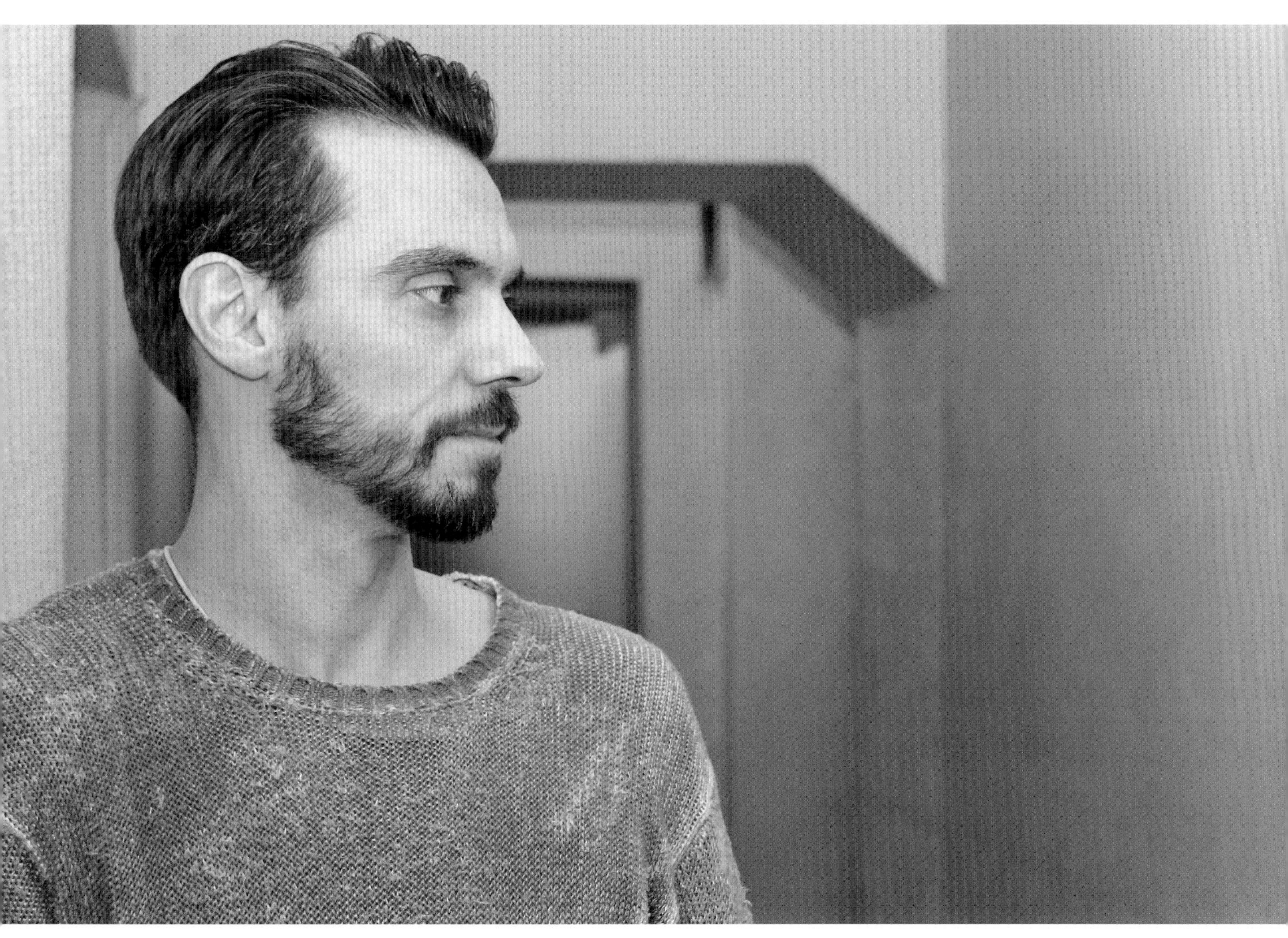

WOLFRAM

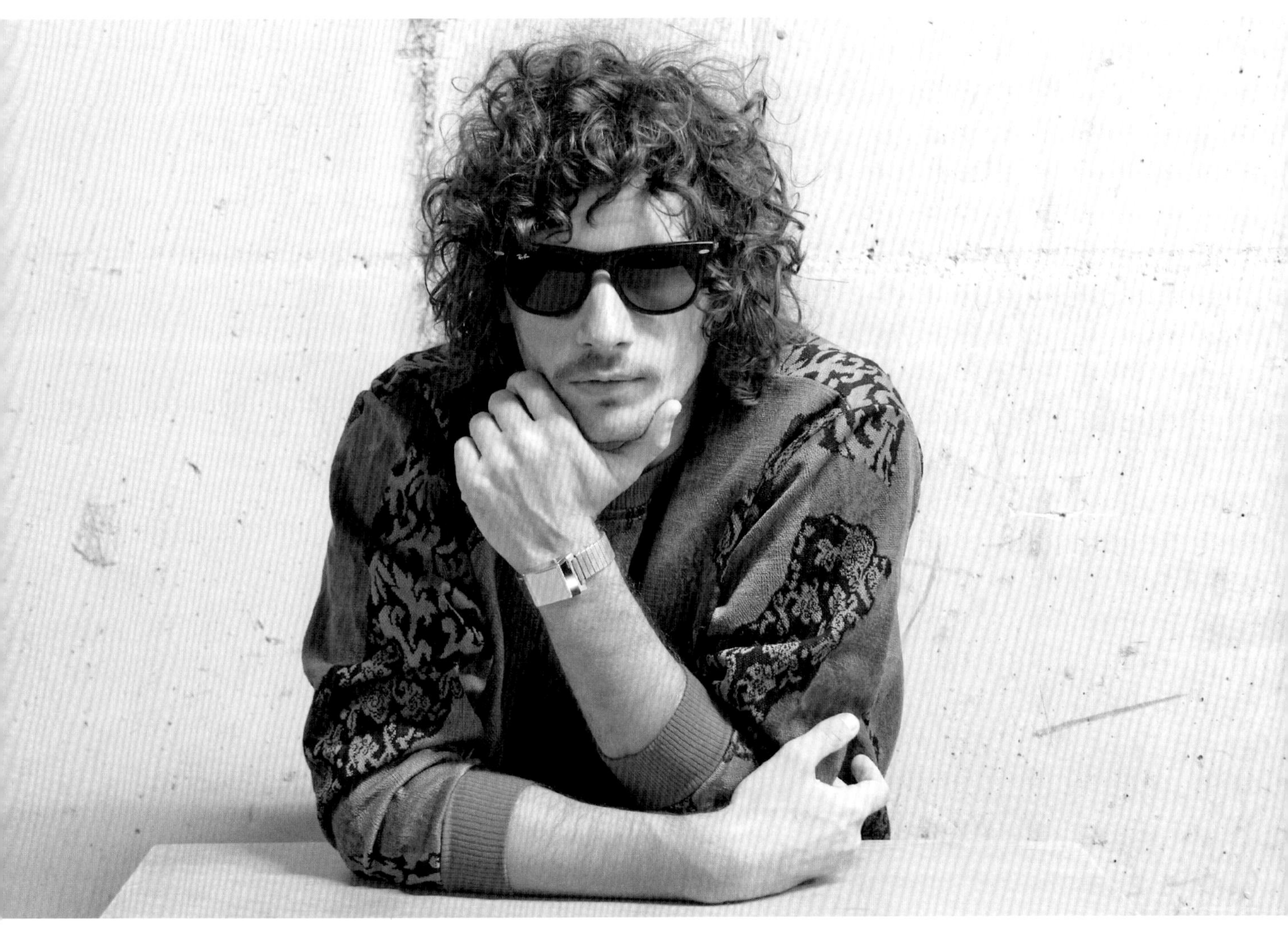

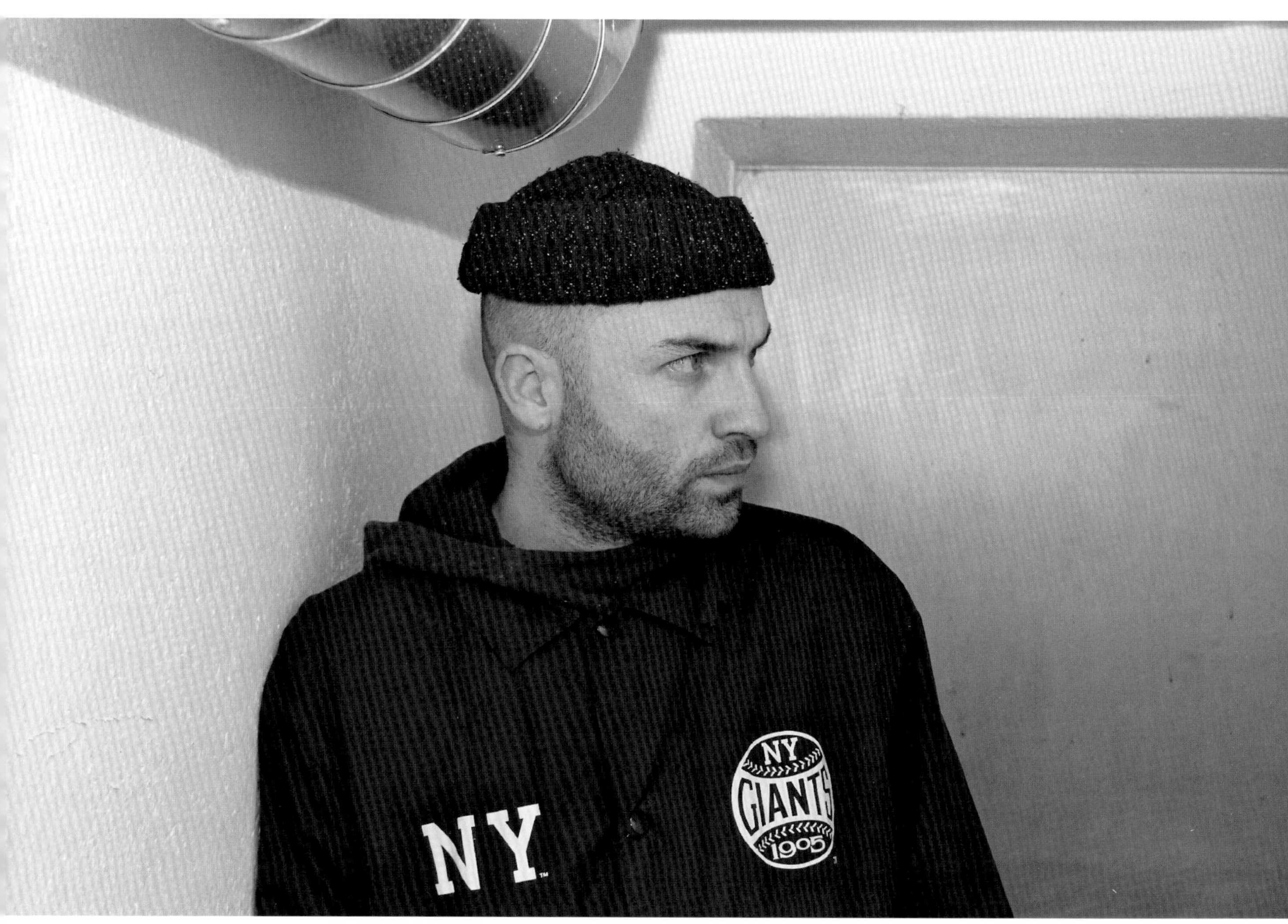

DARKSTAR

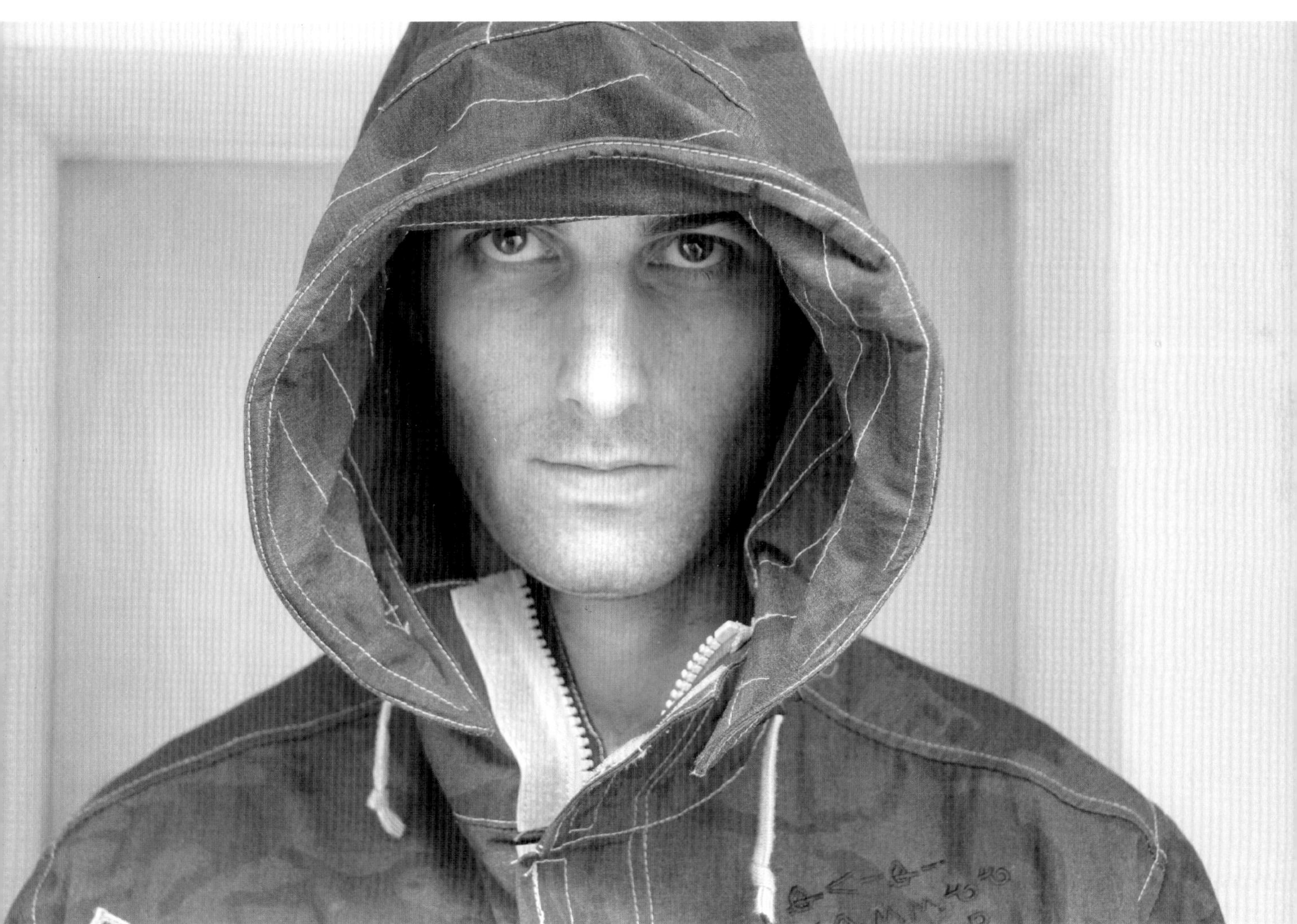

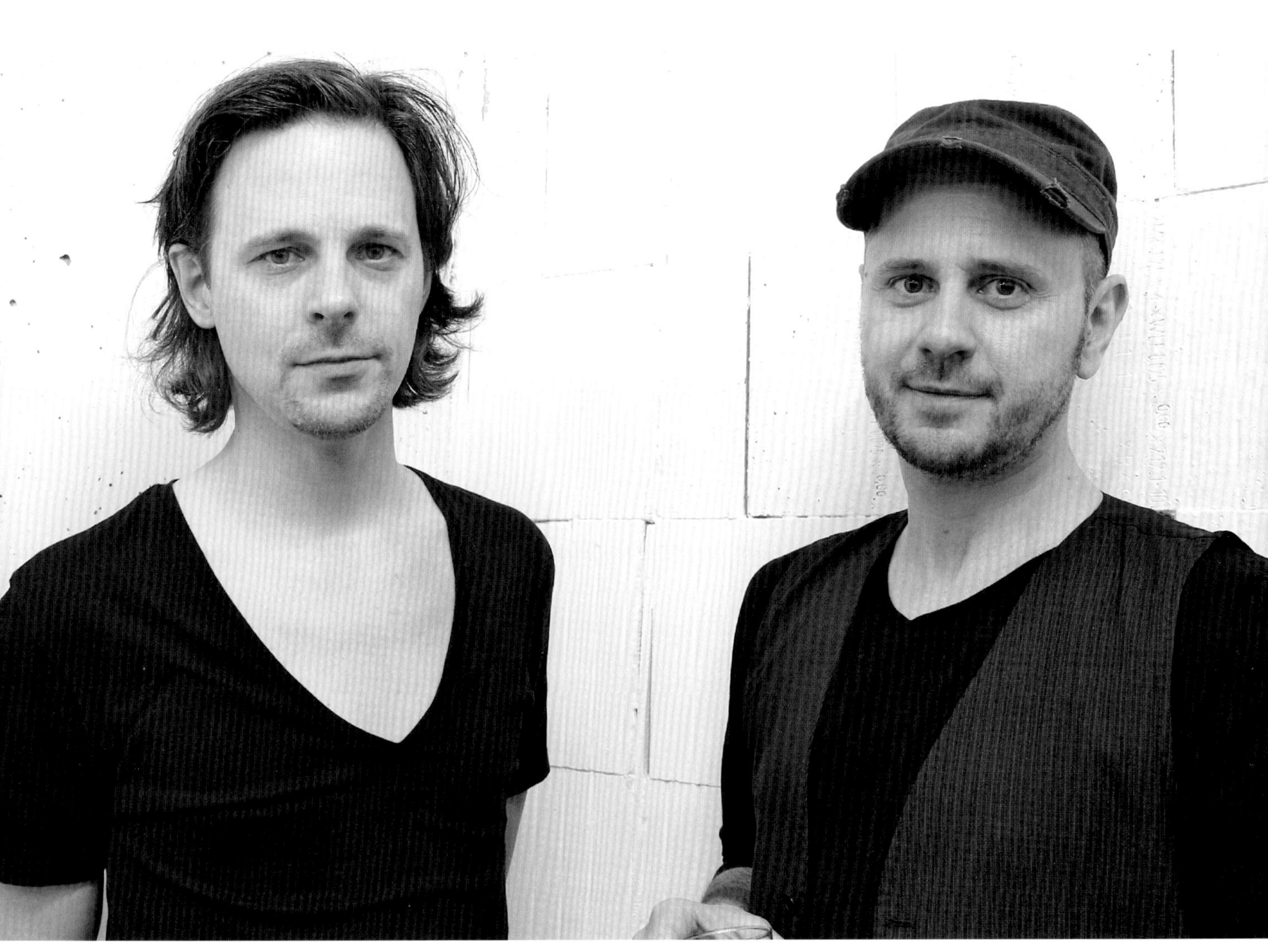

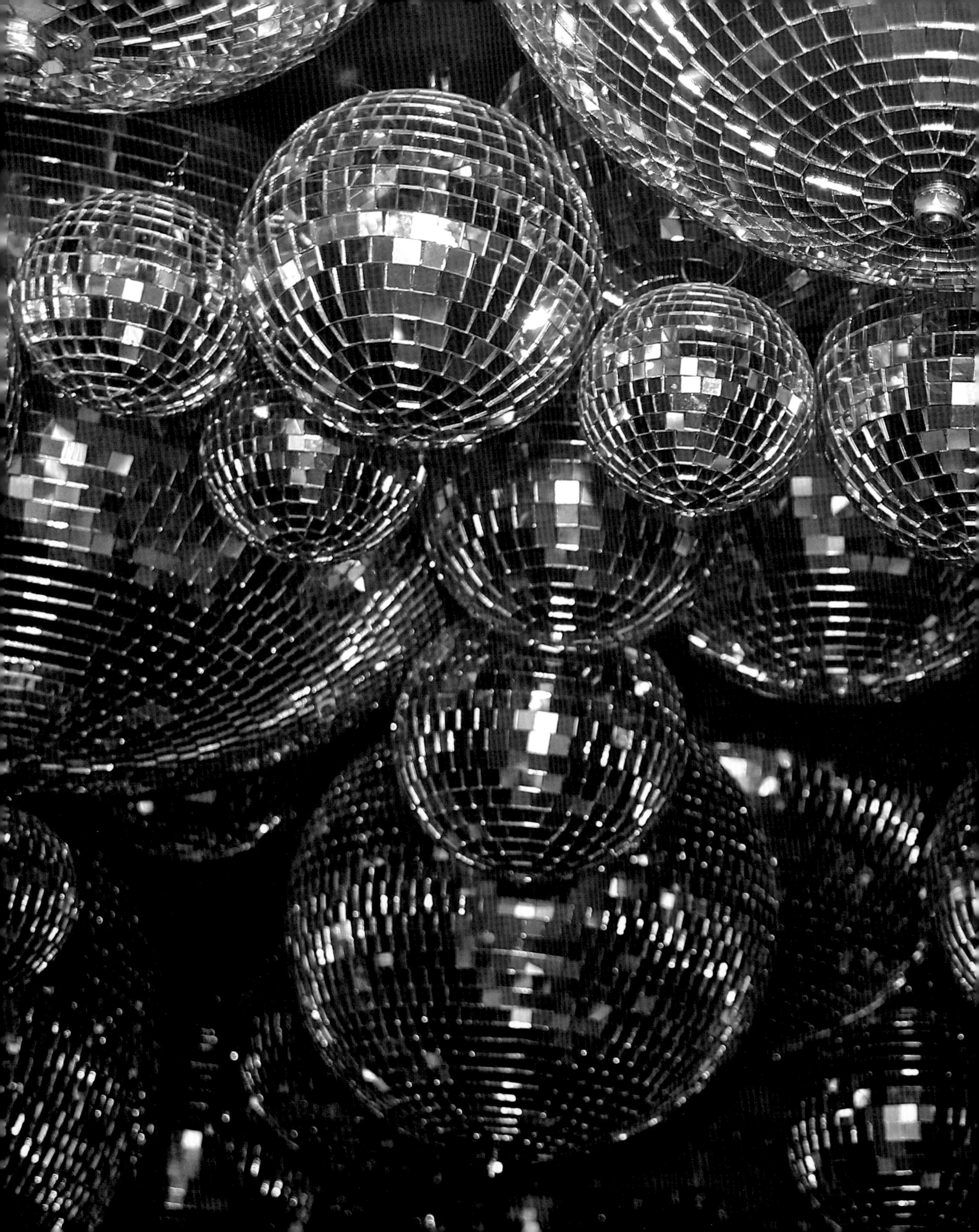

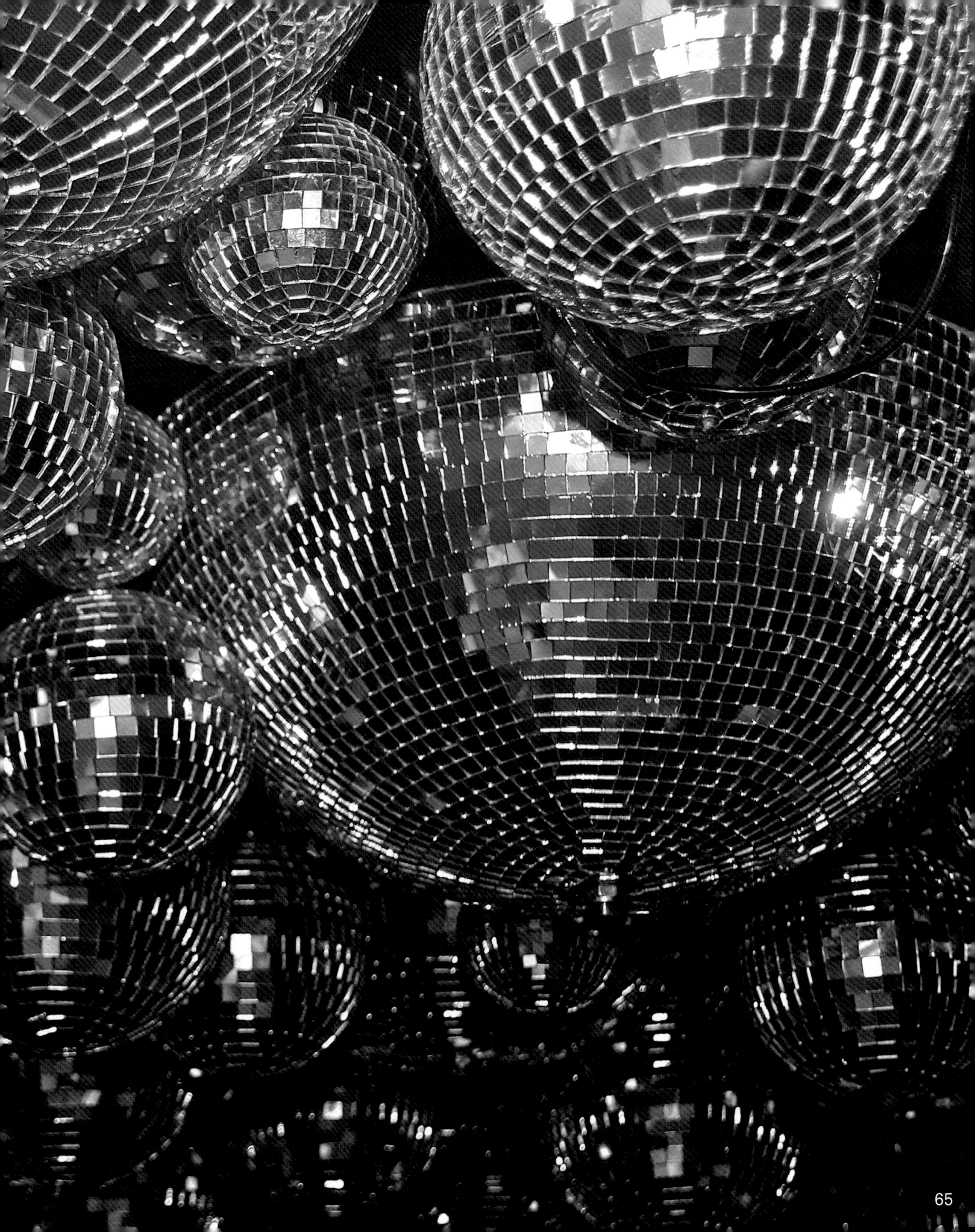

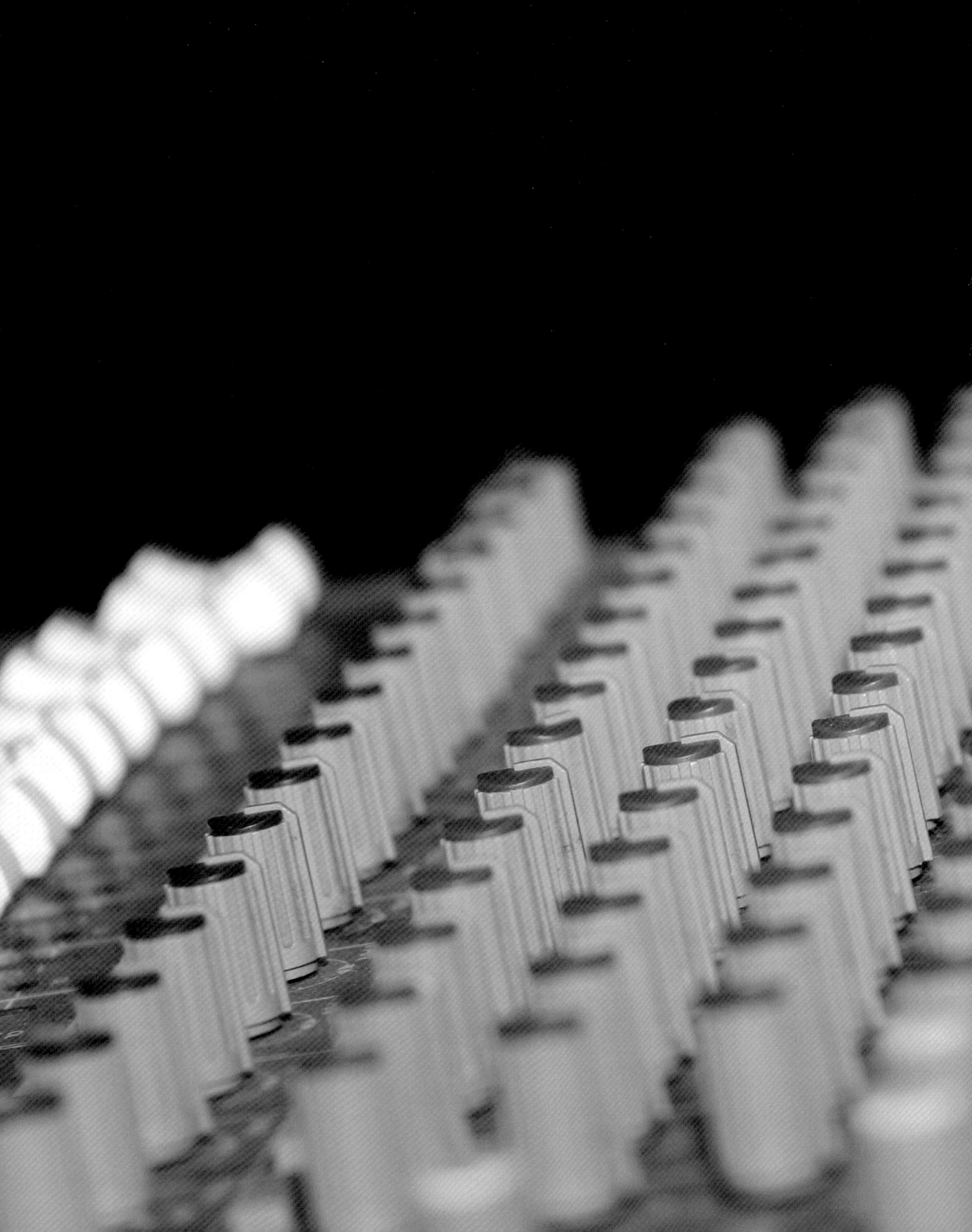

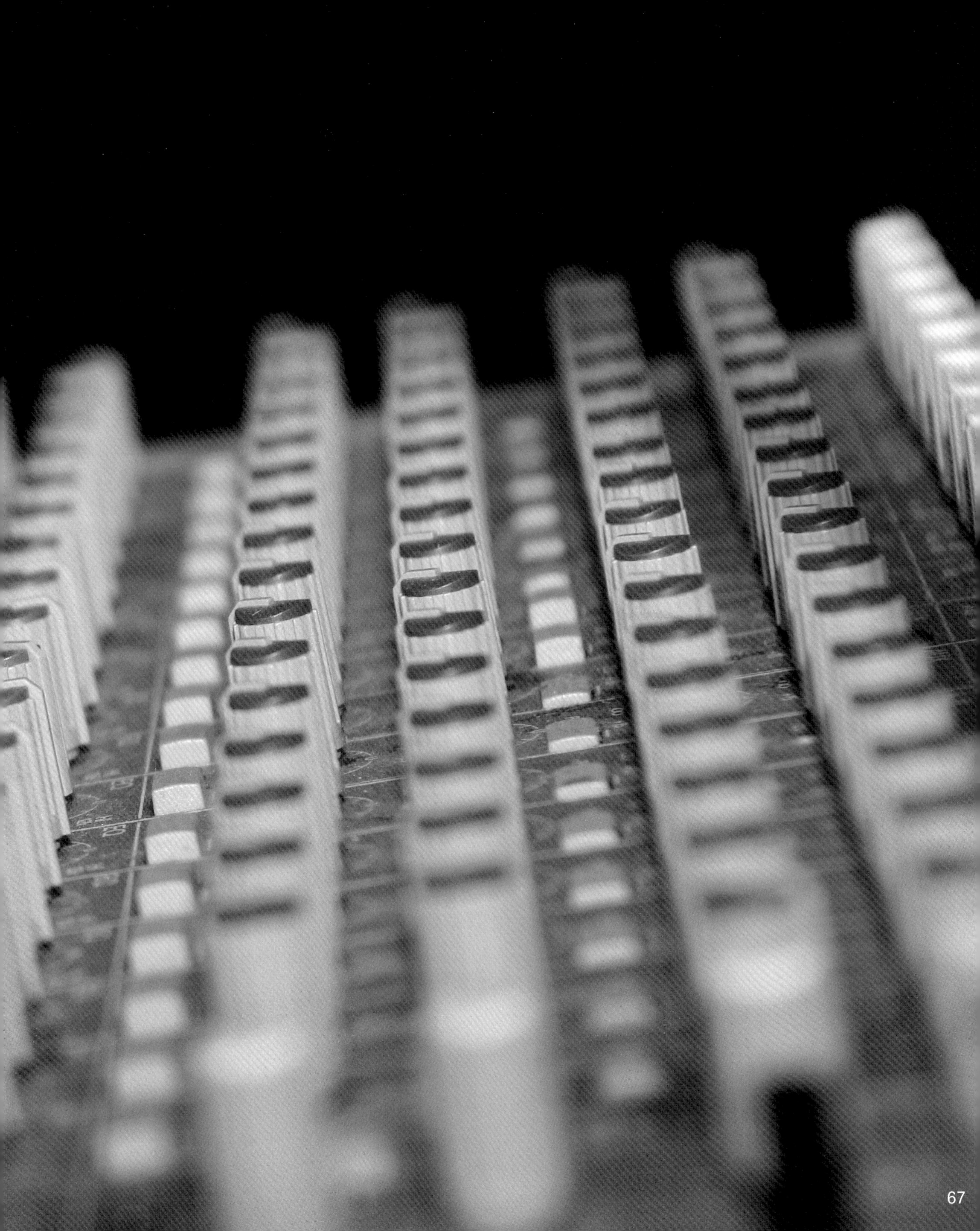

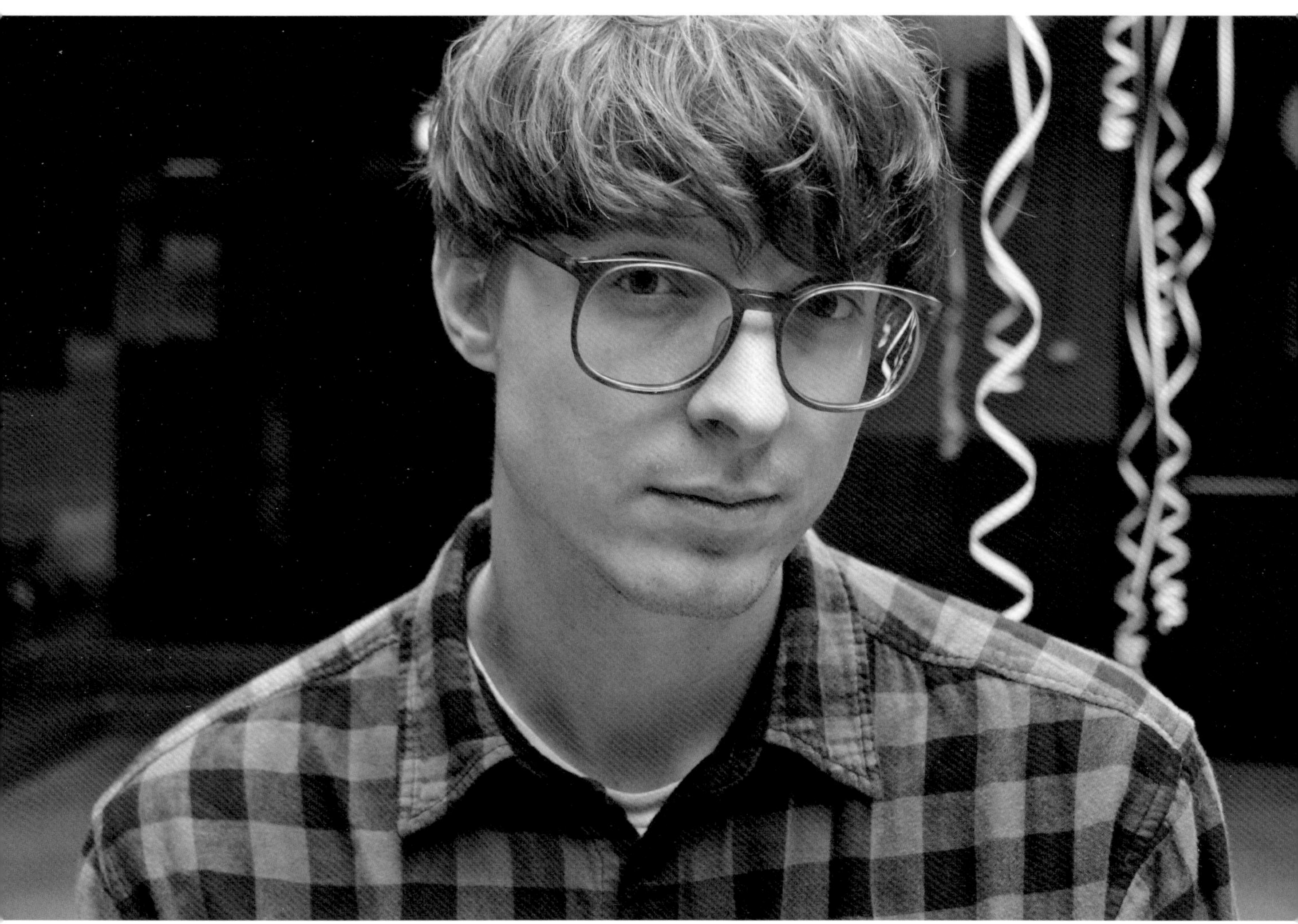

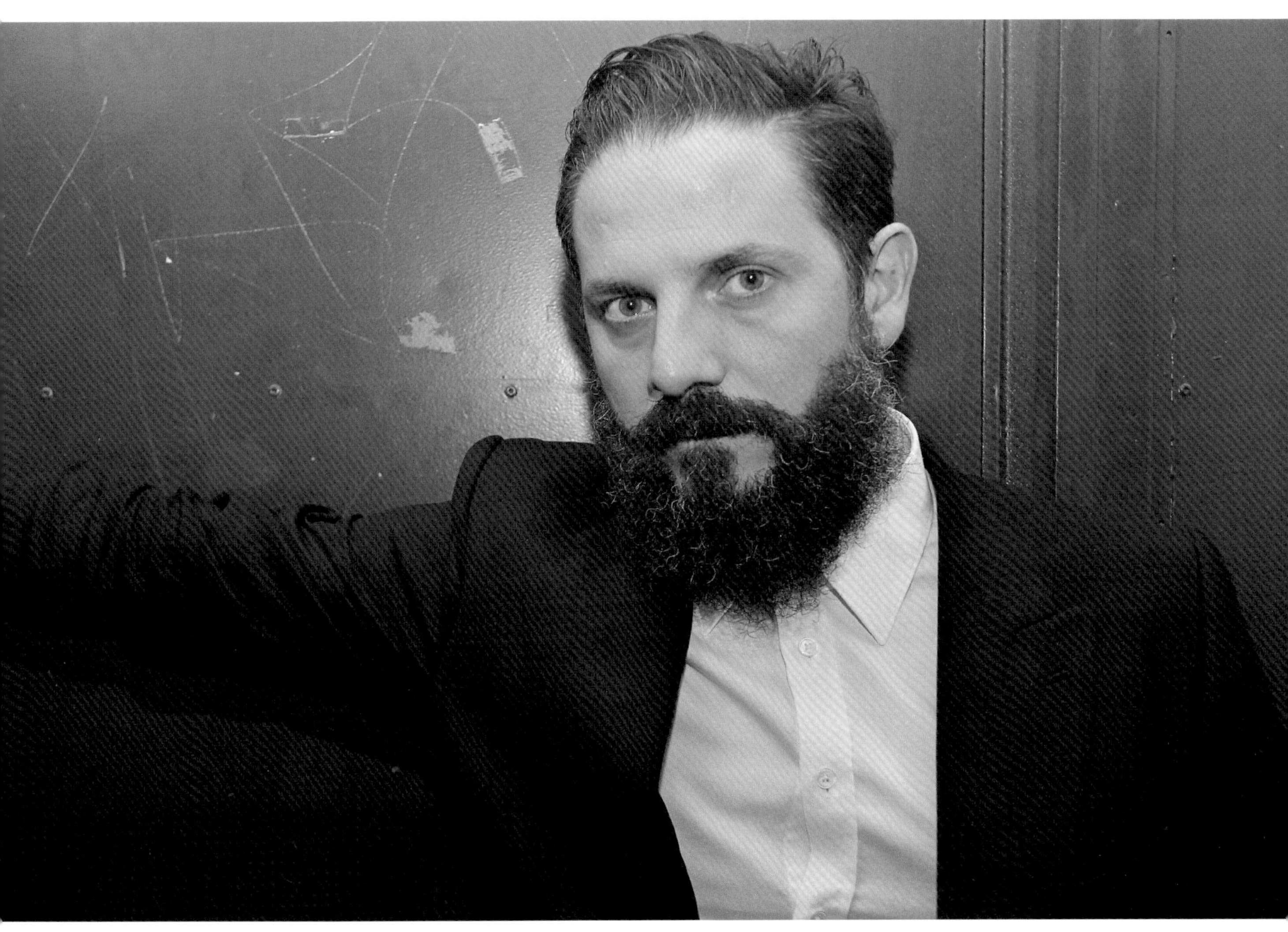

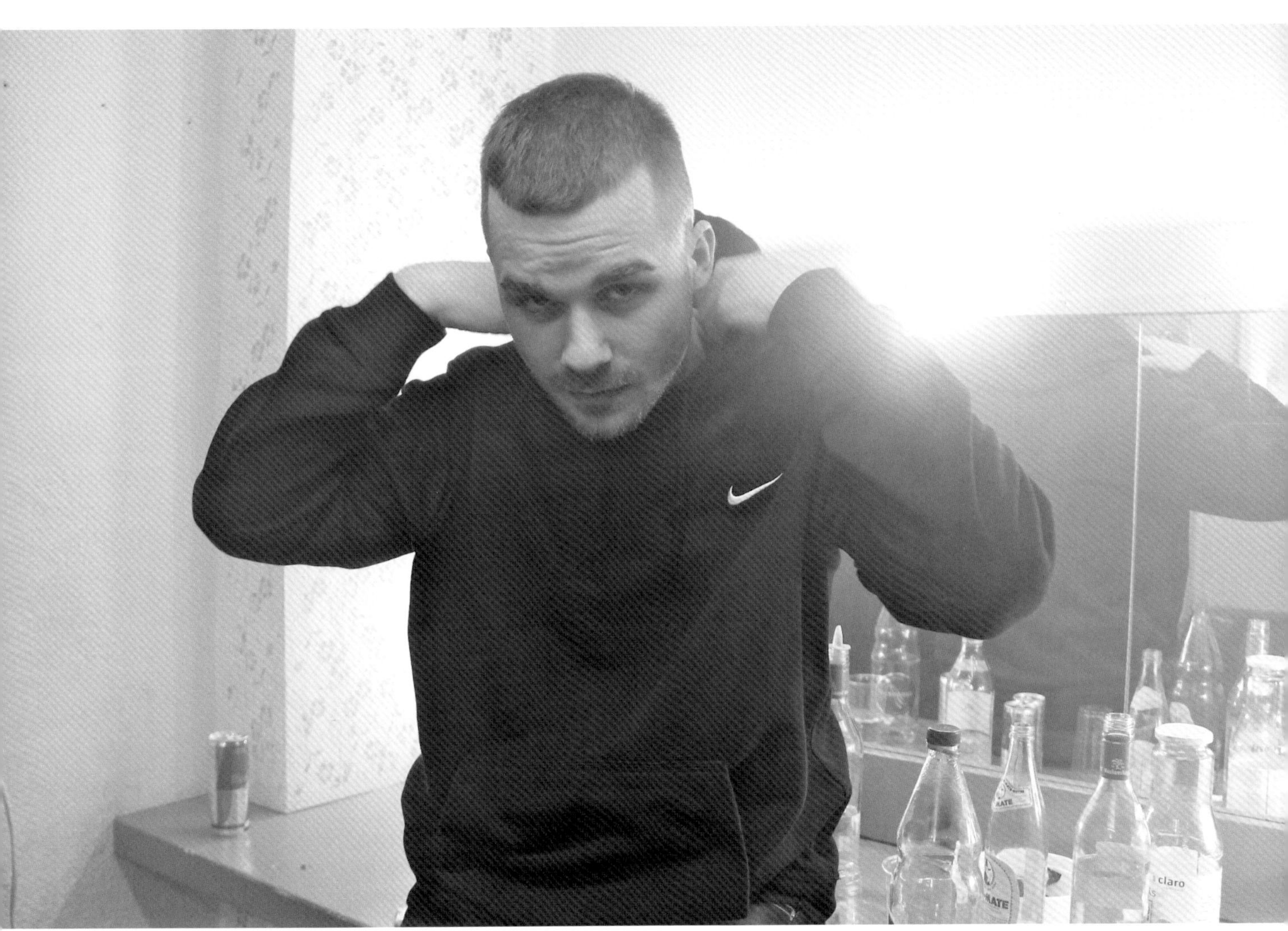
claro

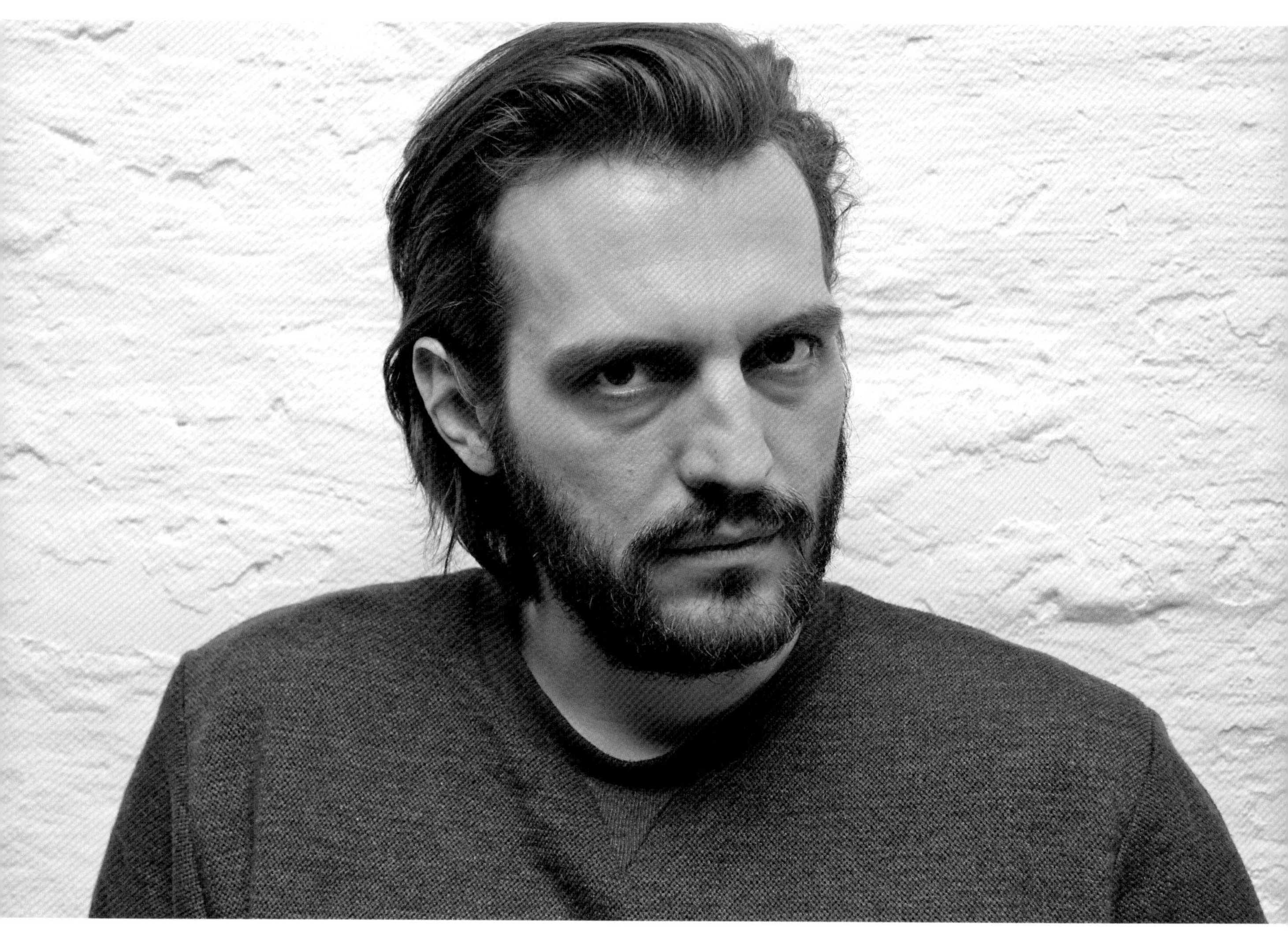

GHEIST

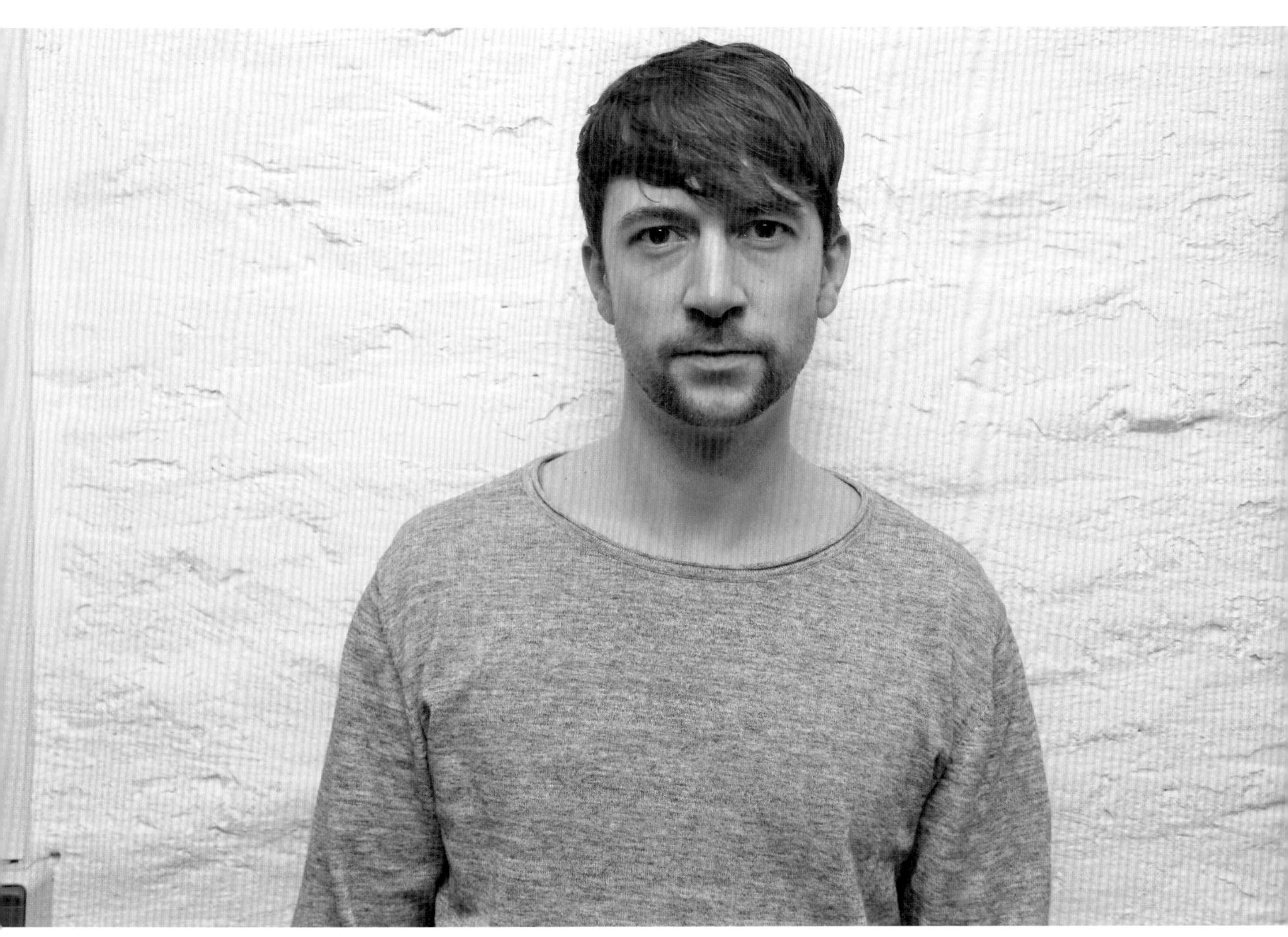

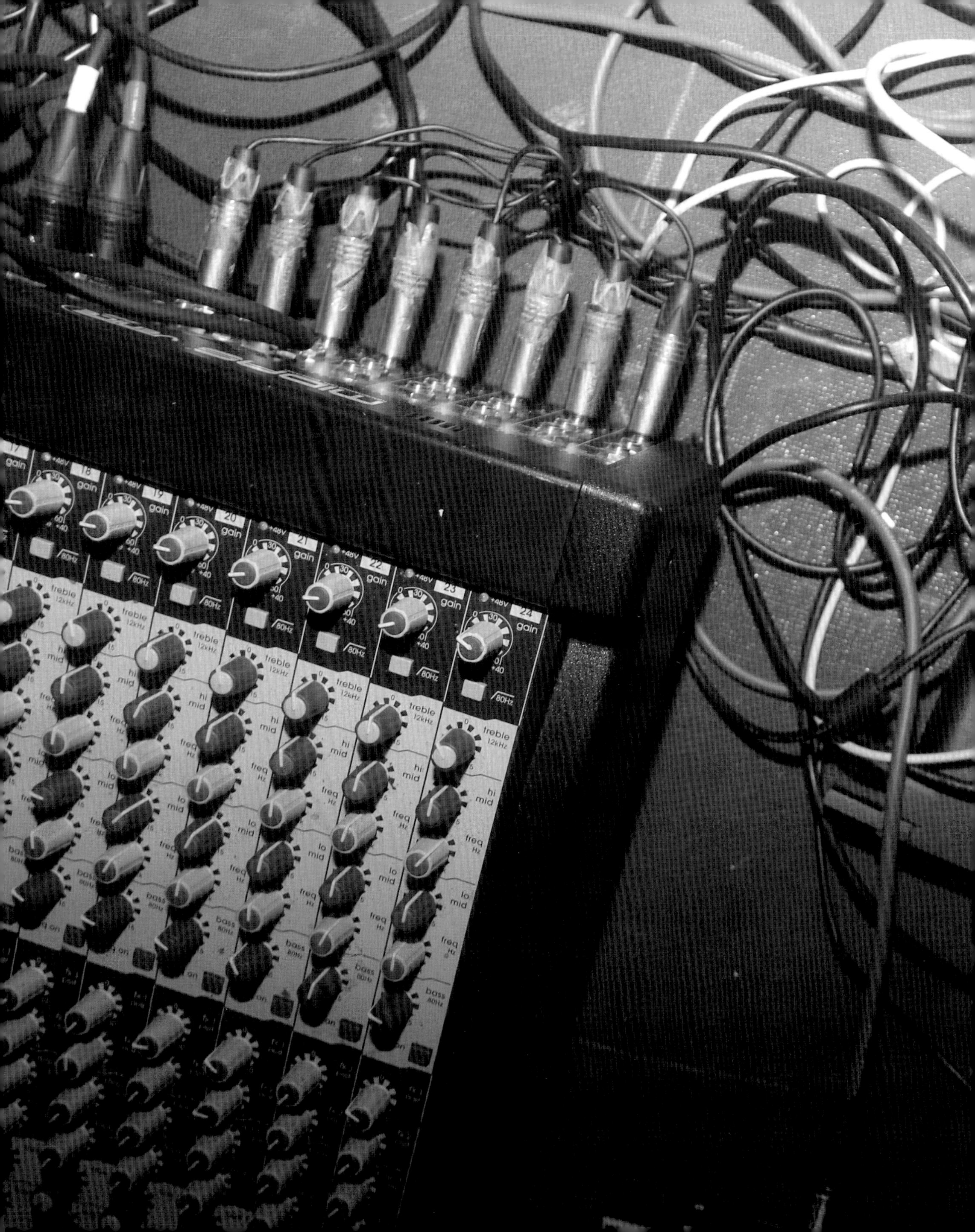

17
18
19
20
21
22
23
24
+48V
gain
80Hz
treble
12kHz
hi
mid
freq
Hz
lo
mid
bass
80Hz
on

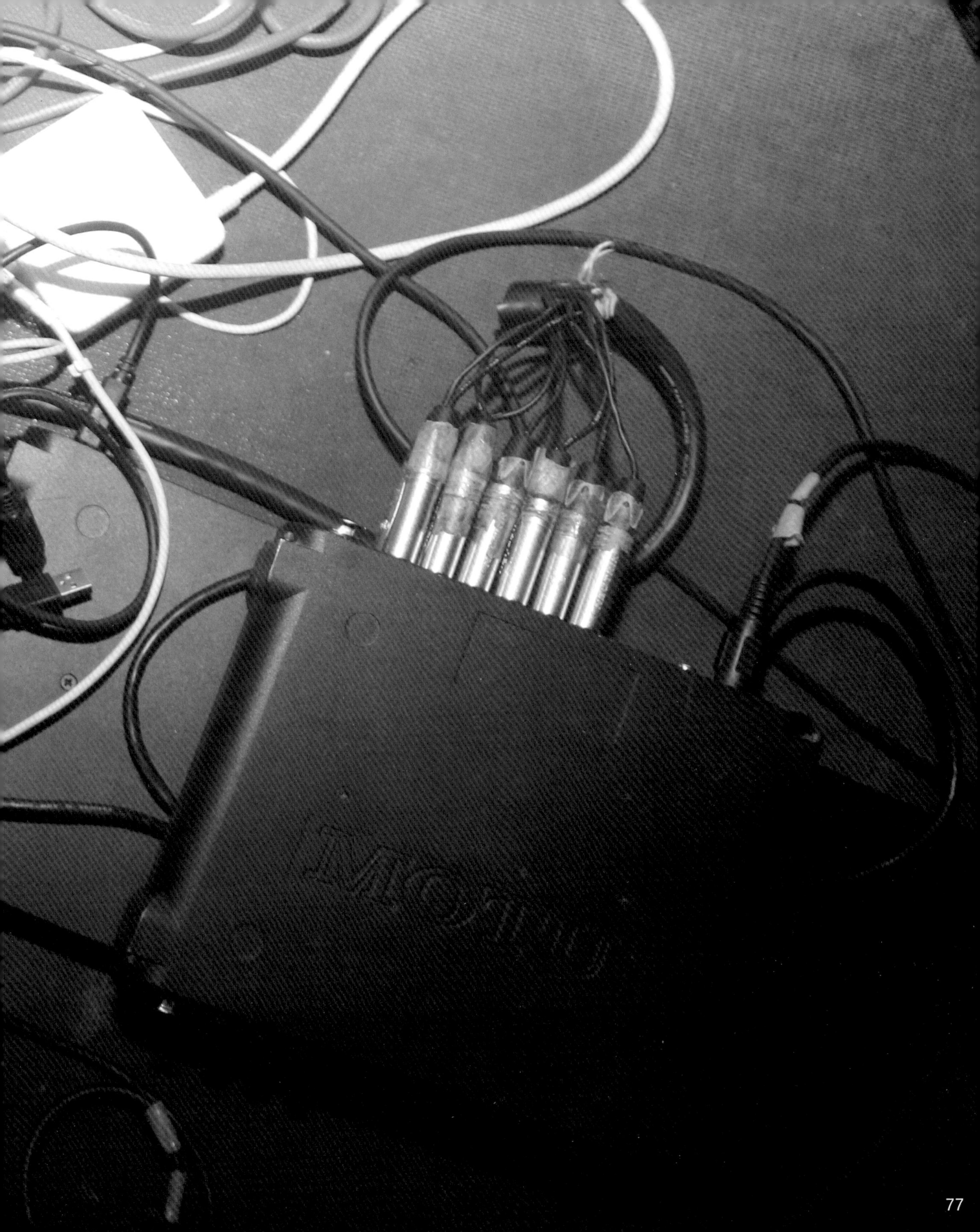

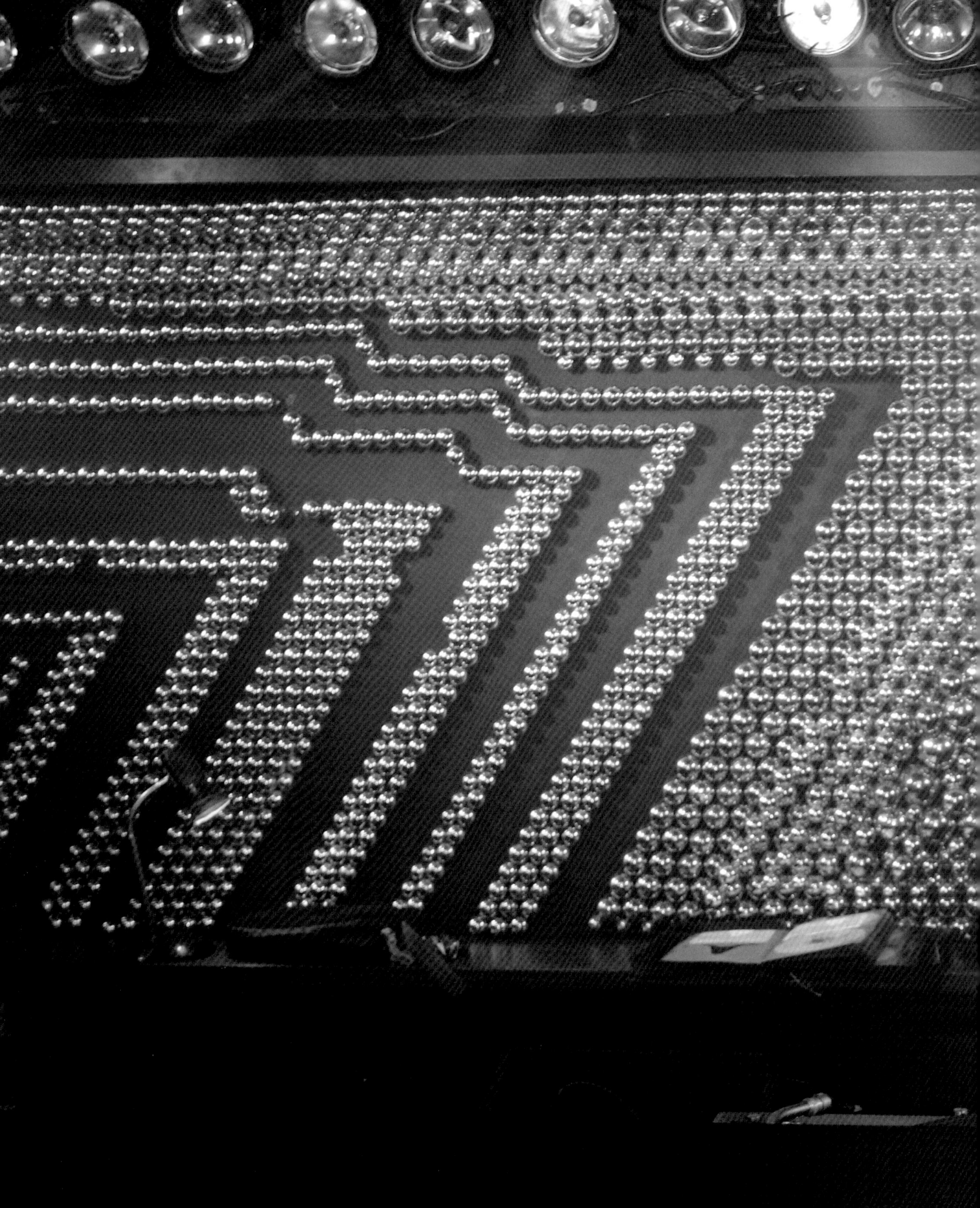

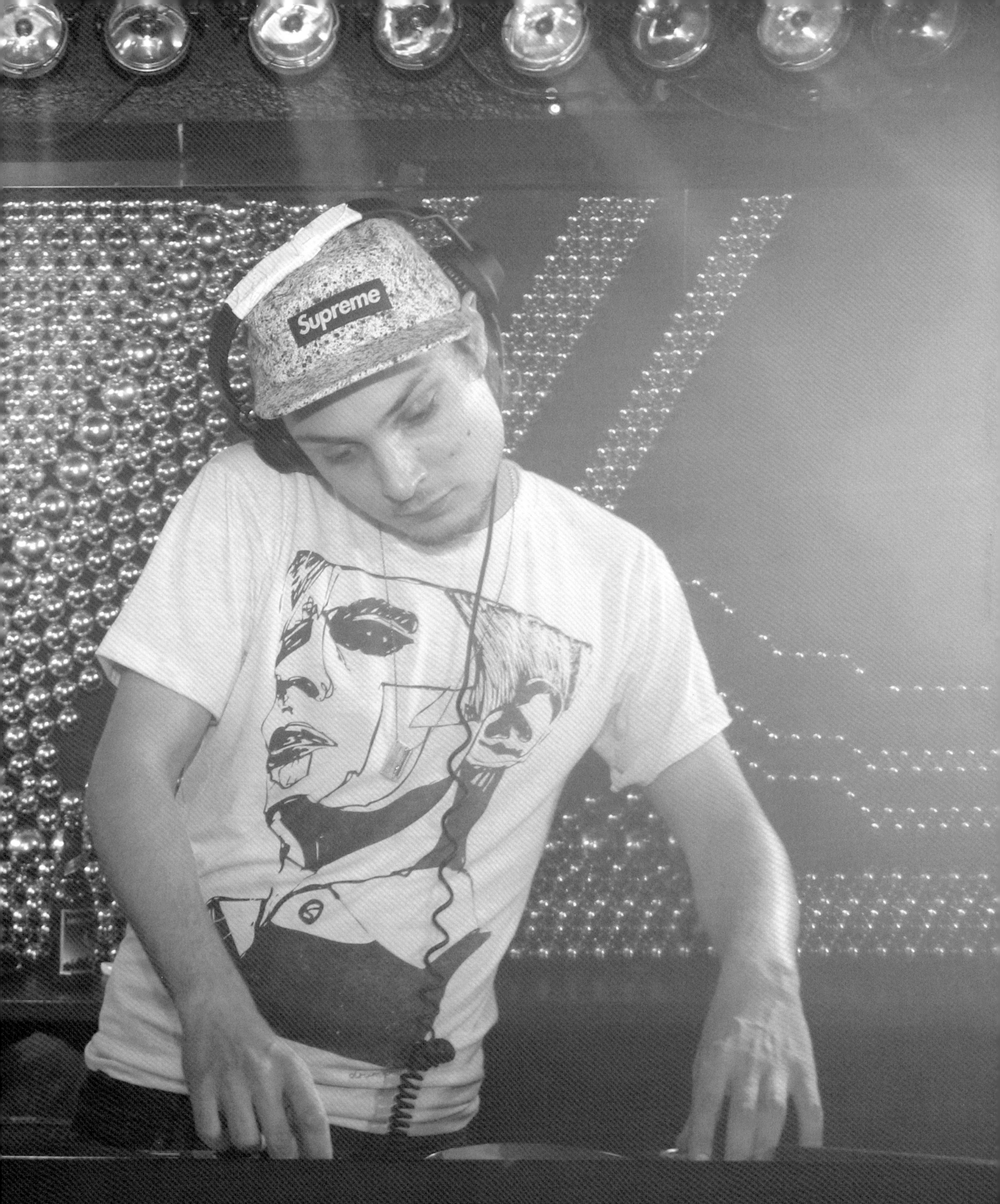
Supreme

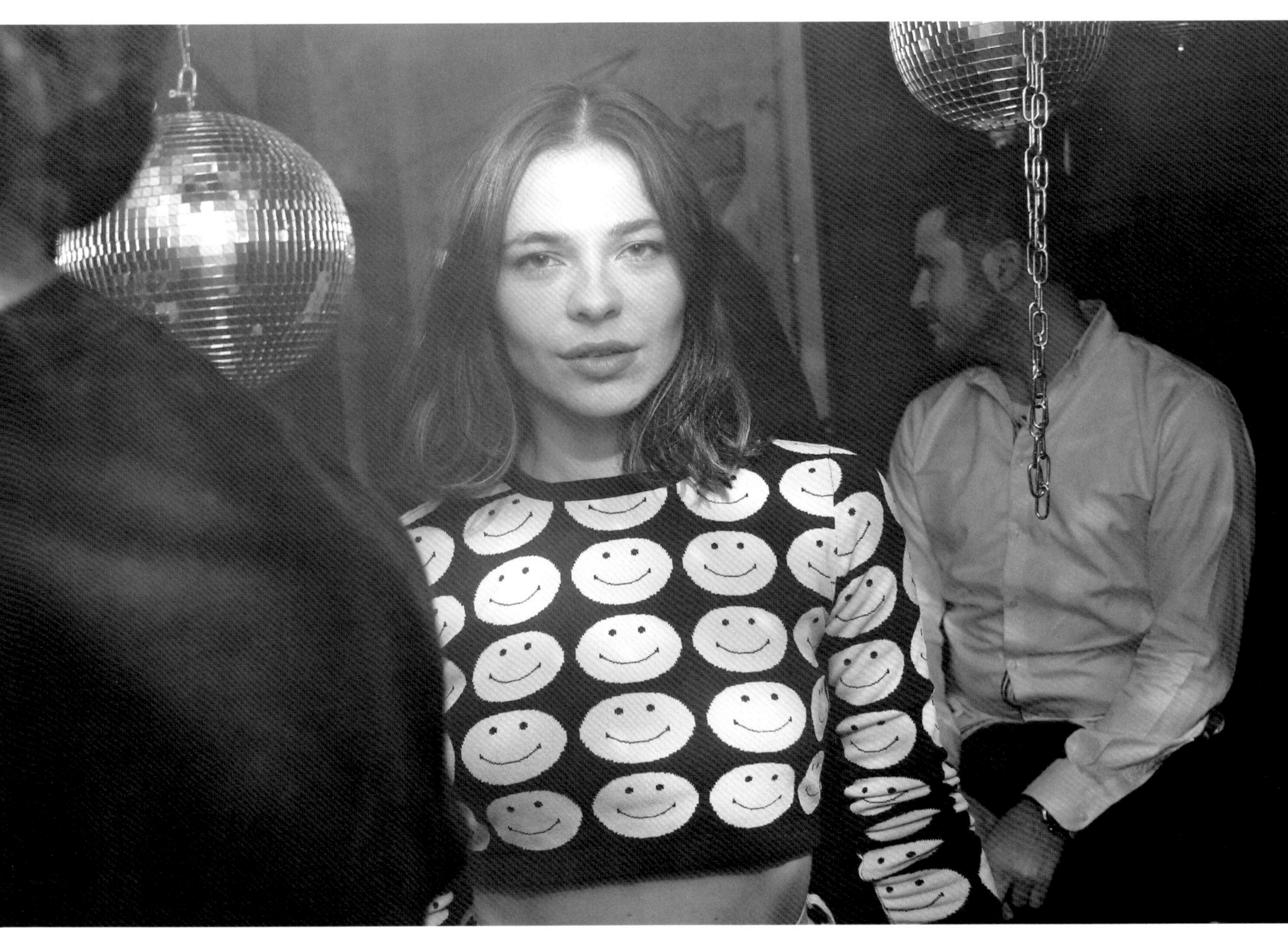

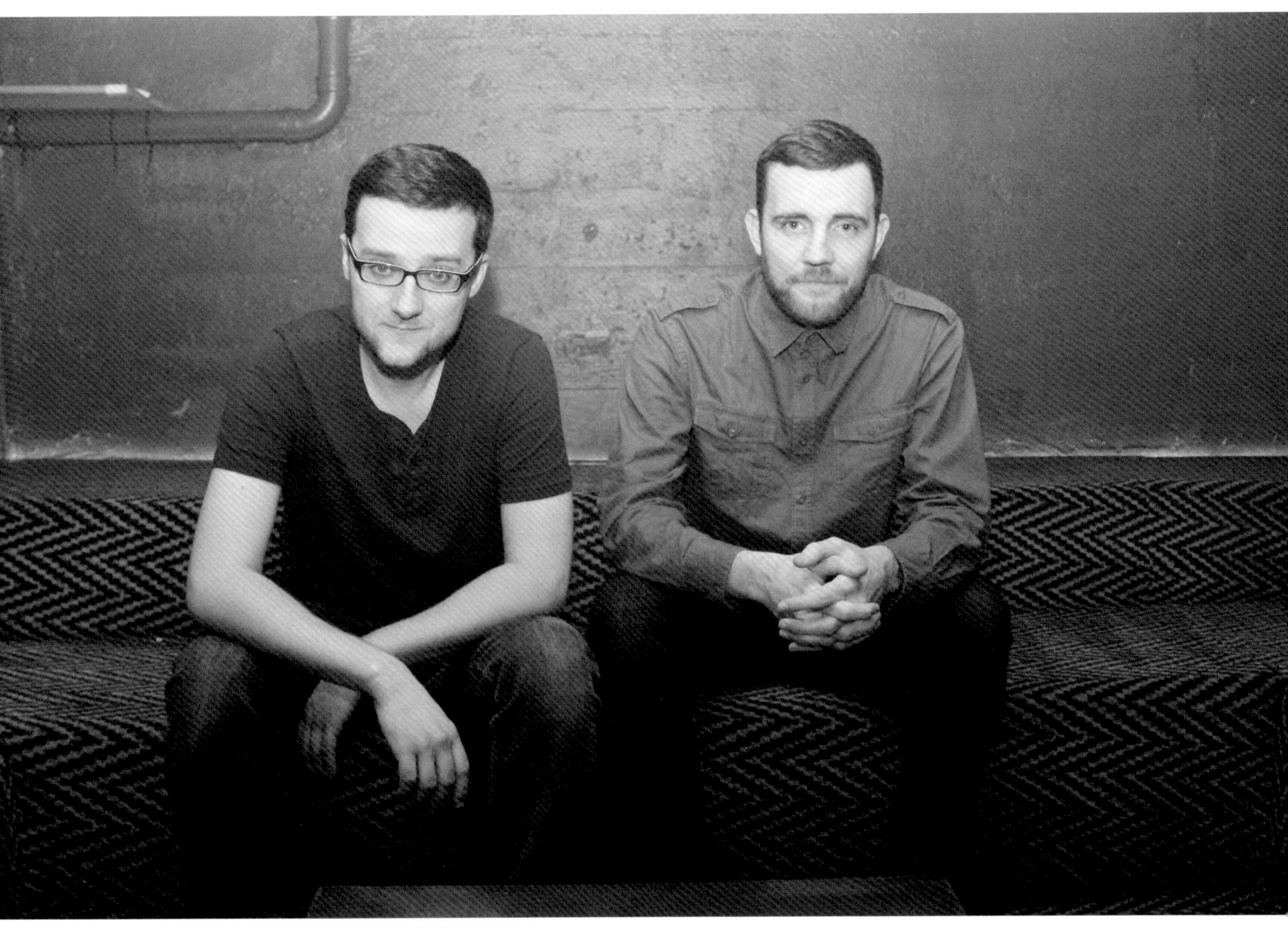

JESPER DAHLBÄCK

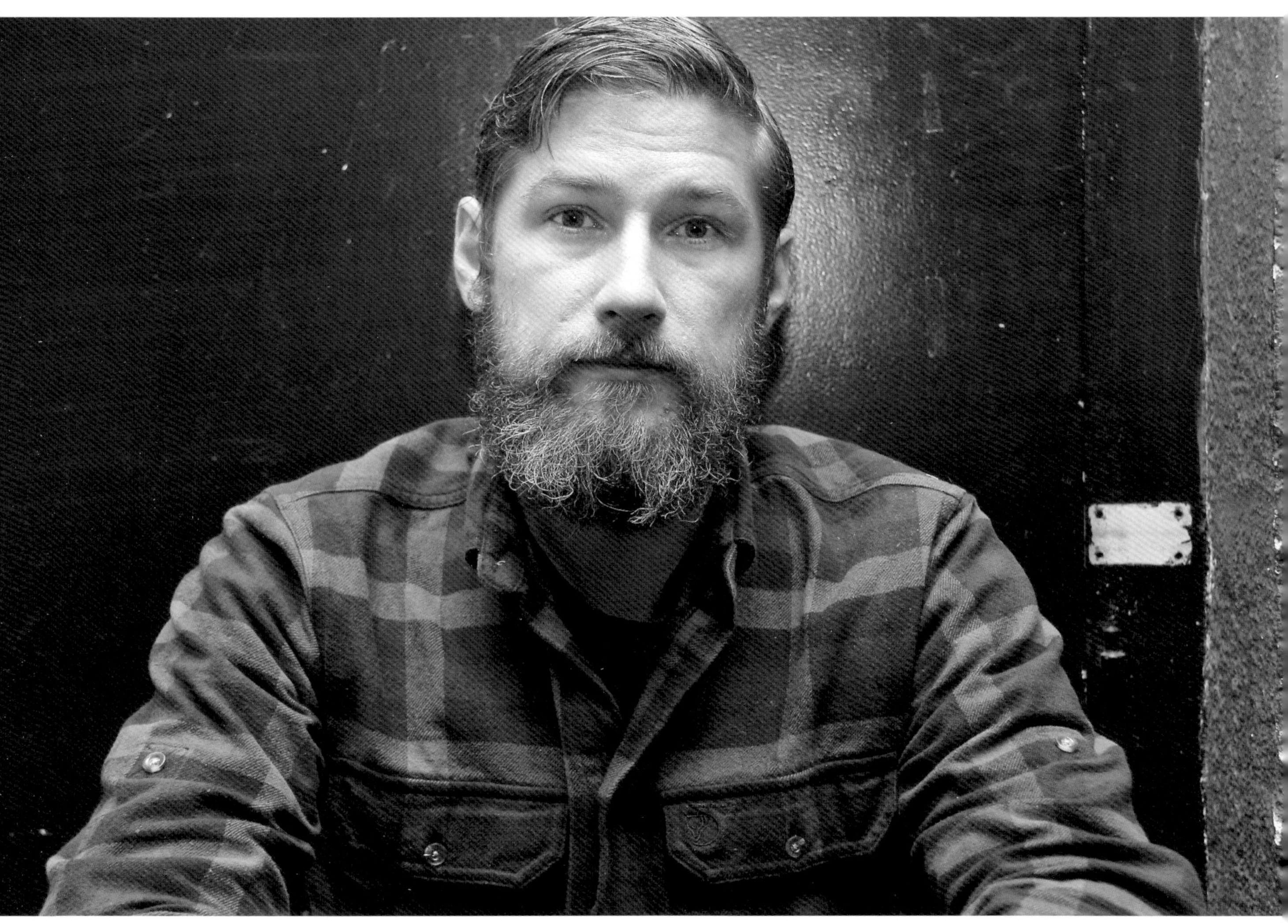

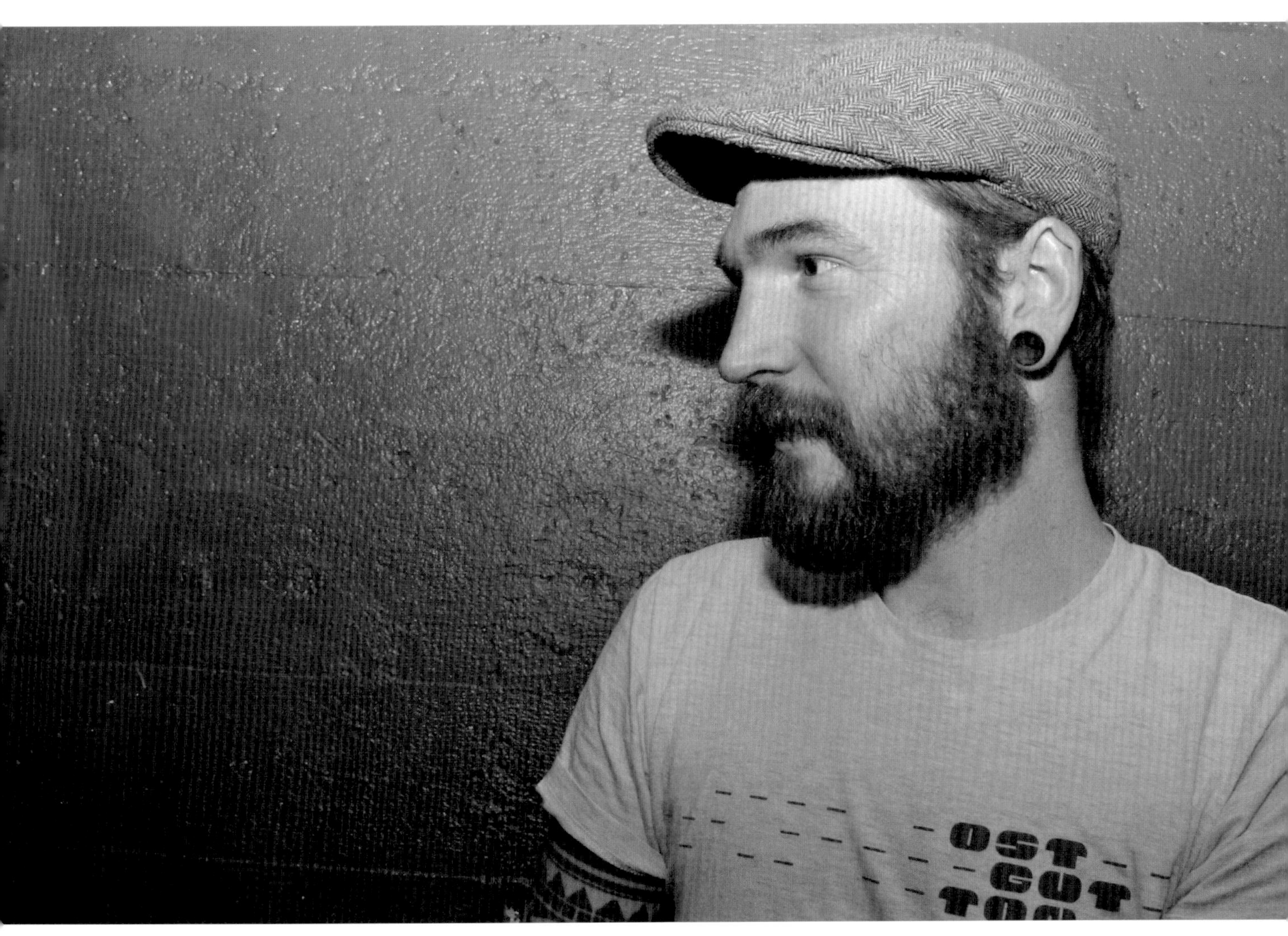
OST
GUT

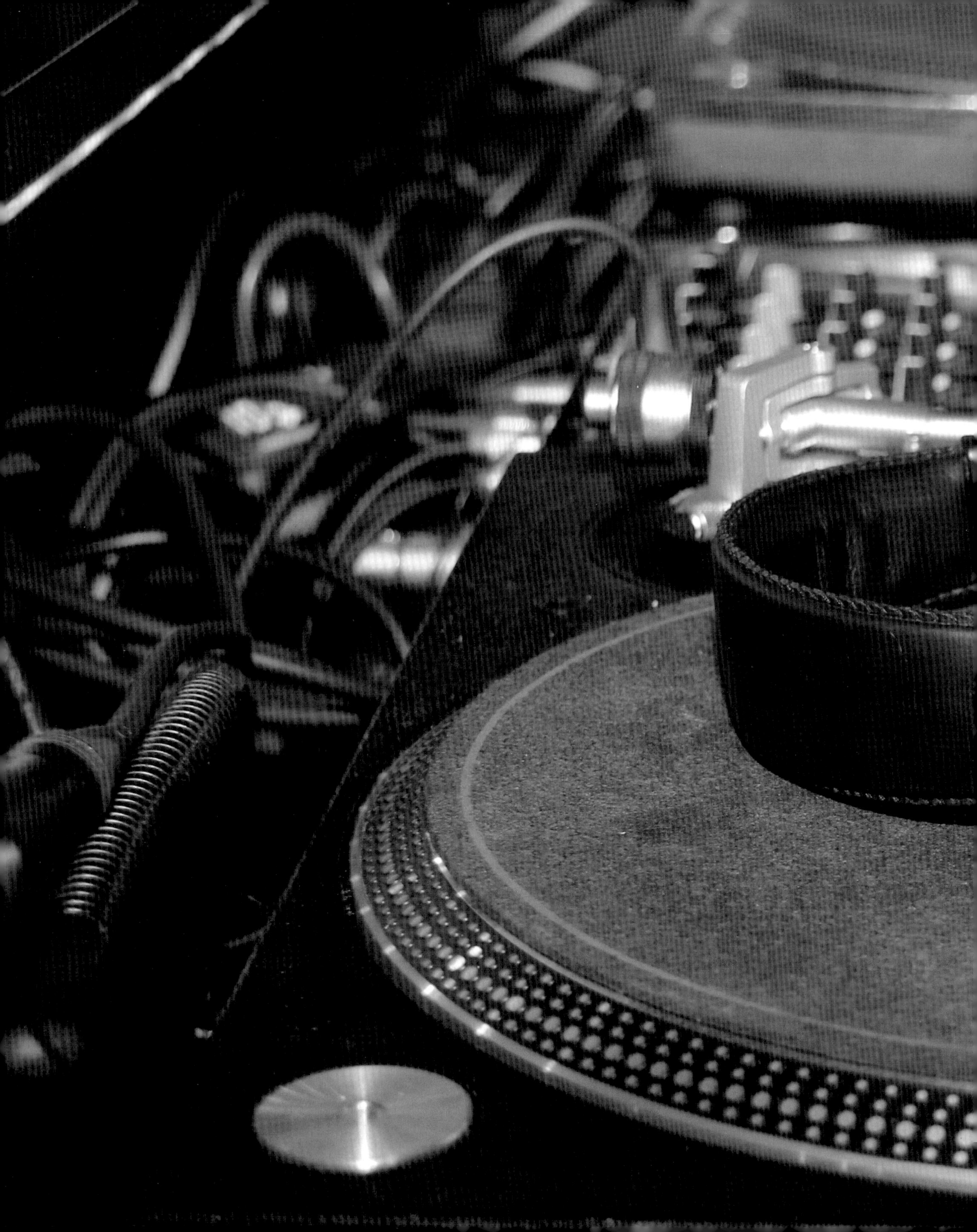

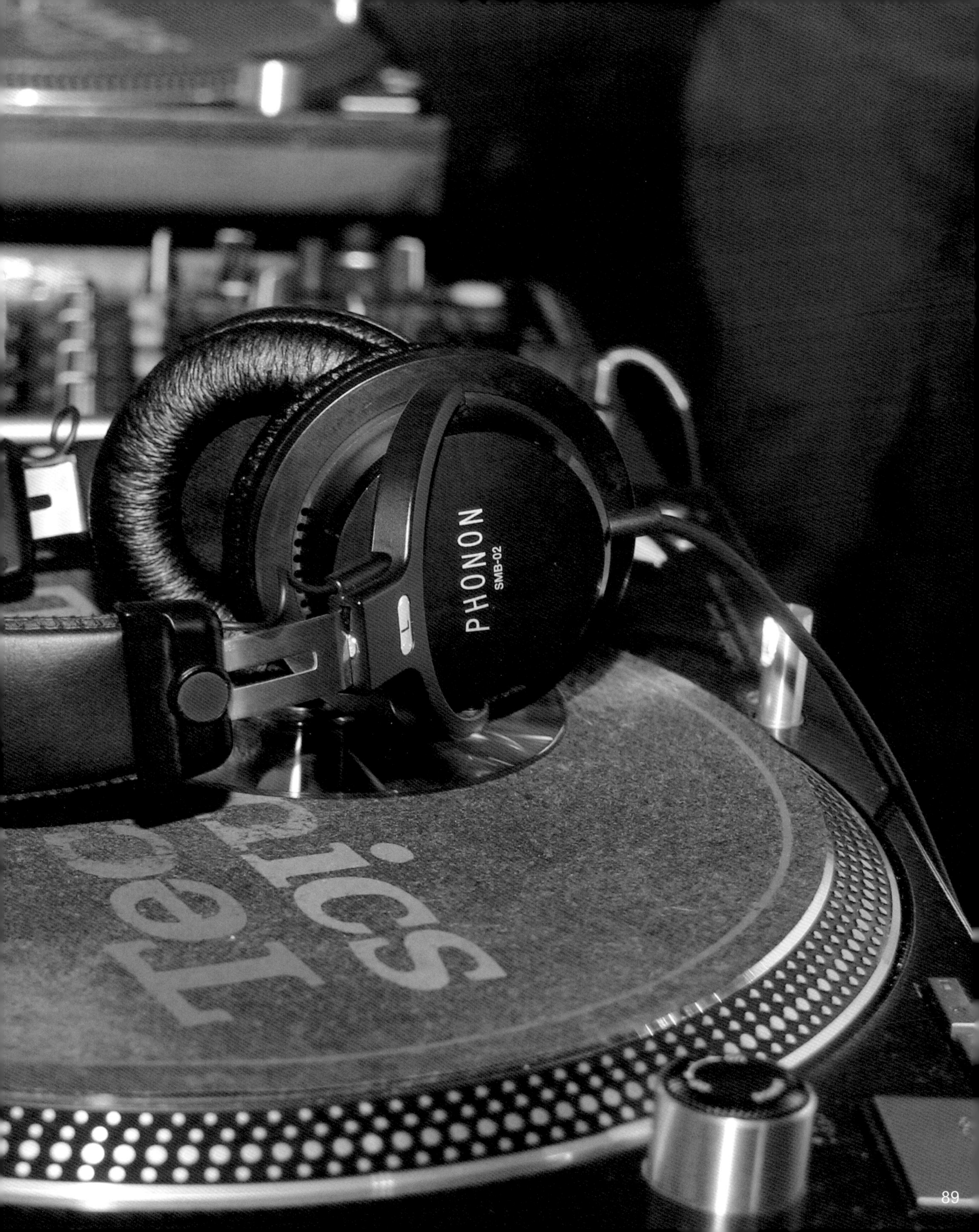

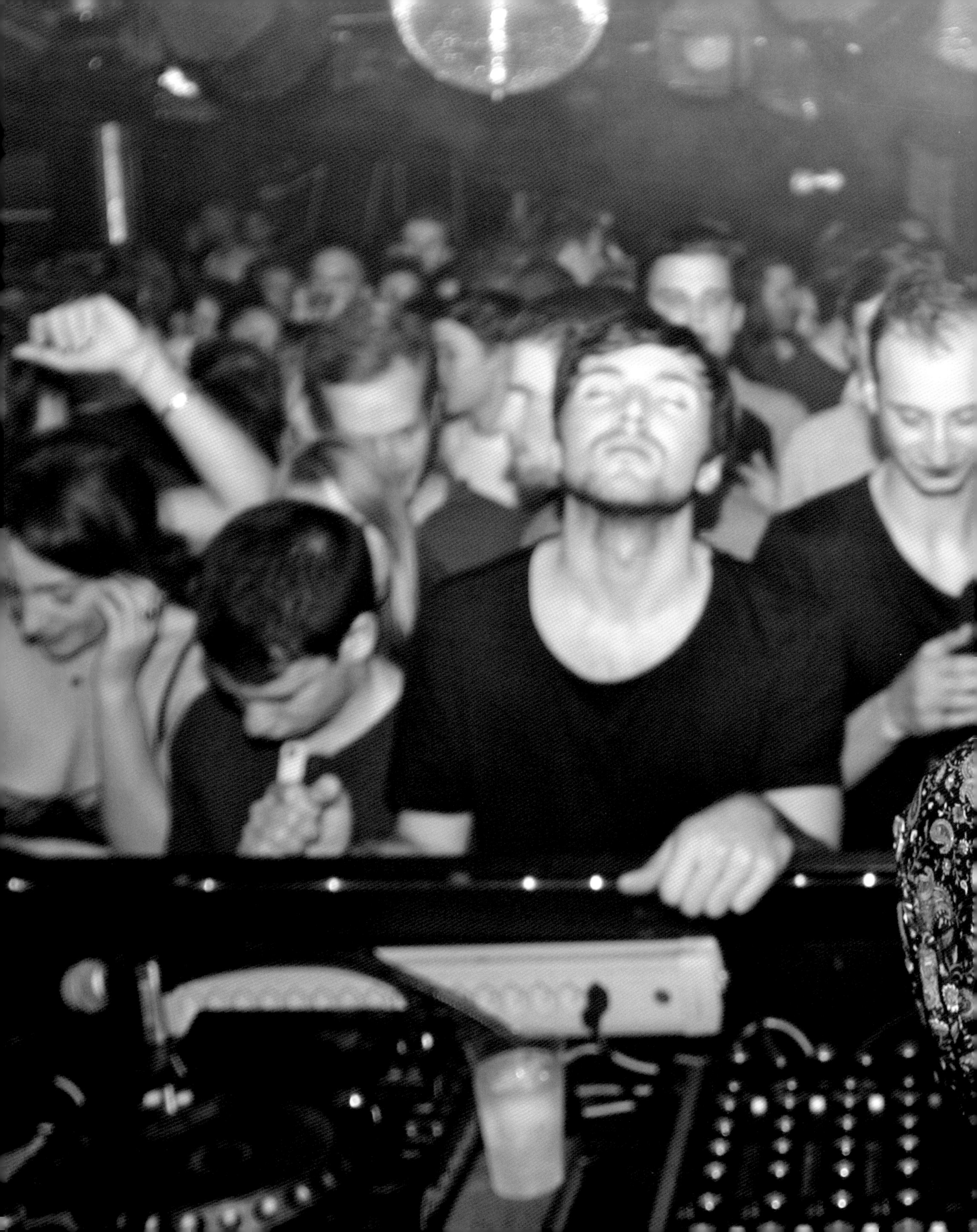

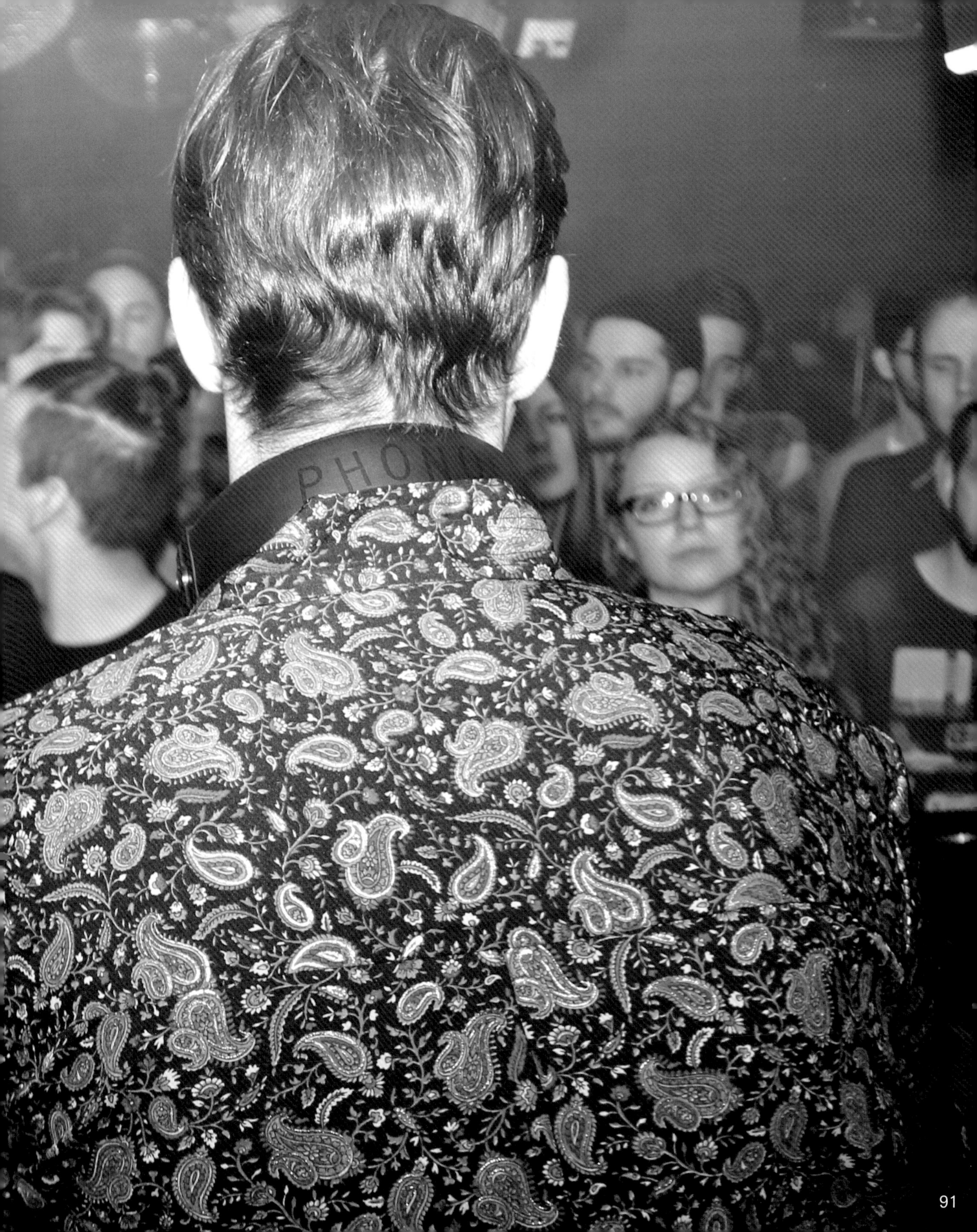
PHO

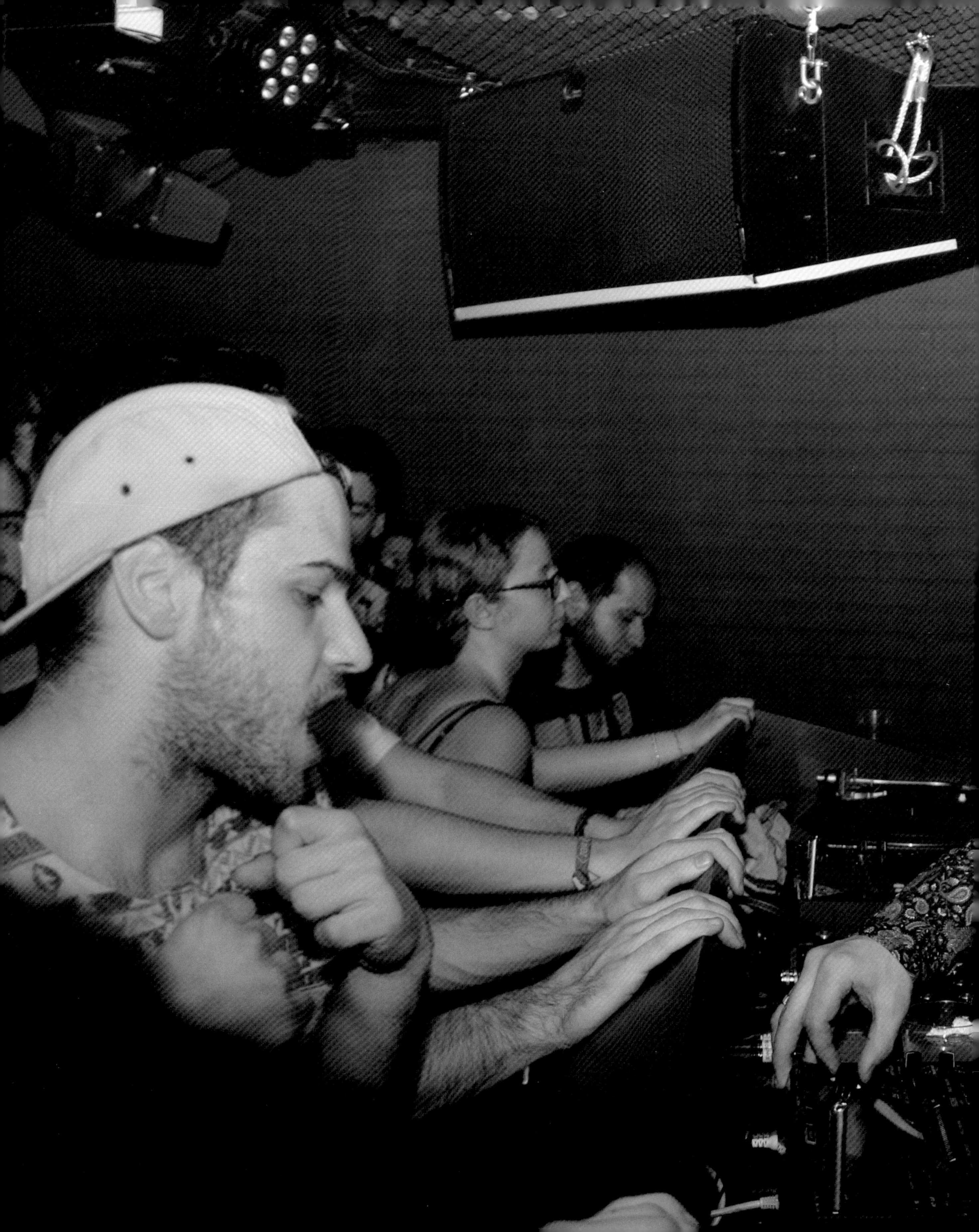

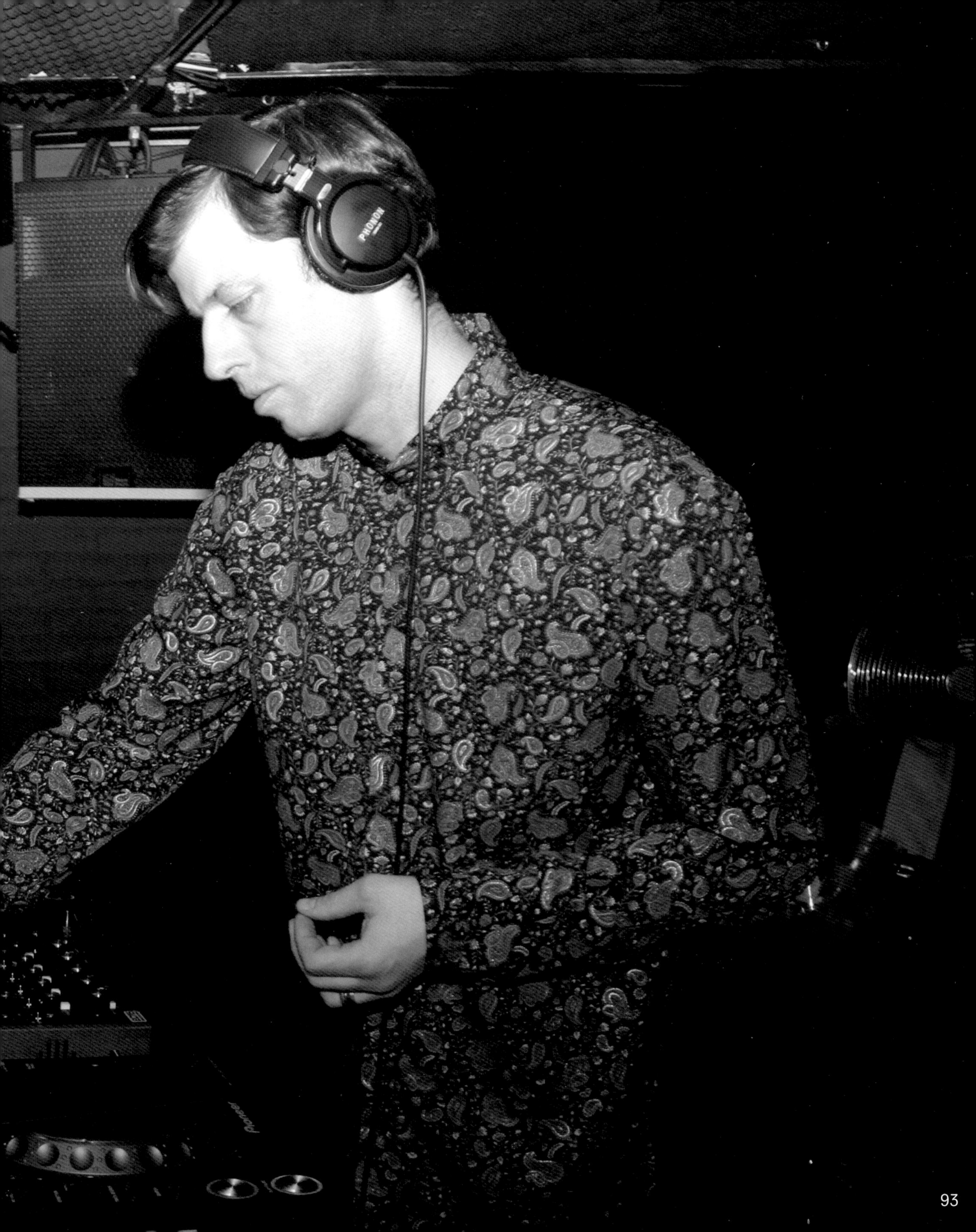
PHONON

TELEPHONES

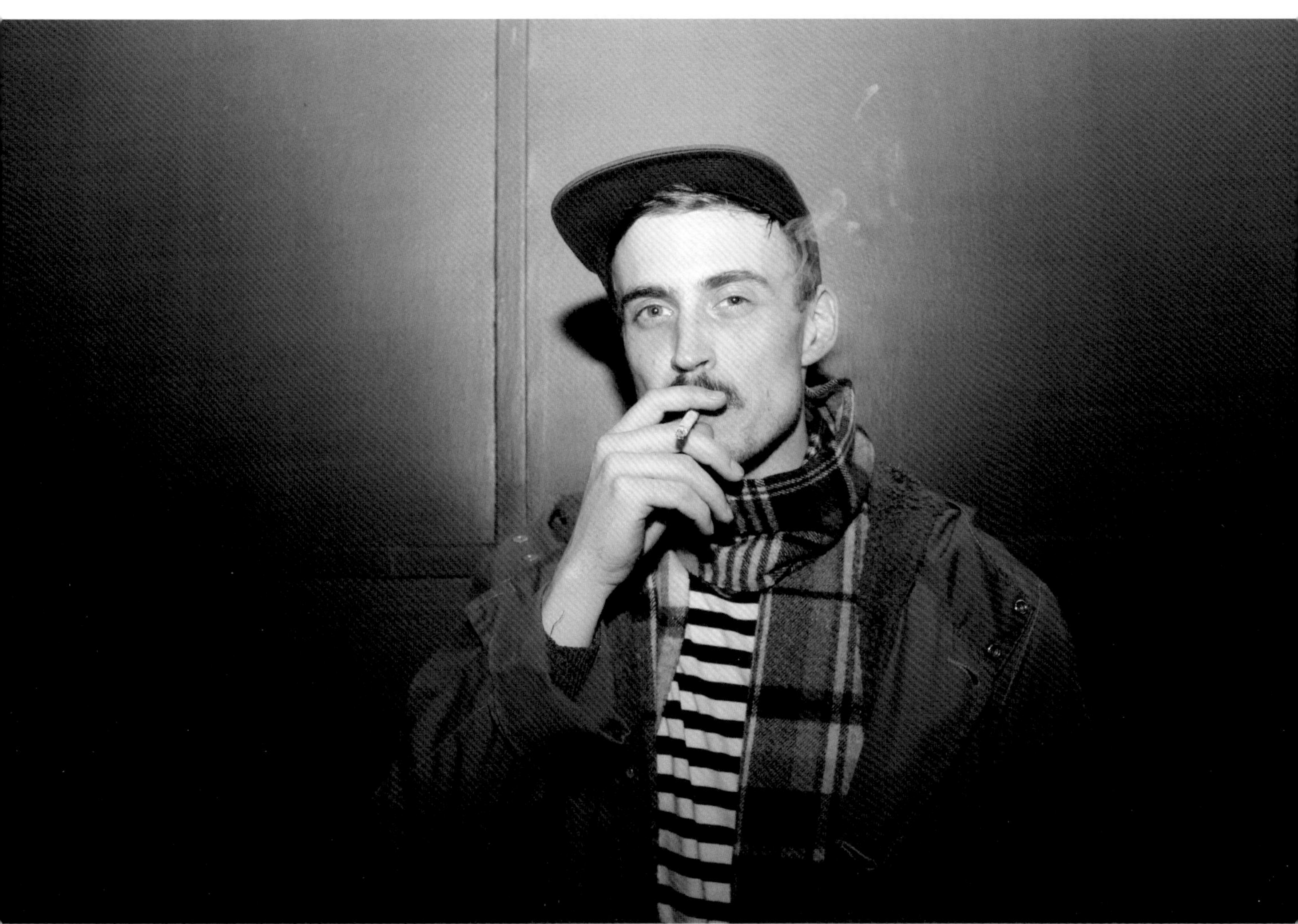

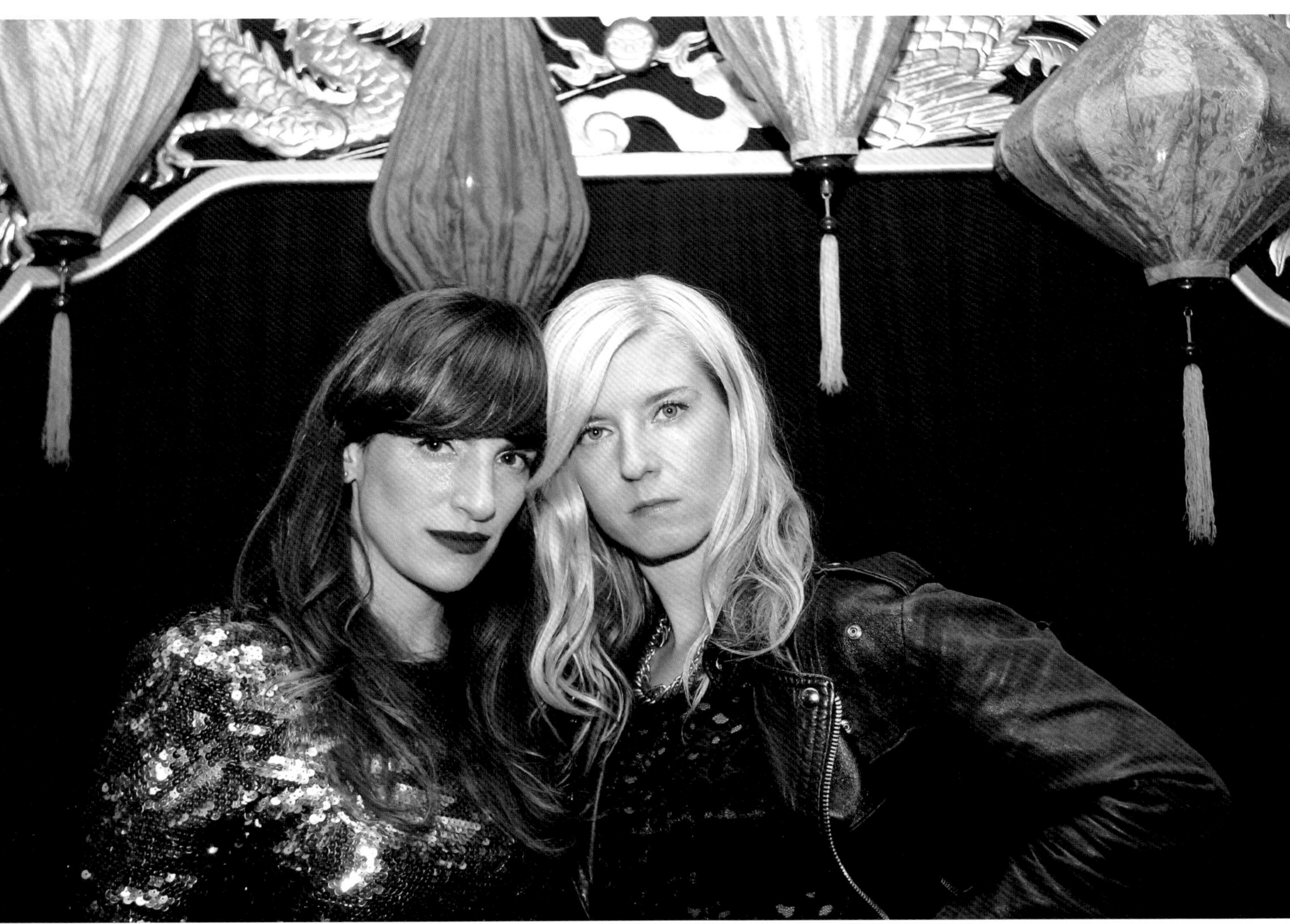

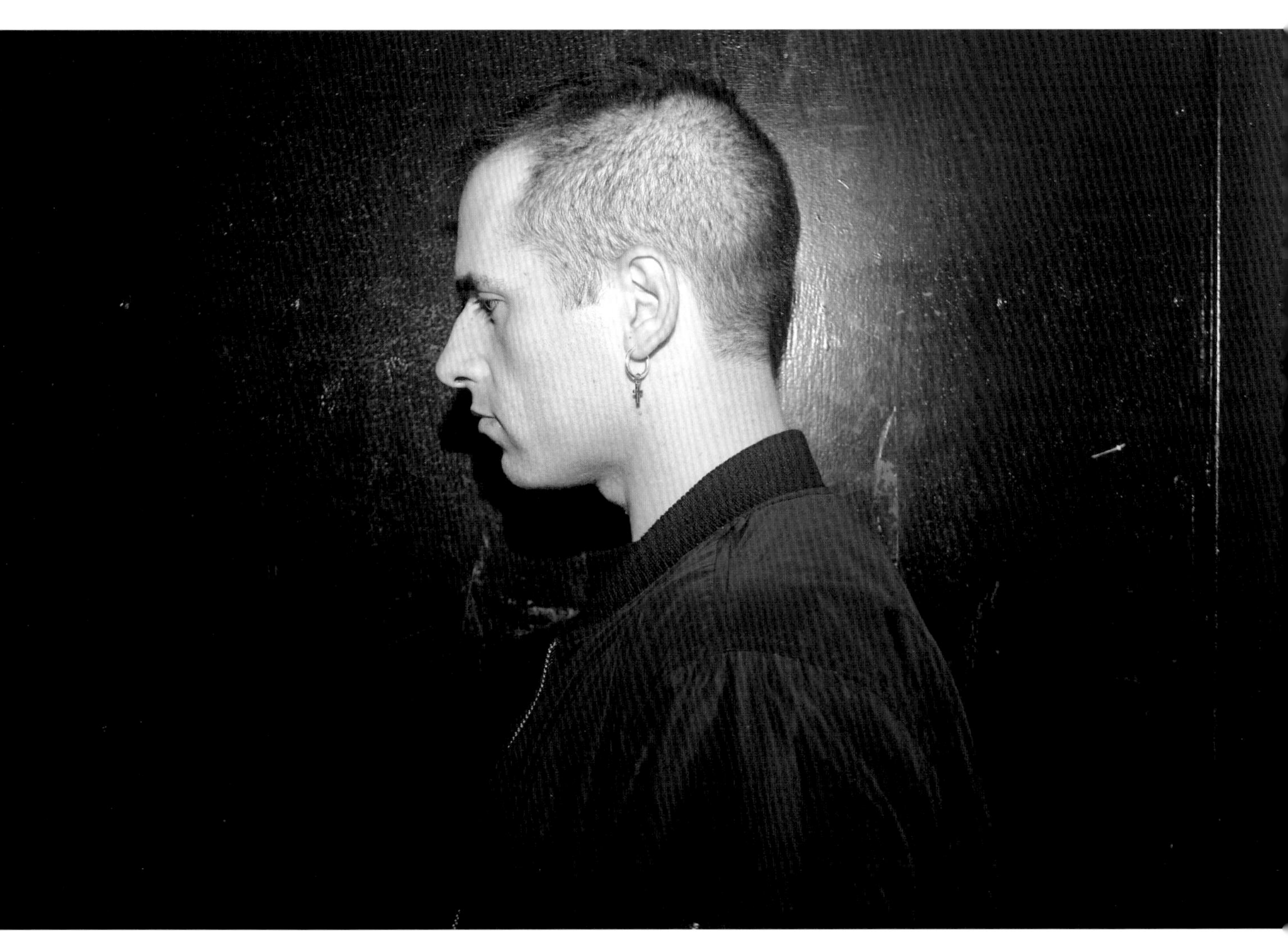

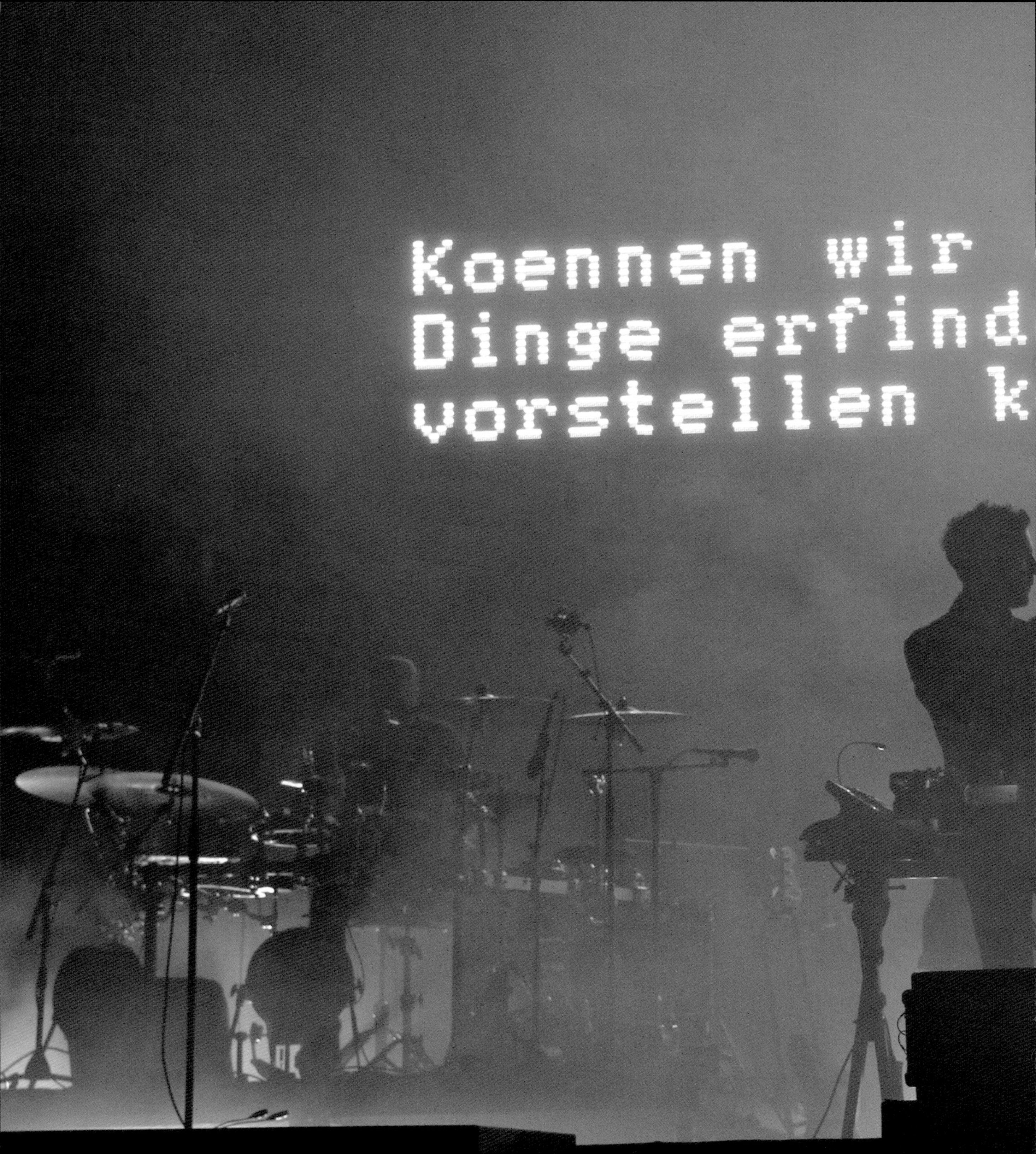

Koennen wir
Dinge erfind
vorstellen k

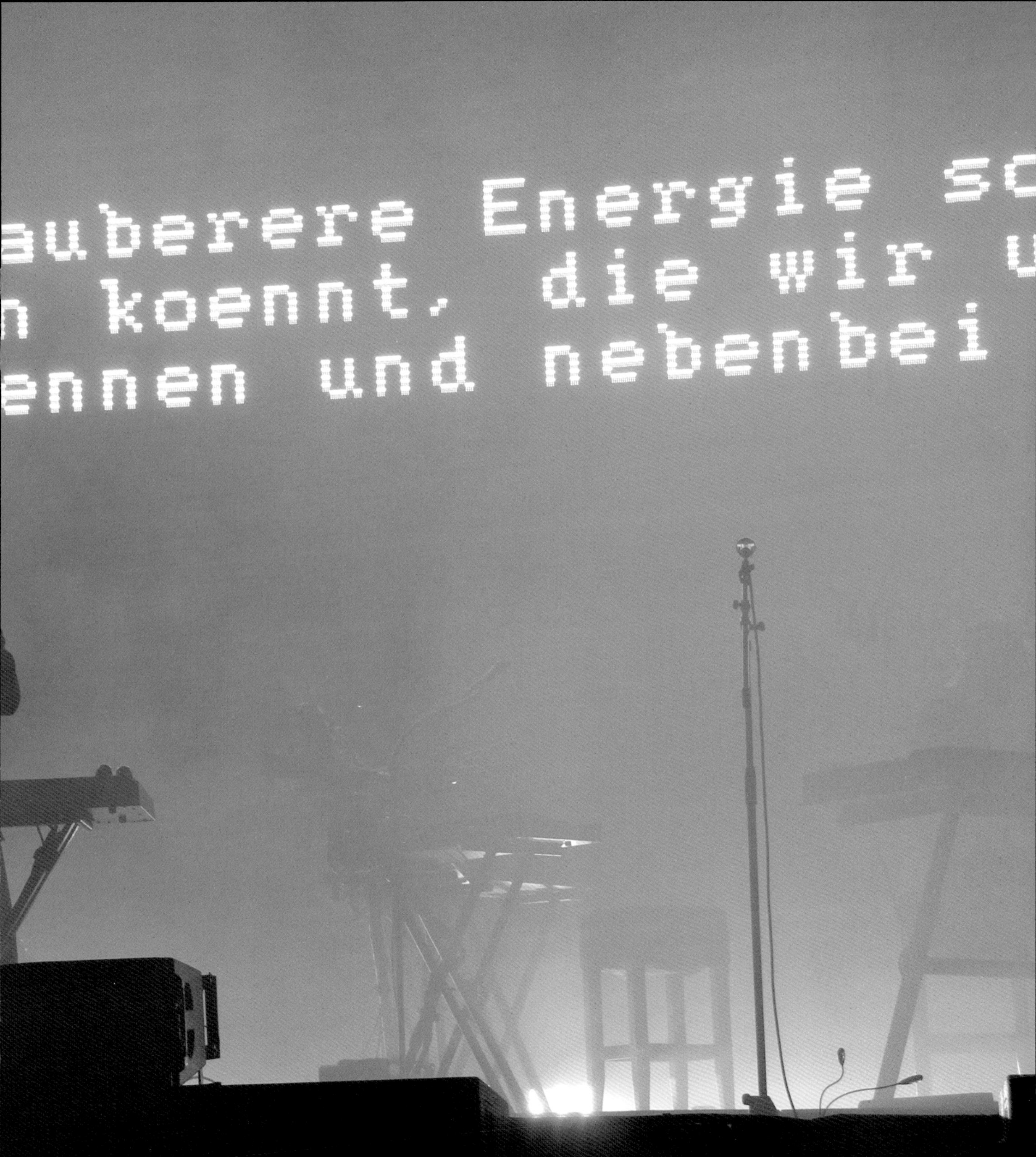

auberere Energie sc
n koennt, die wir u
ennen und nebenbei

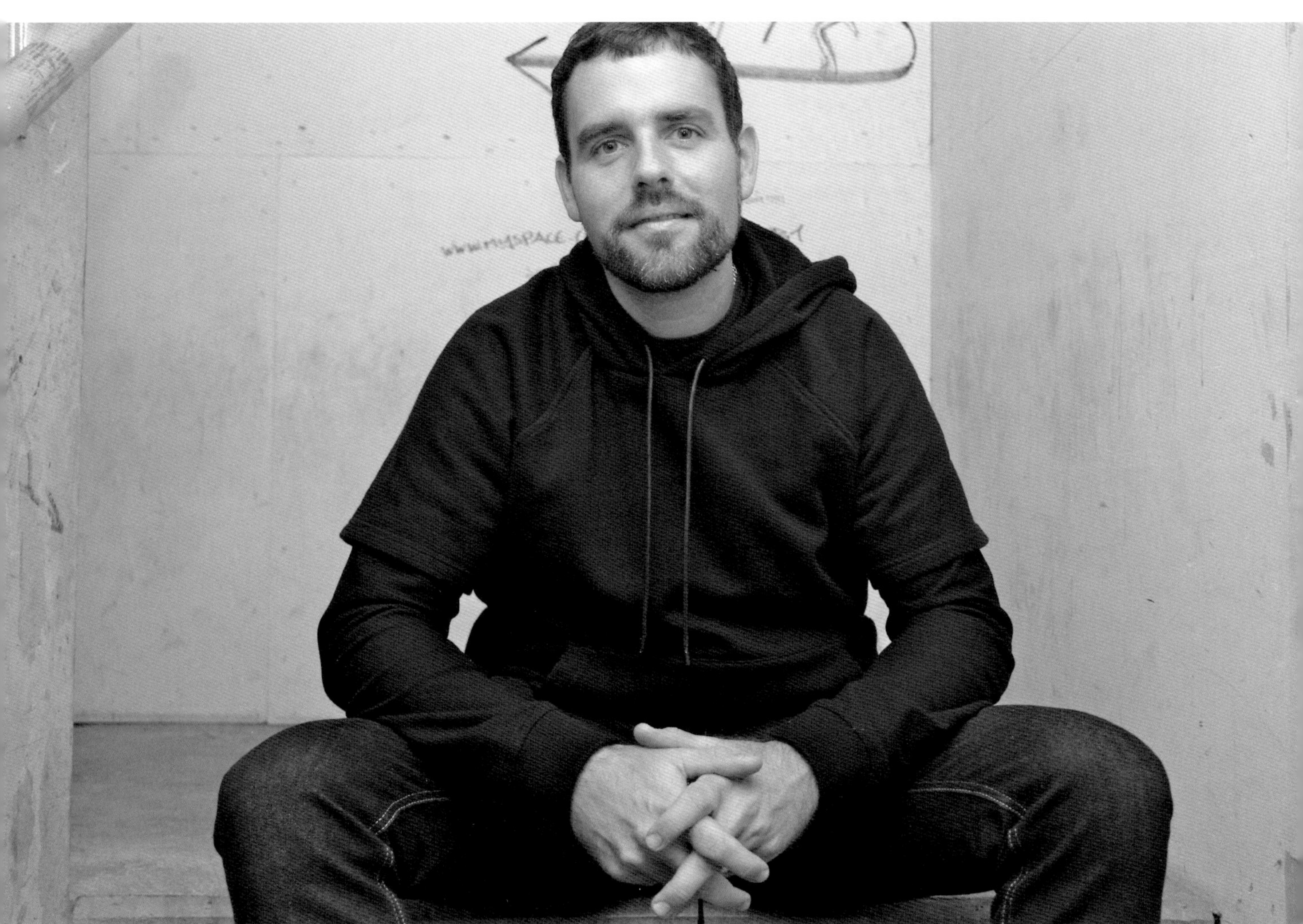

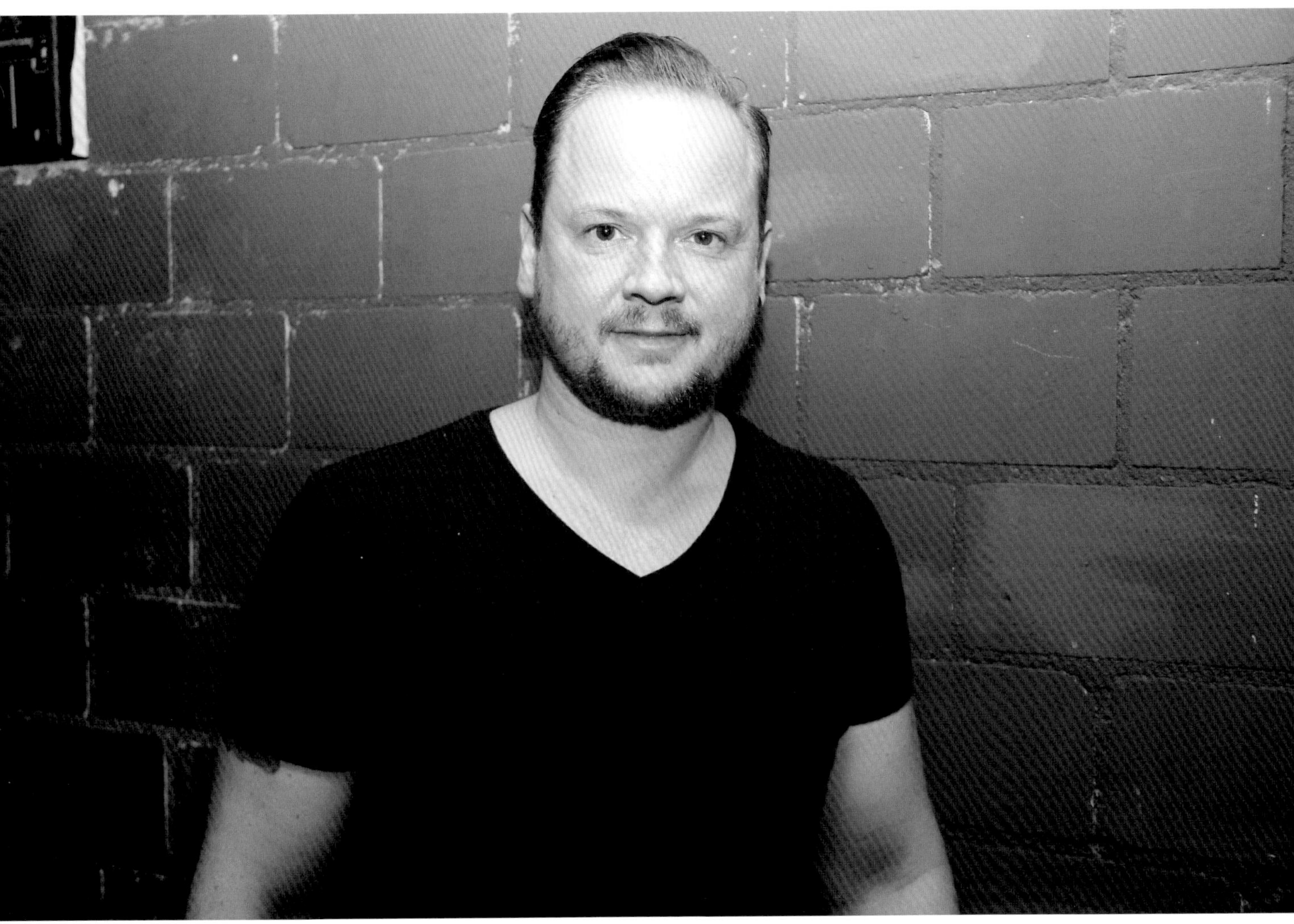

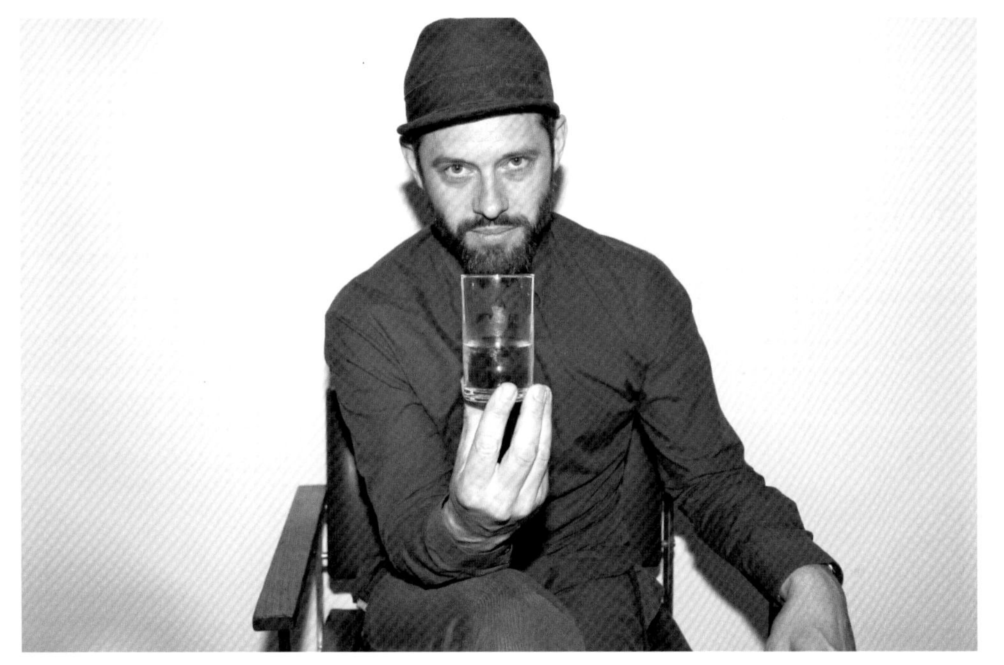

BON HOMME (WHOMADEWHO)

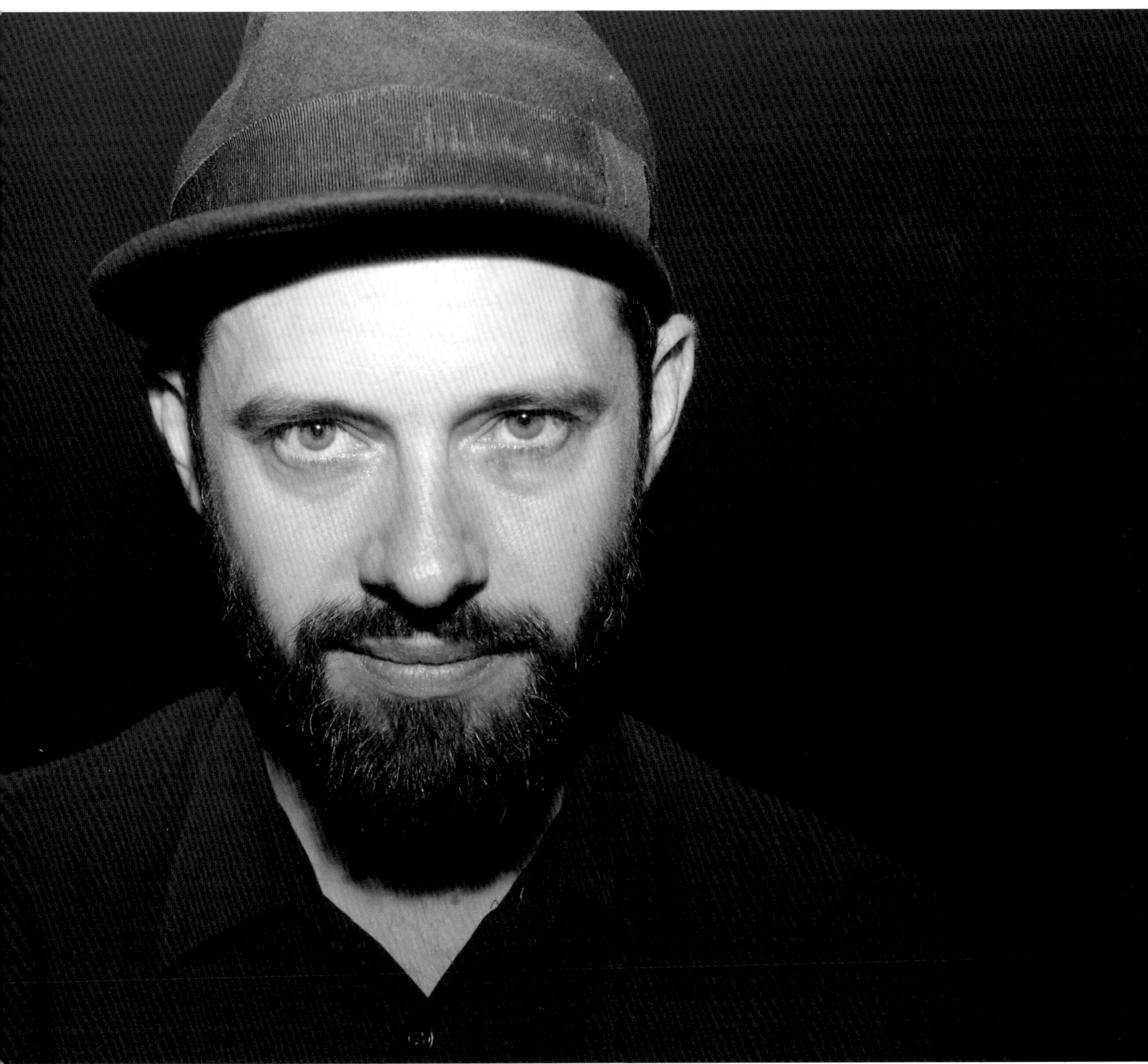

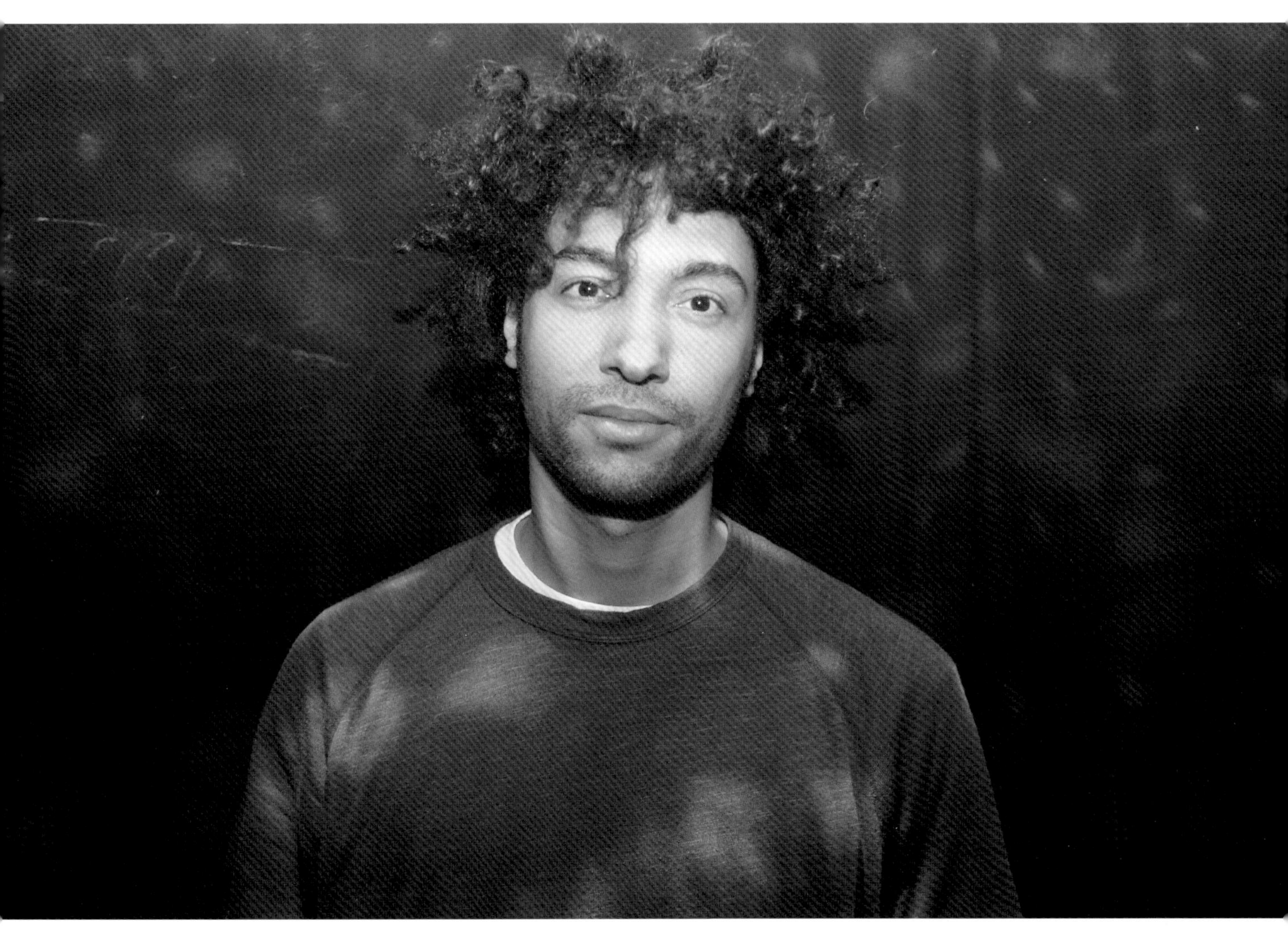

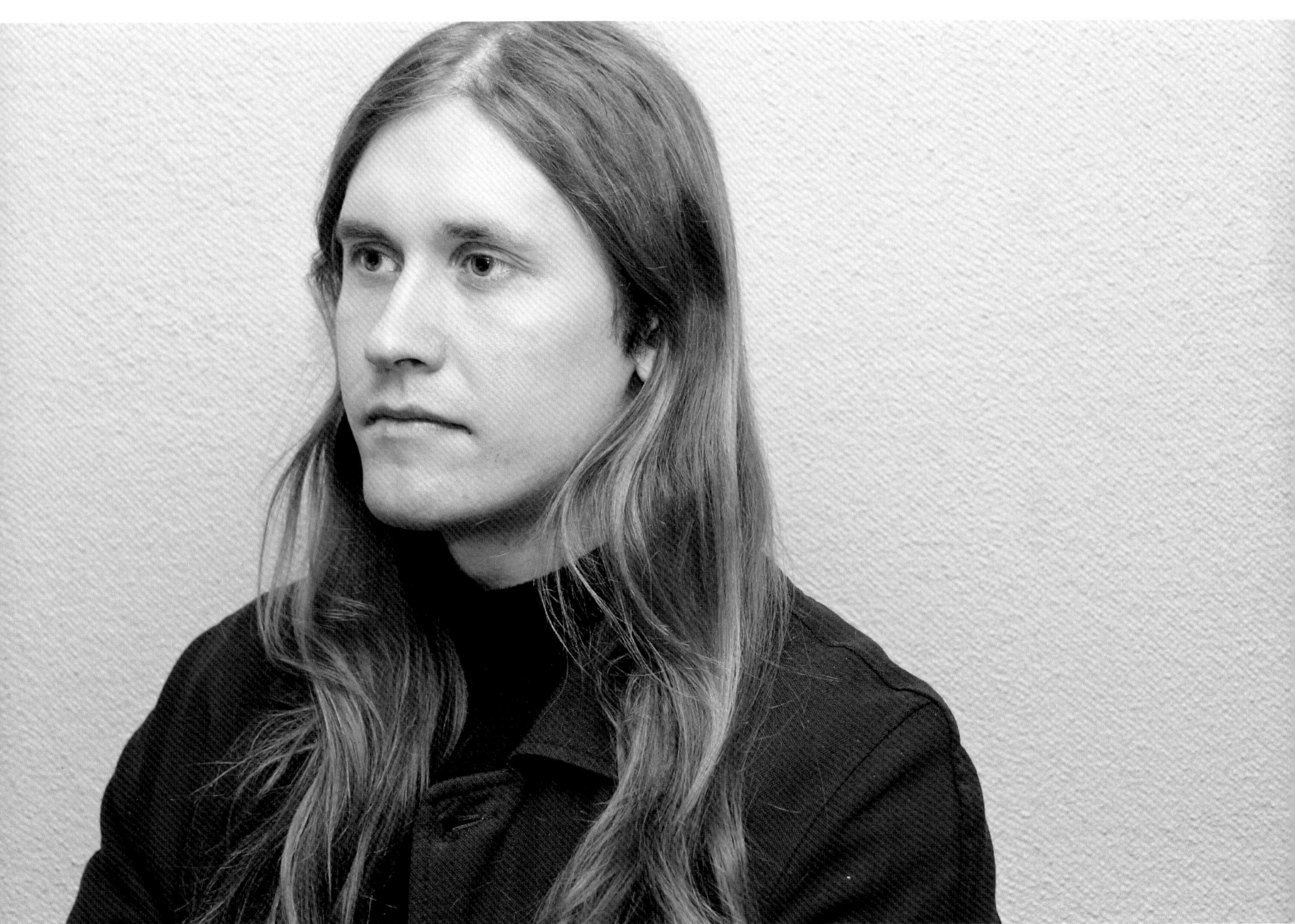

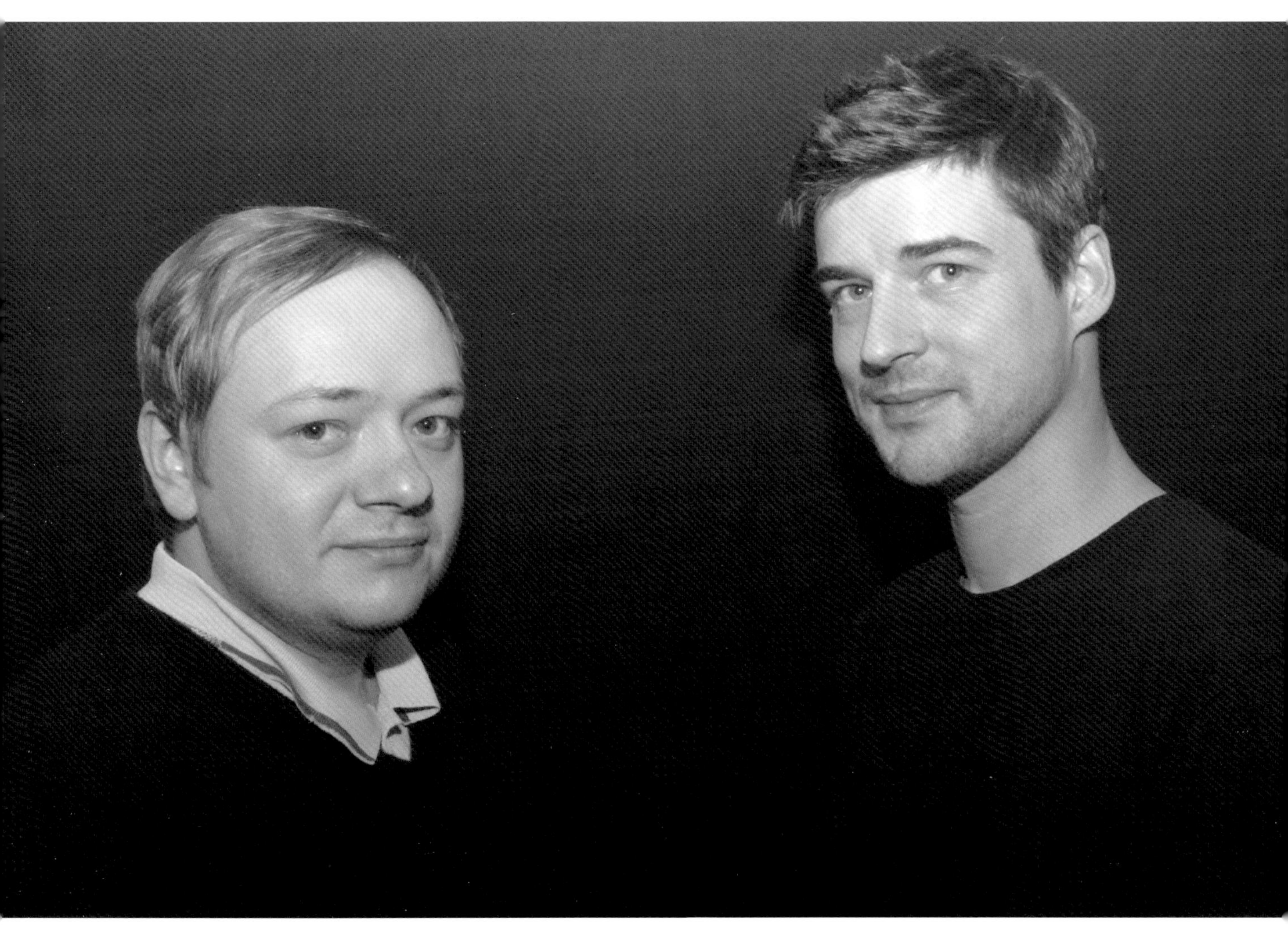

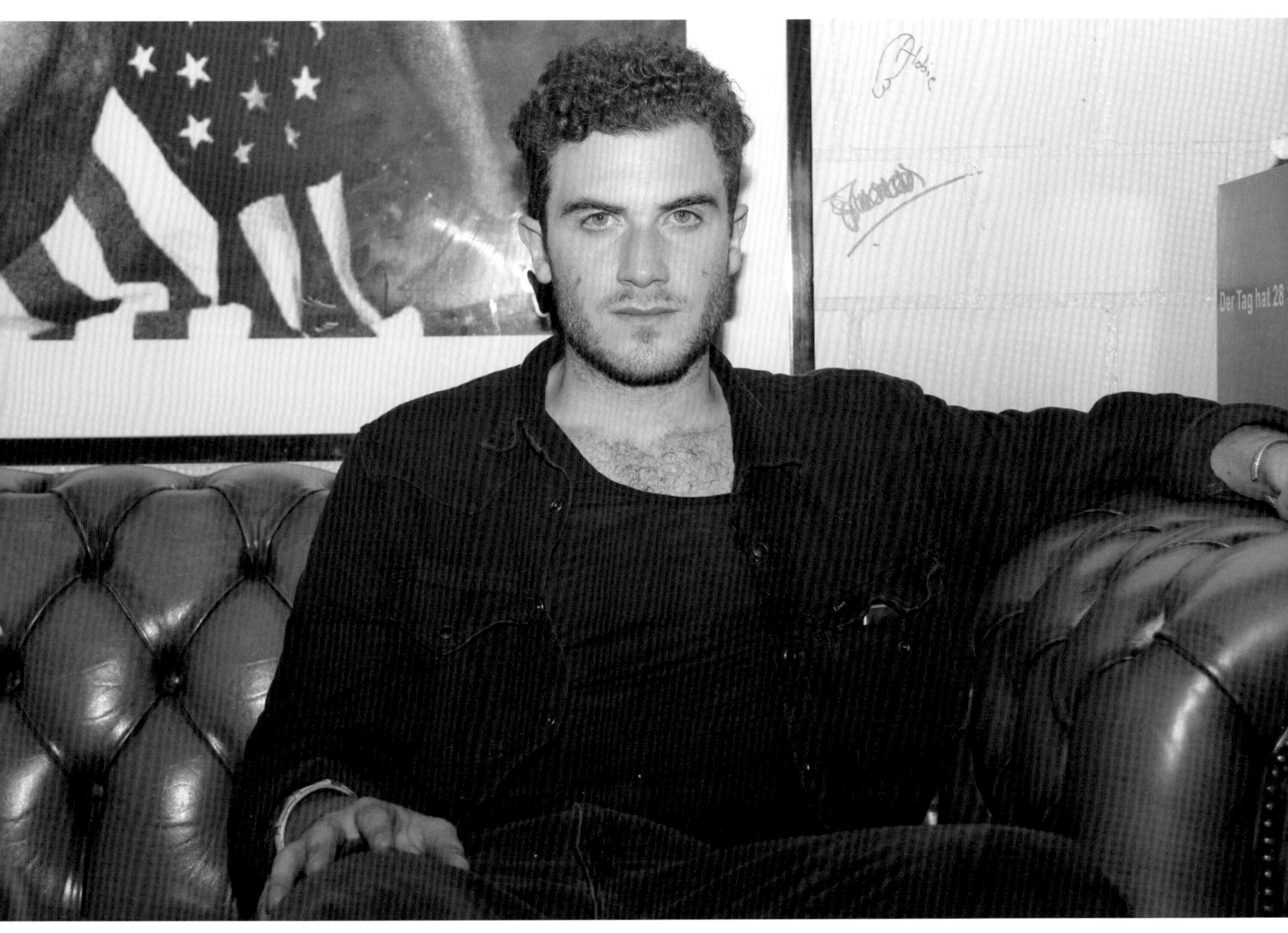
Der Tag hat 28

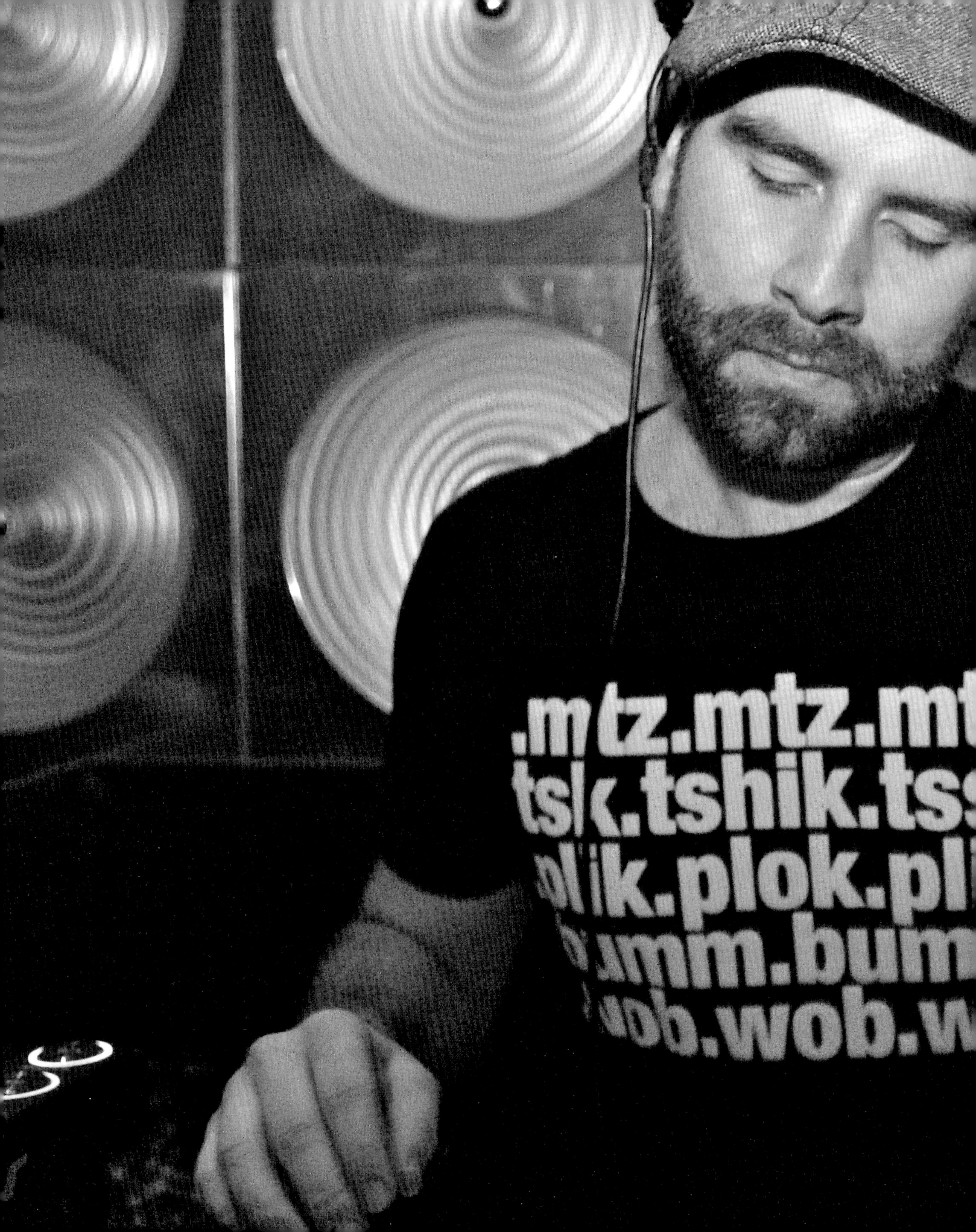
tz.mtz.mt
.tshik.ts
k.plok.pl
mm.bum
ob.wob.w

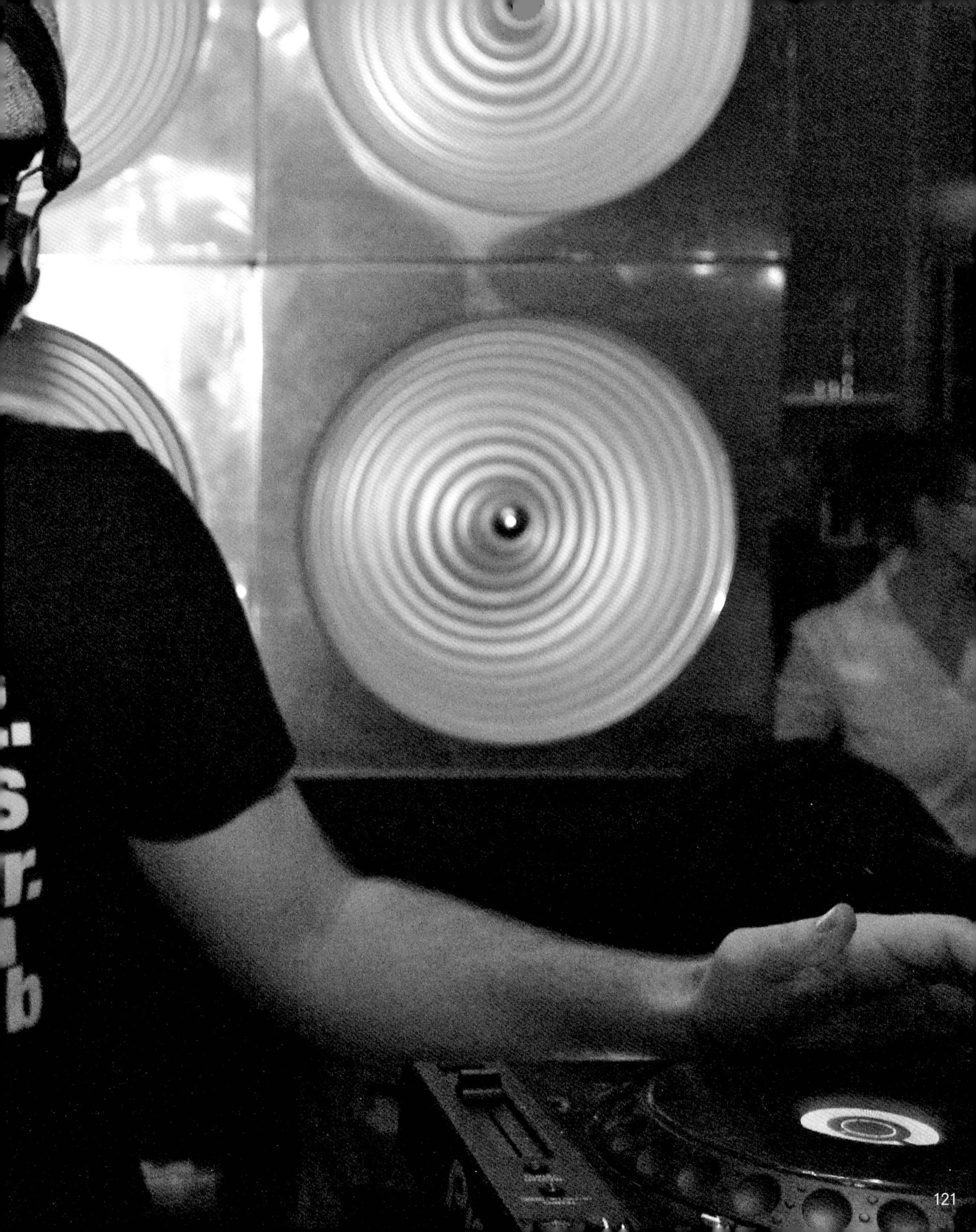

DAVID AUGUST

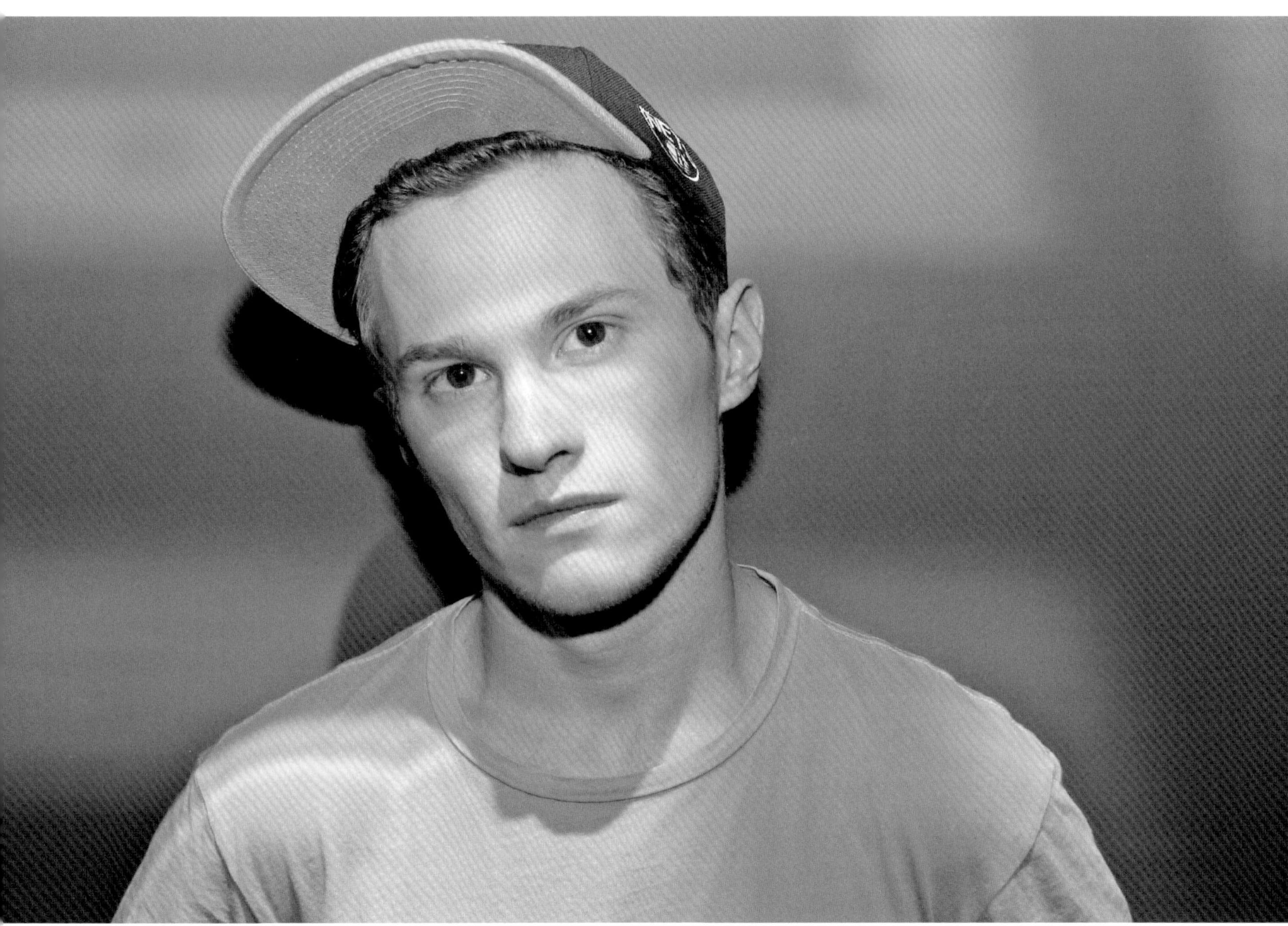

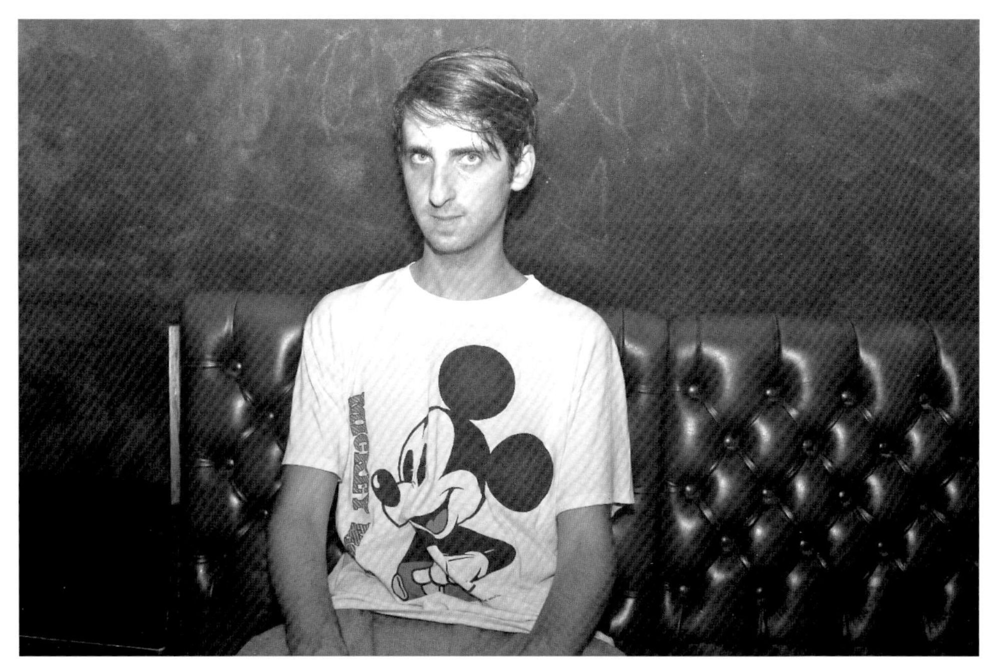

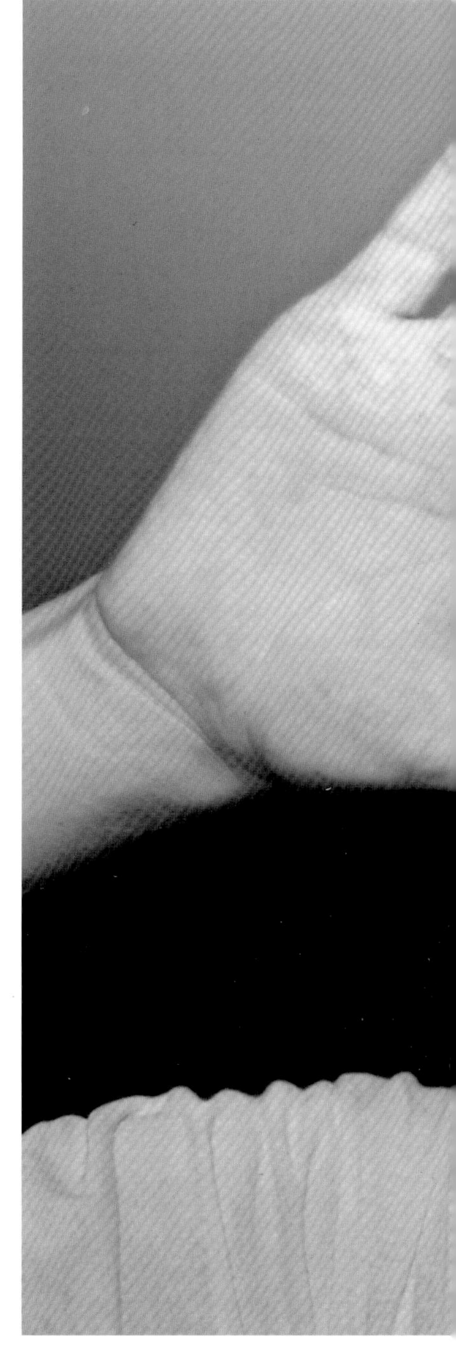

JAMES HOLDEN

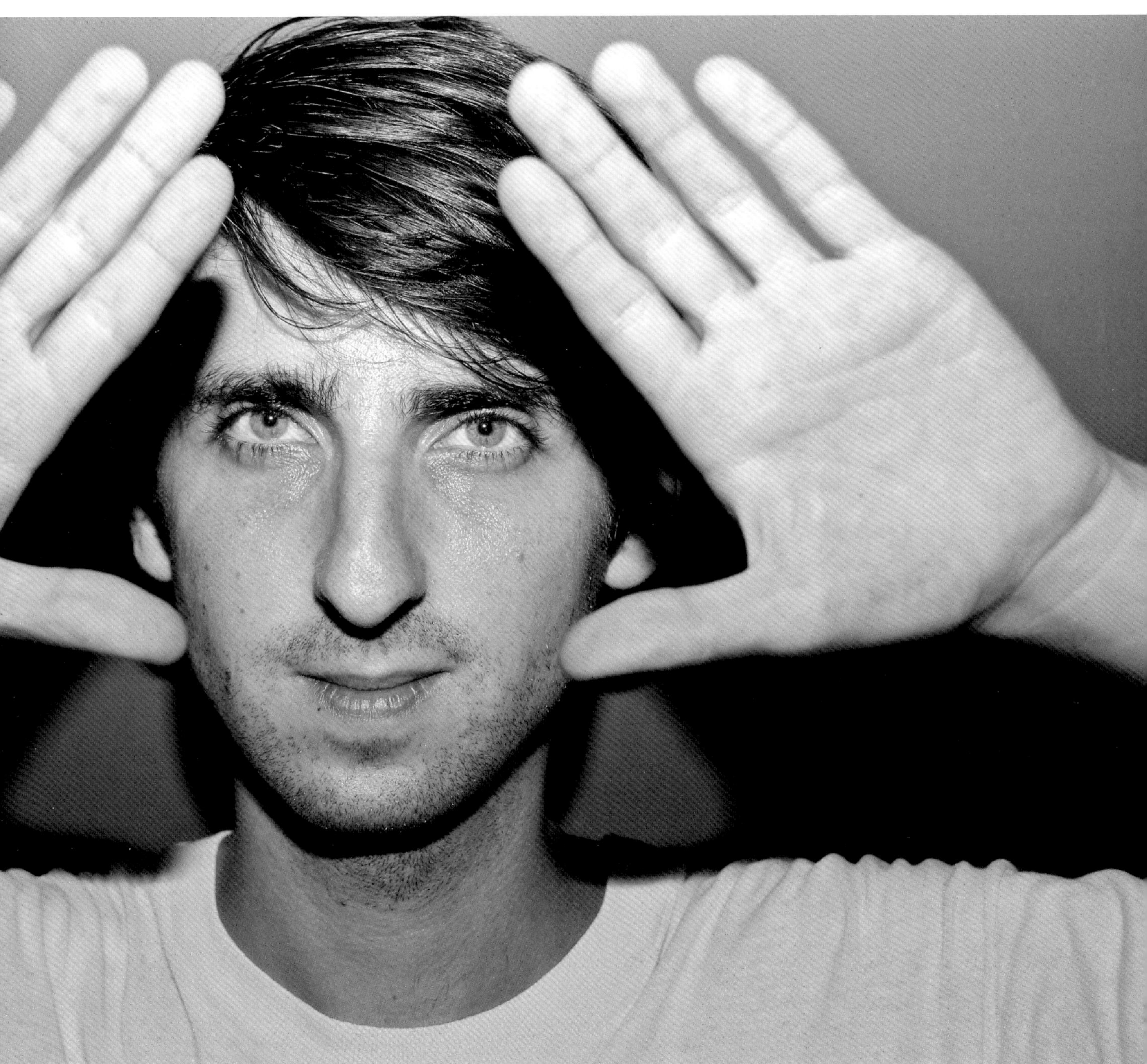

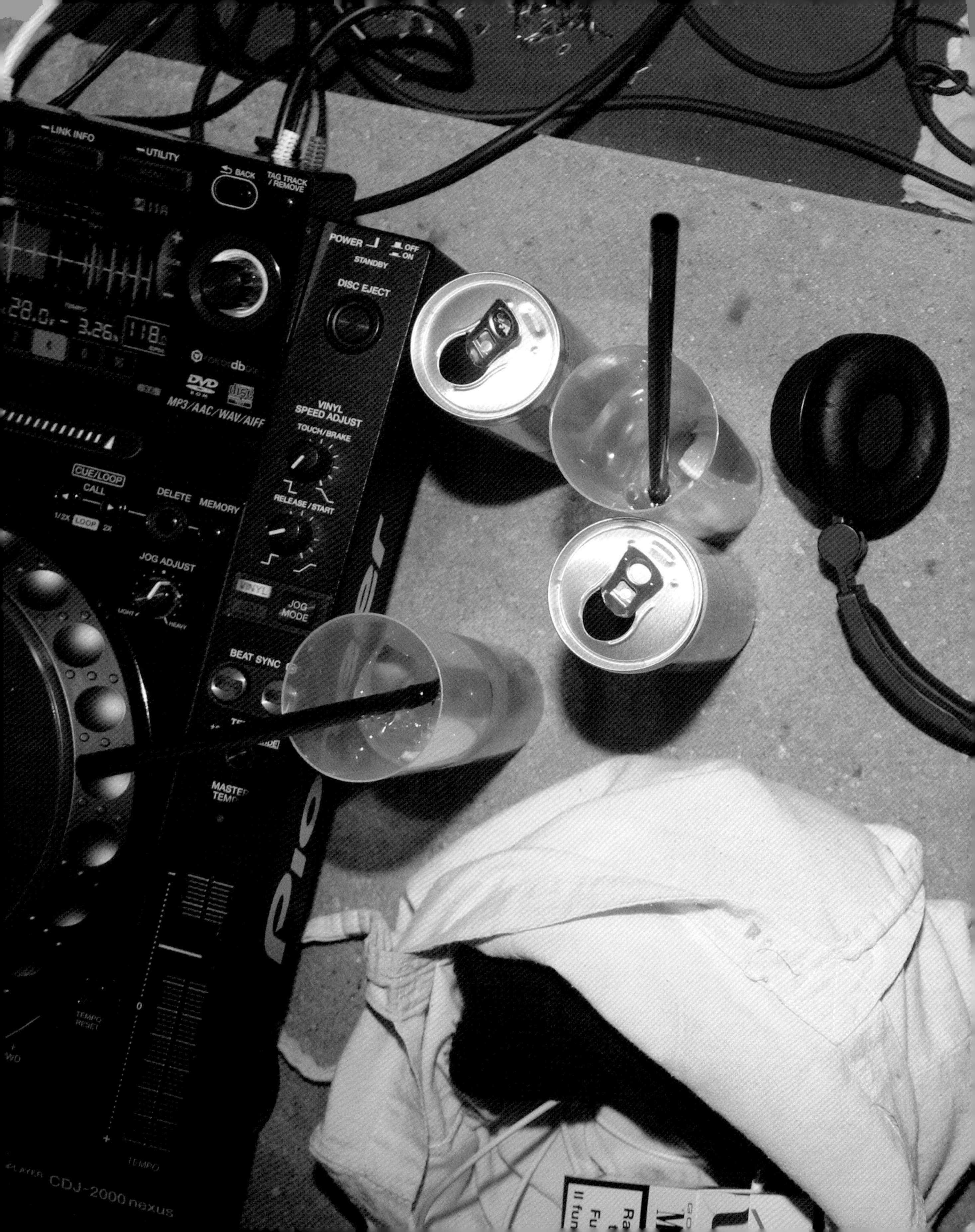
LINK INFO
UTILITY
BACK
TAG TRACK / REMOVE
POWER
OFF
ON
STANDBY
DISC EJECT
MP3/AAC/WAV/AIFF
VINYL SPEED ADJUST
TOUCH/BRAKE
RELEASE/START
CUE/LOOP
CALL
DELETE
MEMORY
1/2X
LOOP
2X
JOG ADJUST
VINYL
JOG MODE
BEAT SYNC
TEMPO RESET
TEMPO
CDJ-2000 nexus

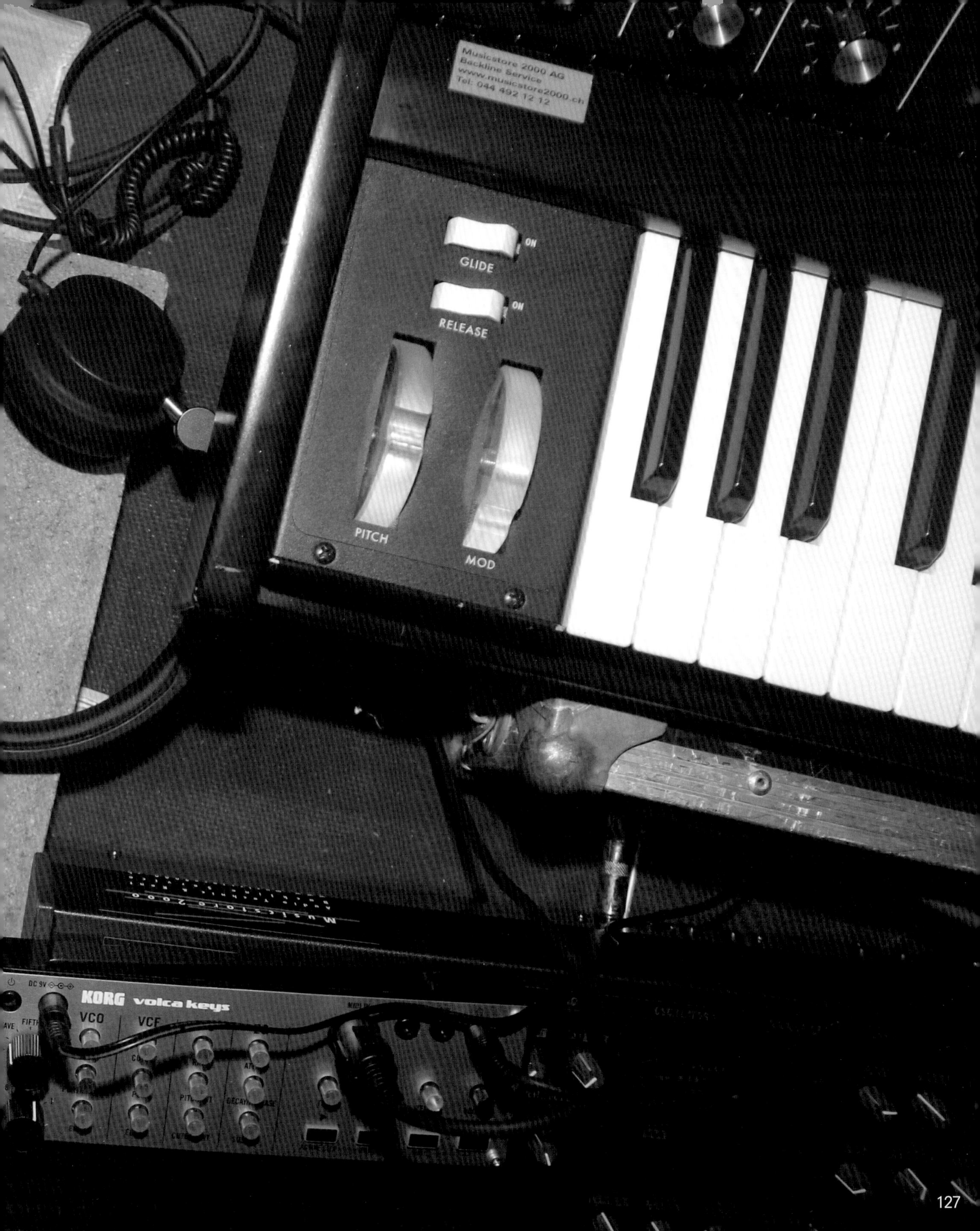
Musicstore 2000 AG
Backline Service
www.musicstore2000.ch
Tel: 044 492 12 12
ON
GLIDE
ON
RELEASE
PITCH
MOD
DC 9V
KORG volca keys
VCO
VCF
FIFTH

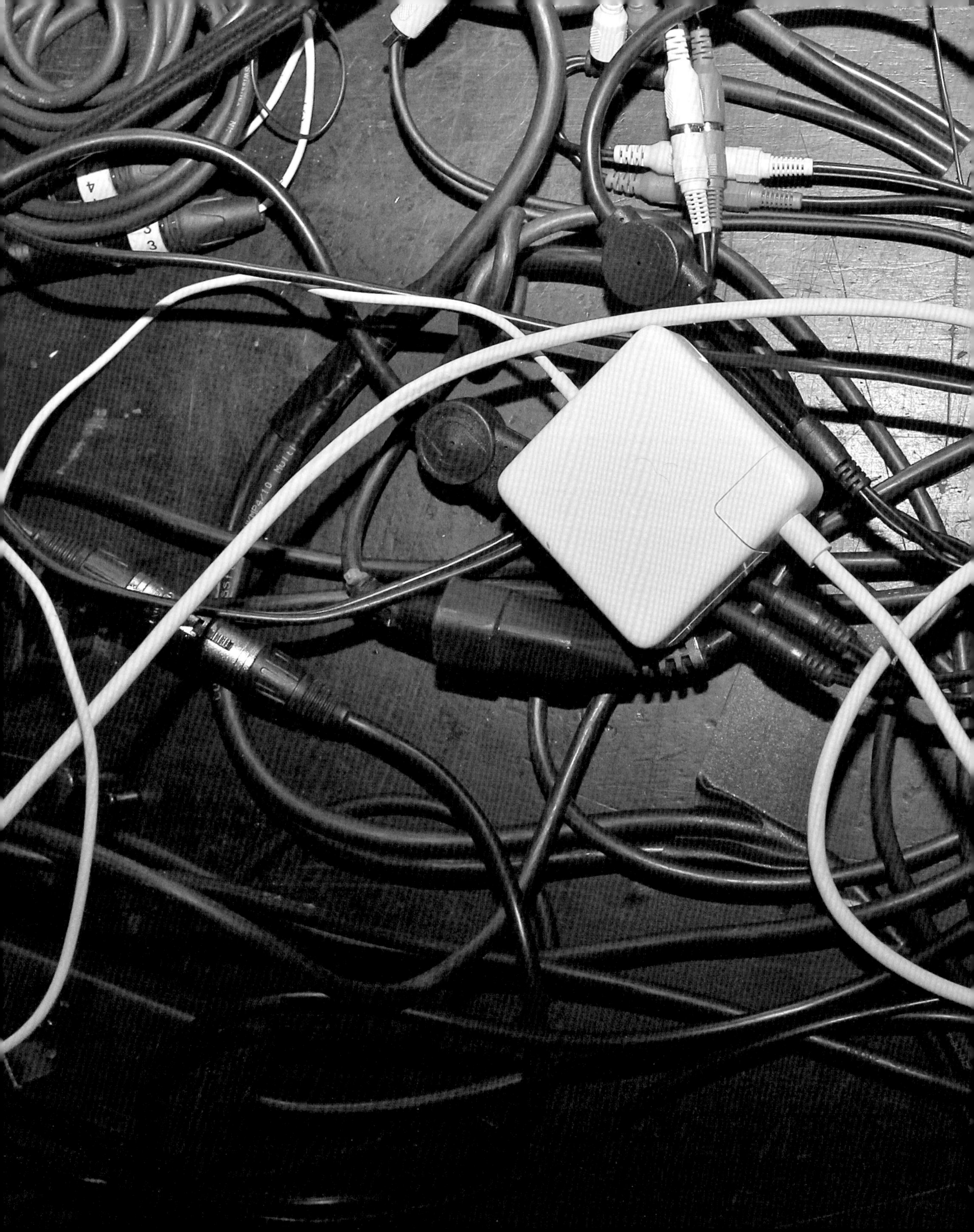
4
3
3

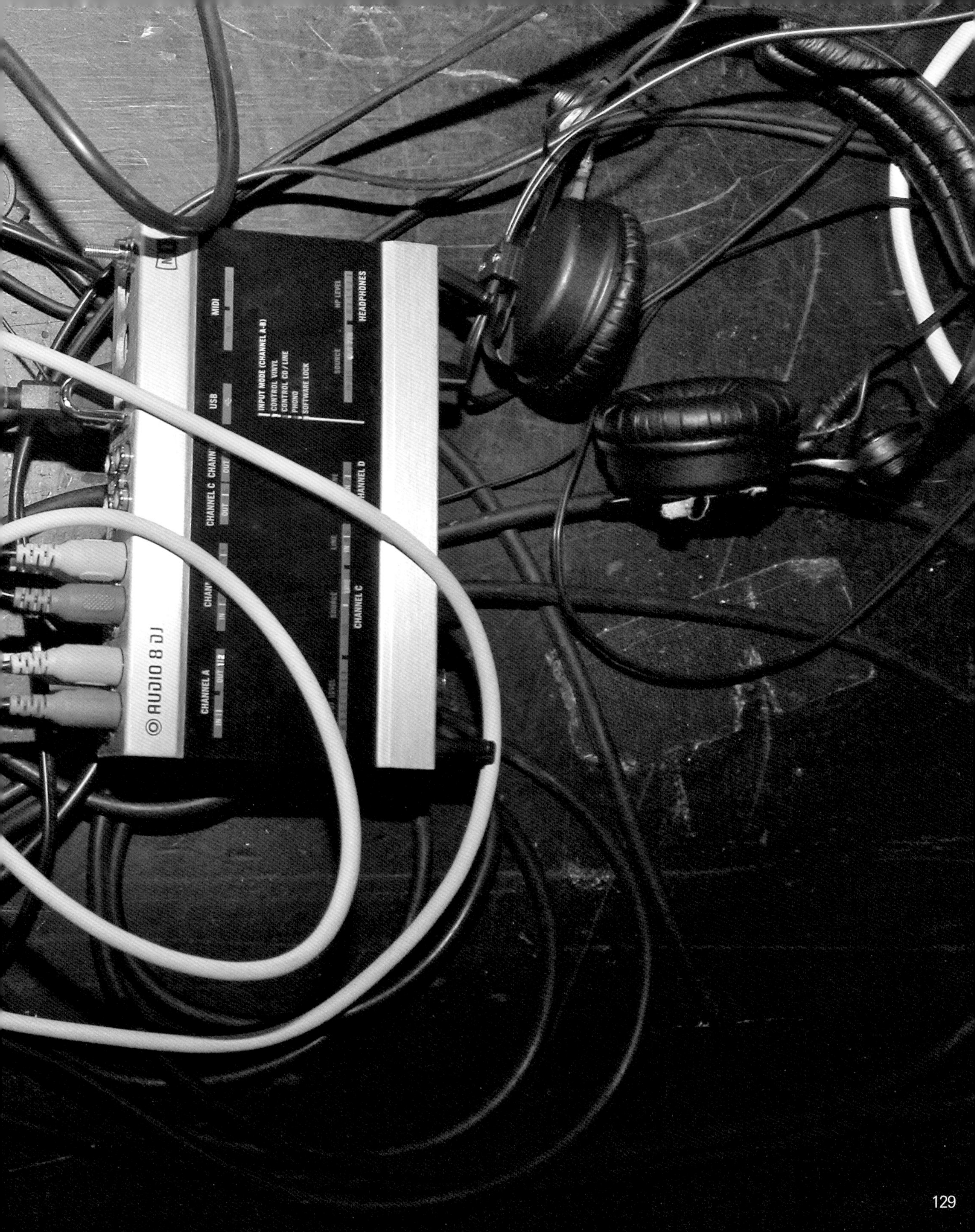
AUDIO 8 DJ
CHANNEL A
CHANNEL C
CHANNEL D
USB
MIDI
INPUT MODE (CHANNEL A-B)
CONTROL VINYL
CONTROL CD / LINE
PHONO
SOFTWARE LOCK
SOURCE
HP LEVEL
HEADPHONES

DJ T

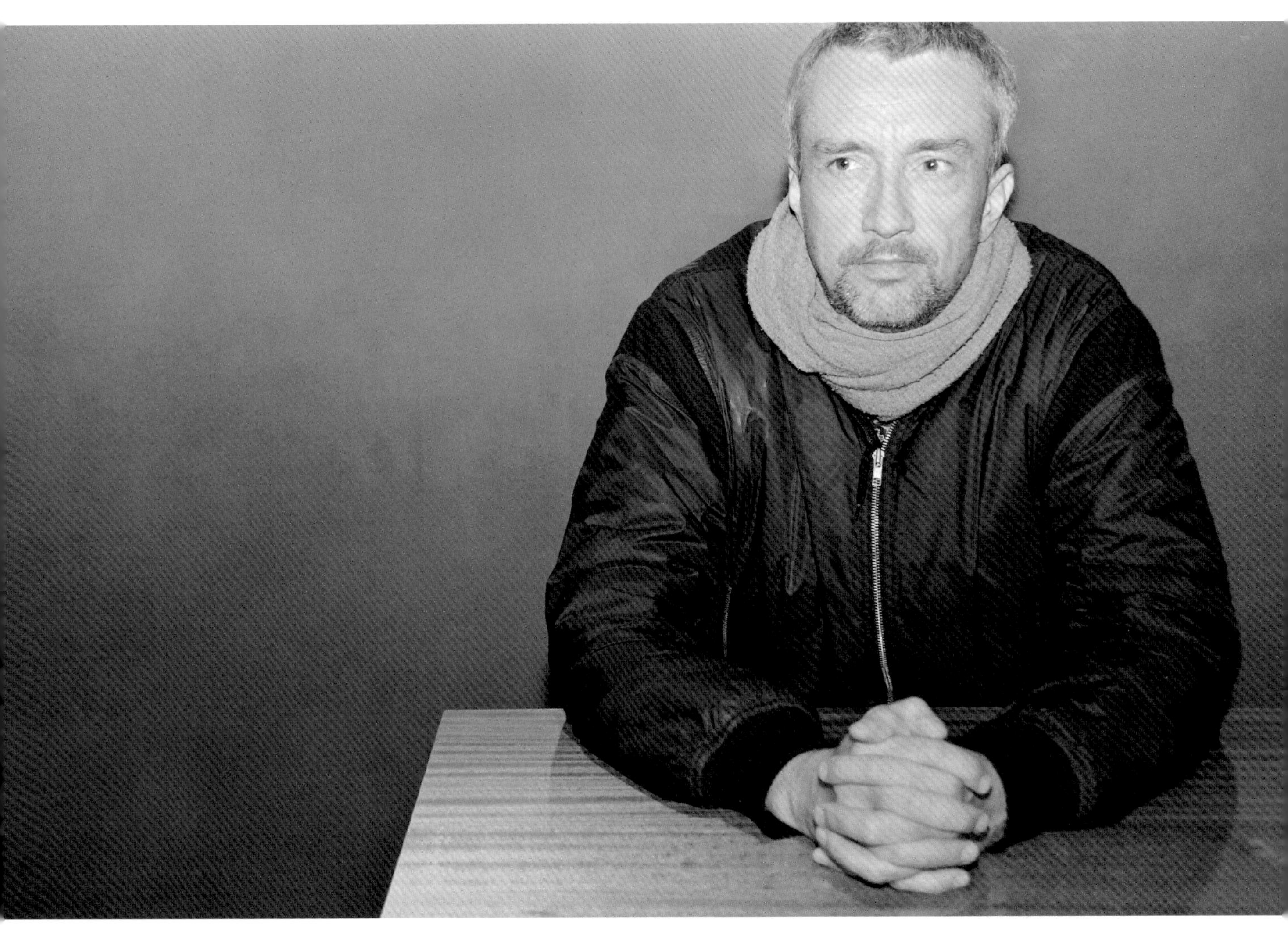

MATTHEW DEAR

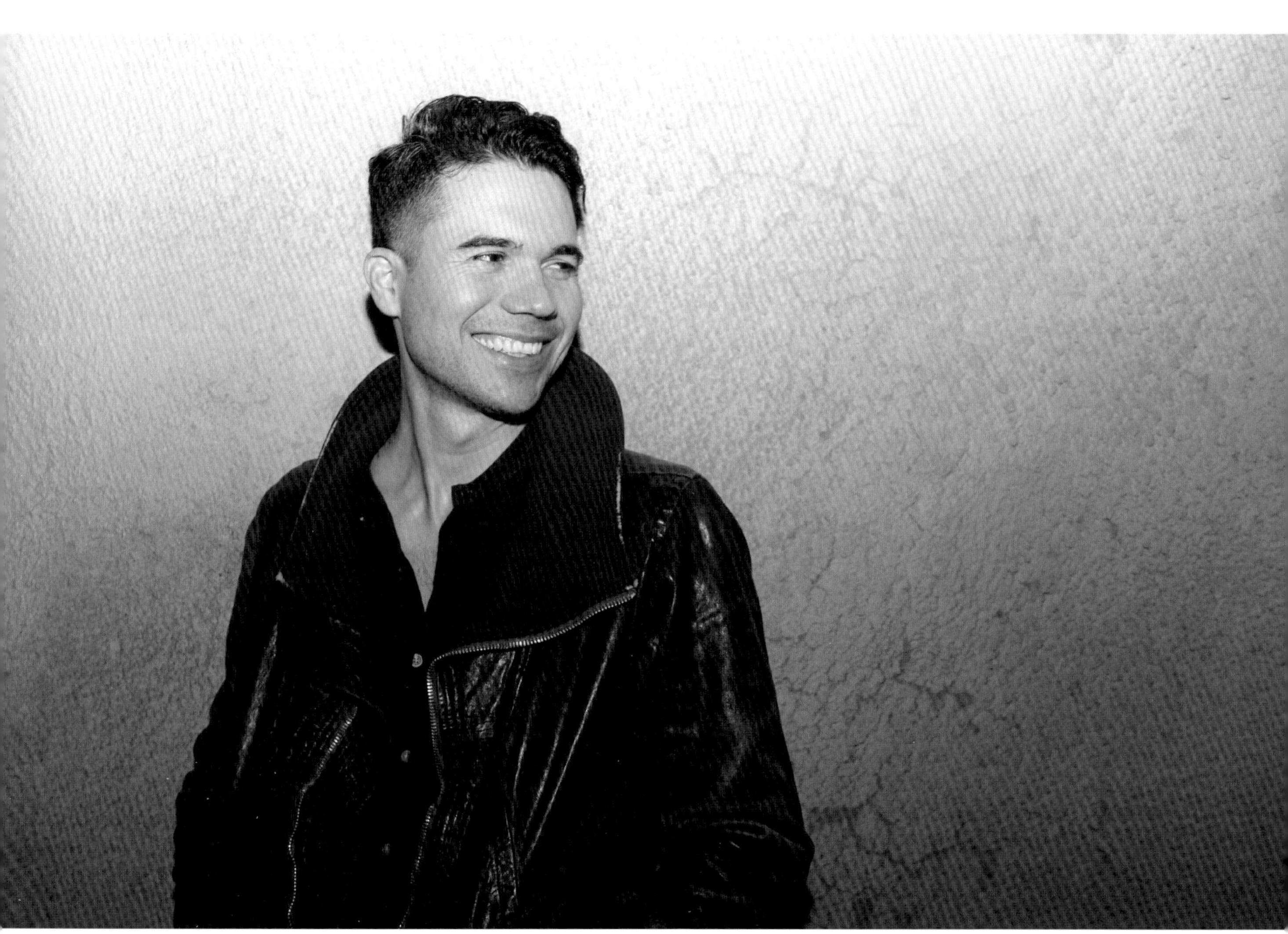

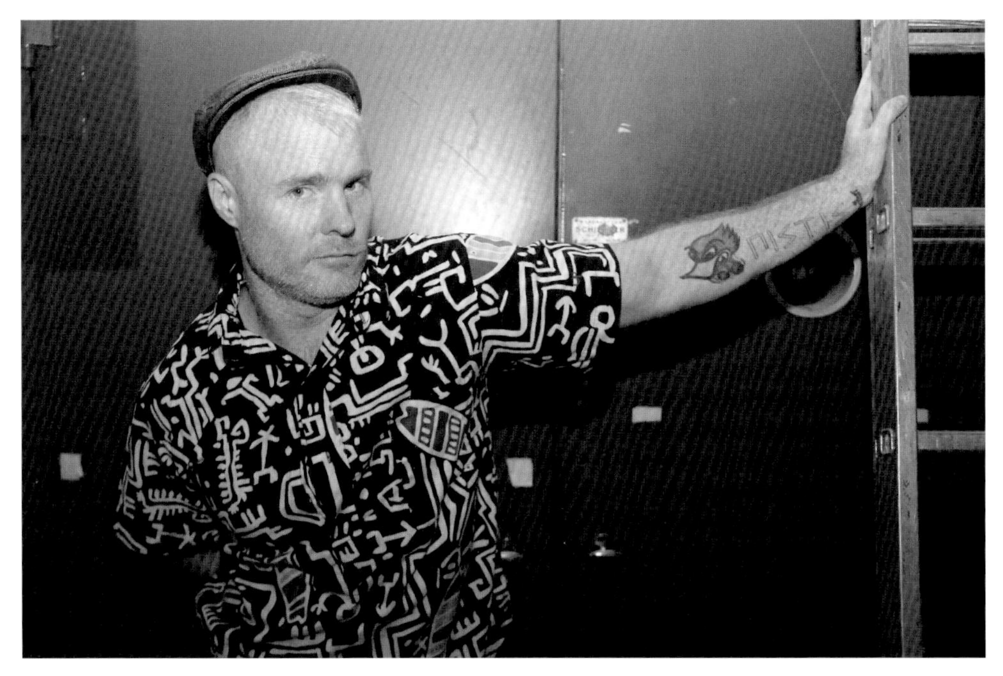

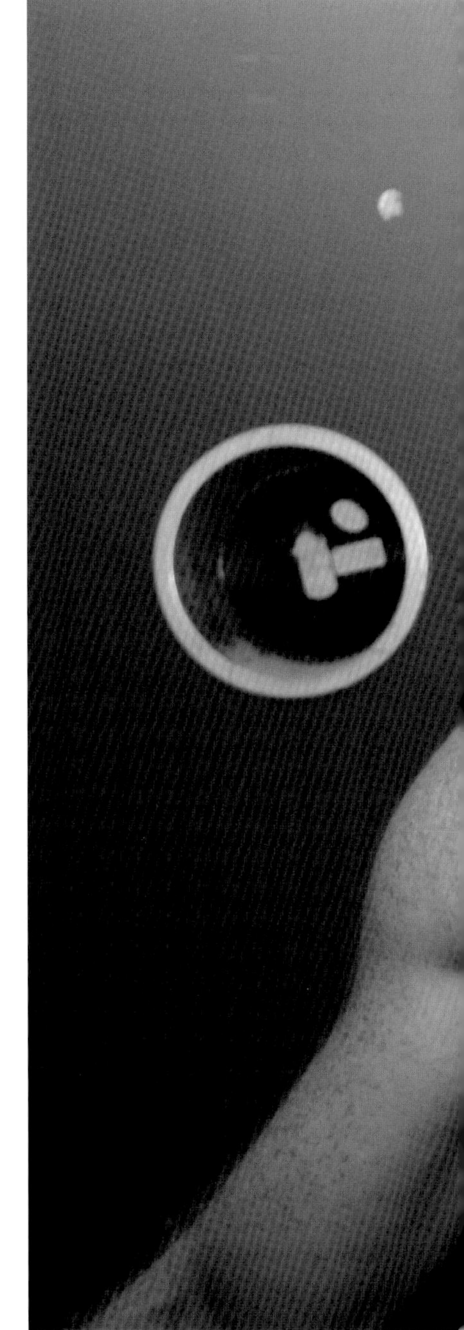

ANDY BUTLER

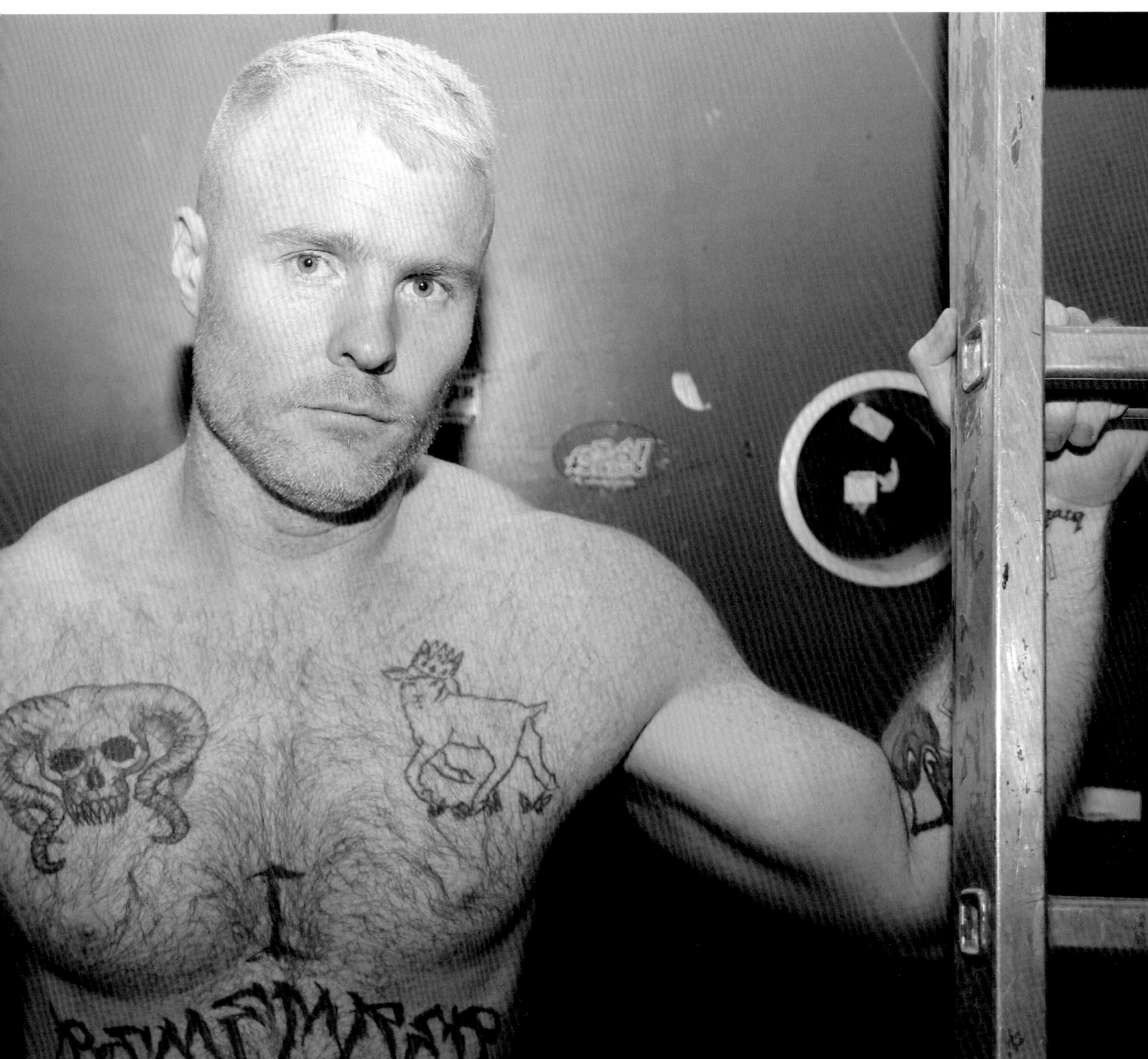

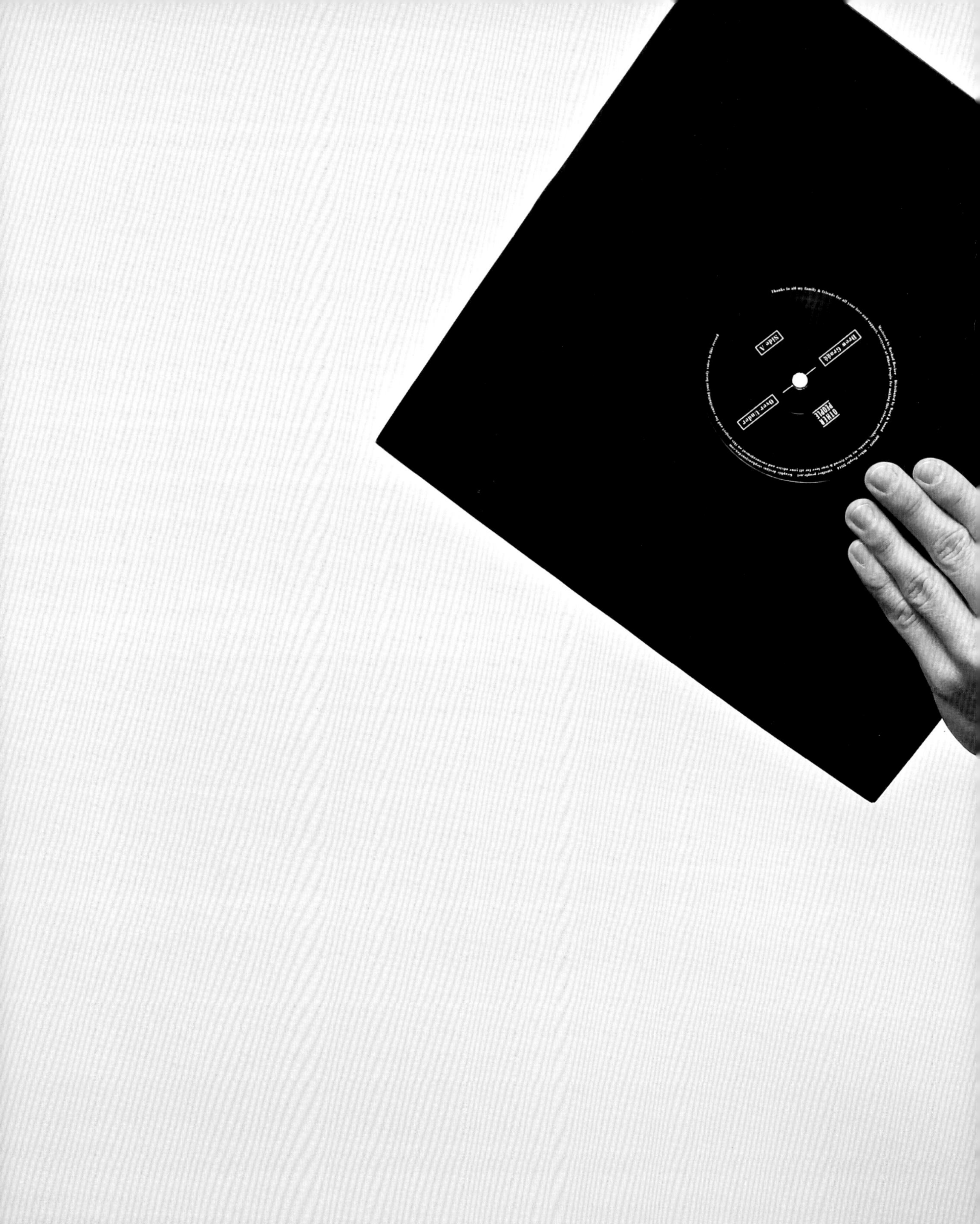
Side A
Drew Gradd
Over Under
OTHER PEOPLE
Thanks to all my family & friends for all your love and support

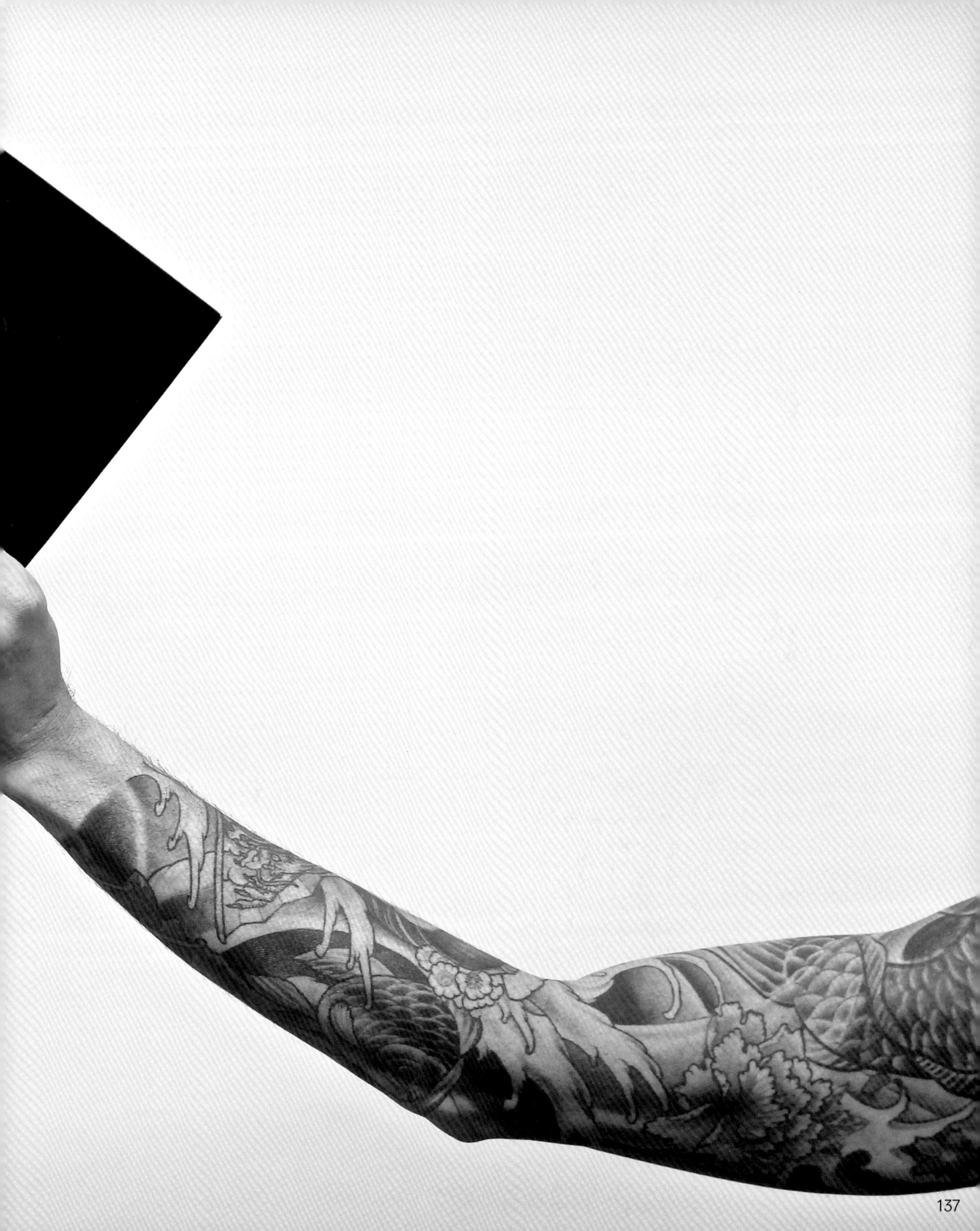

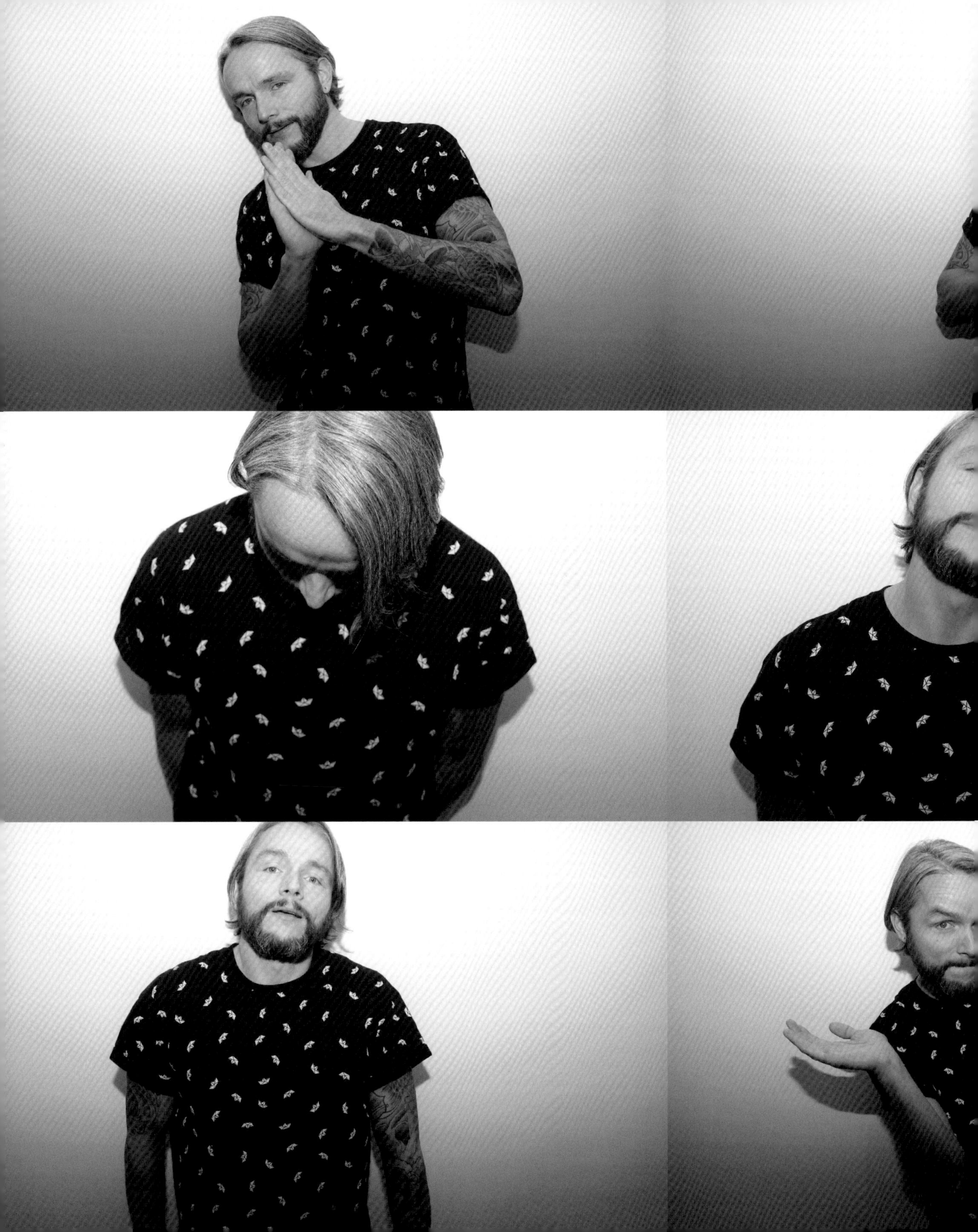

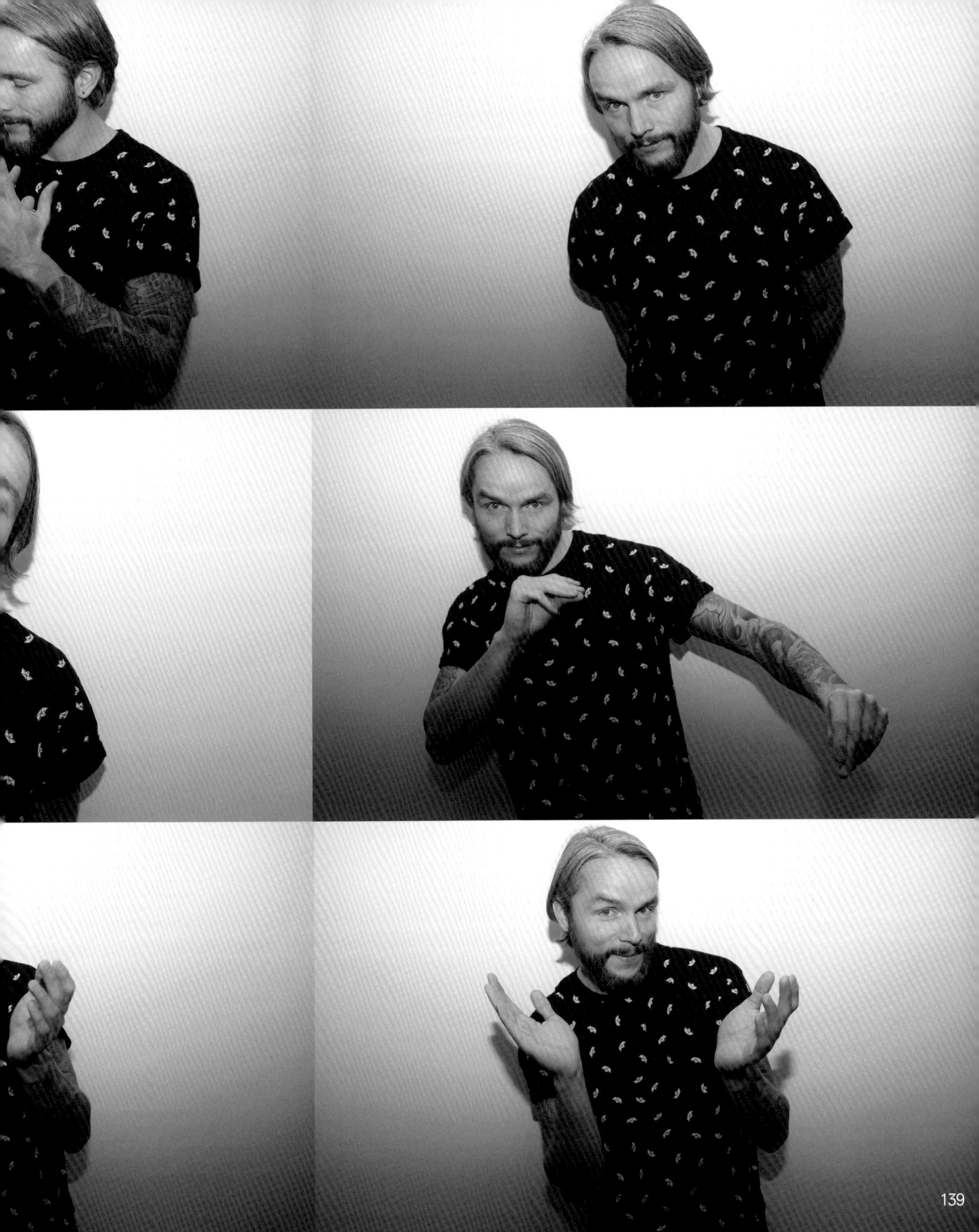

BEN KLOCK

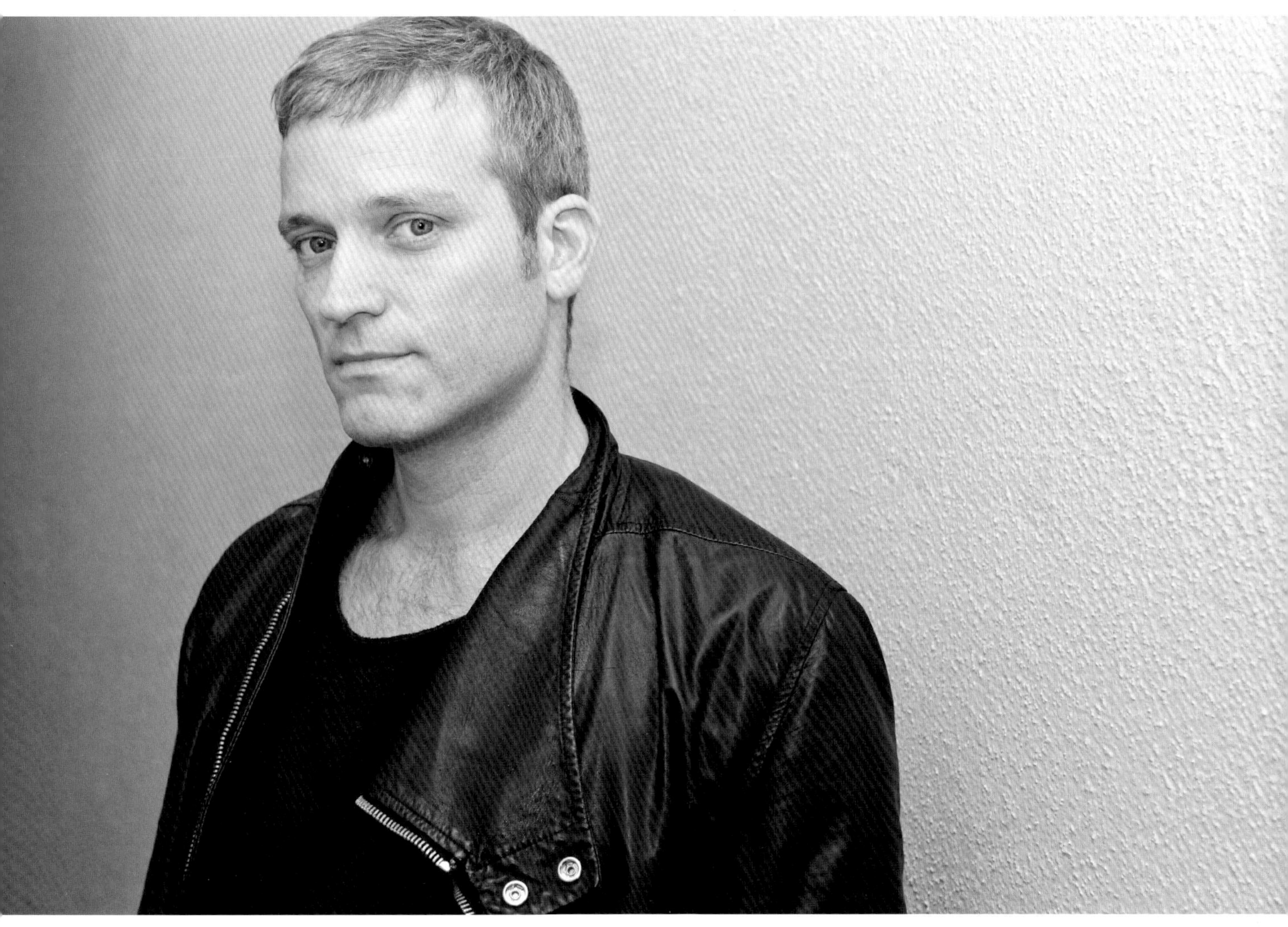

DANIEL BORTZ

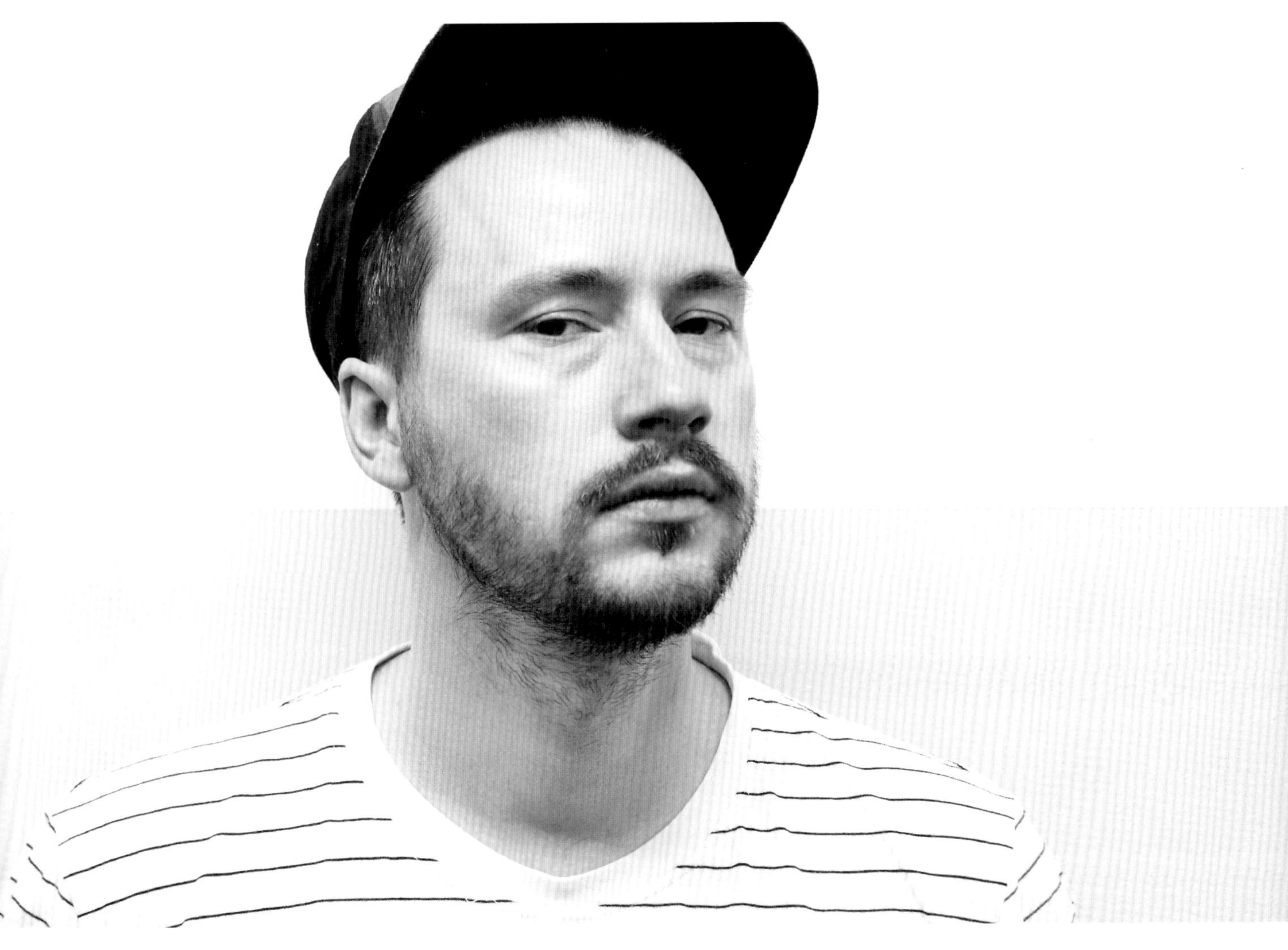

ROMAN FLÜGEL

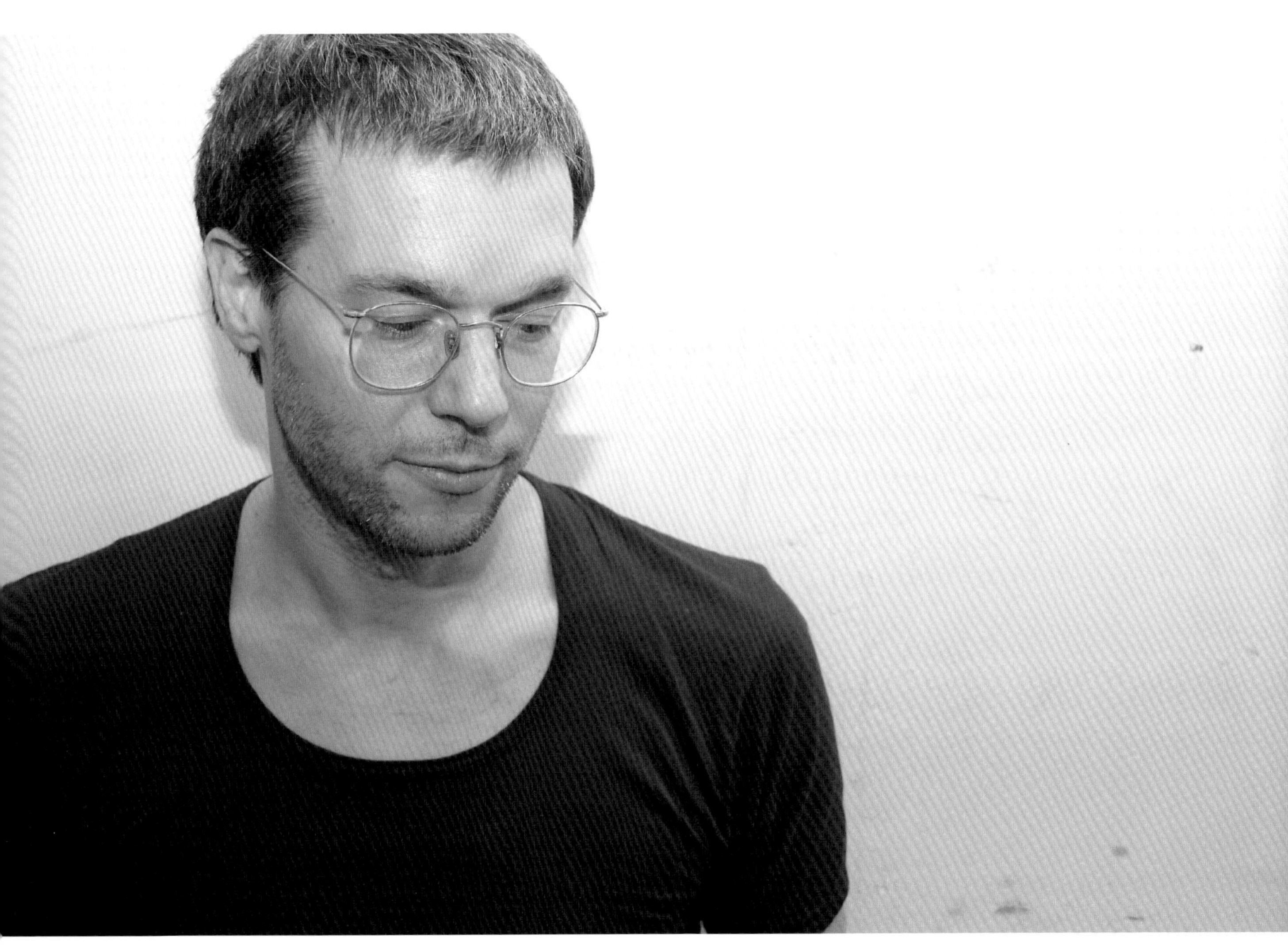

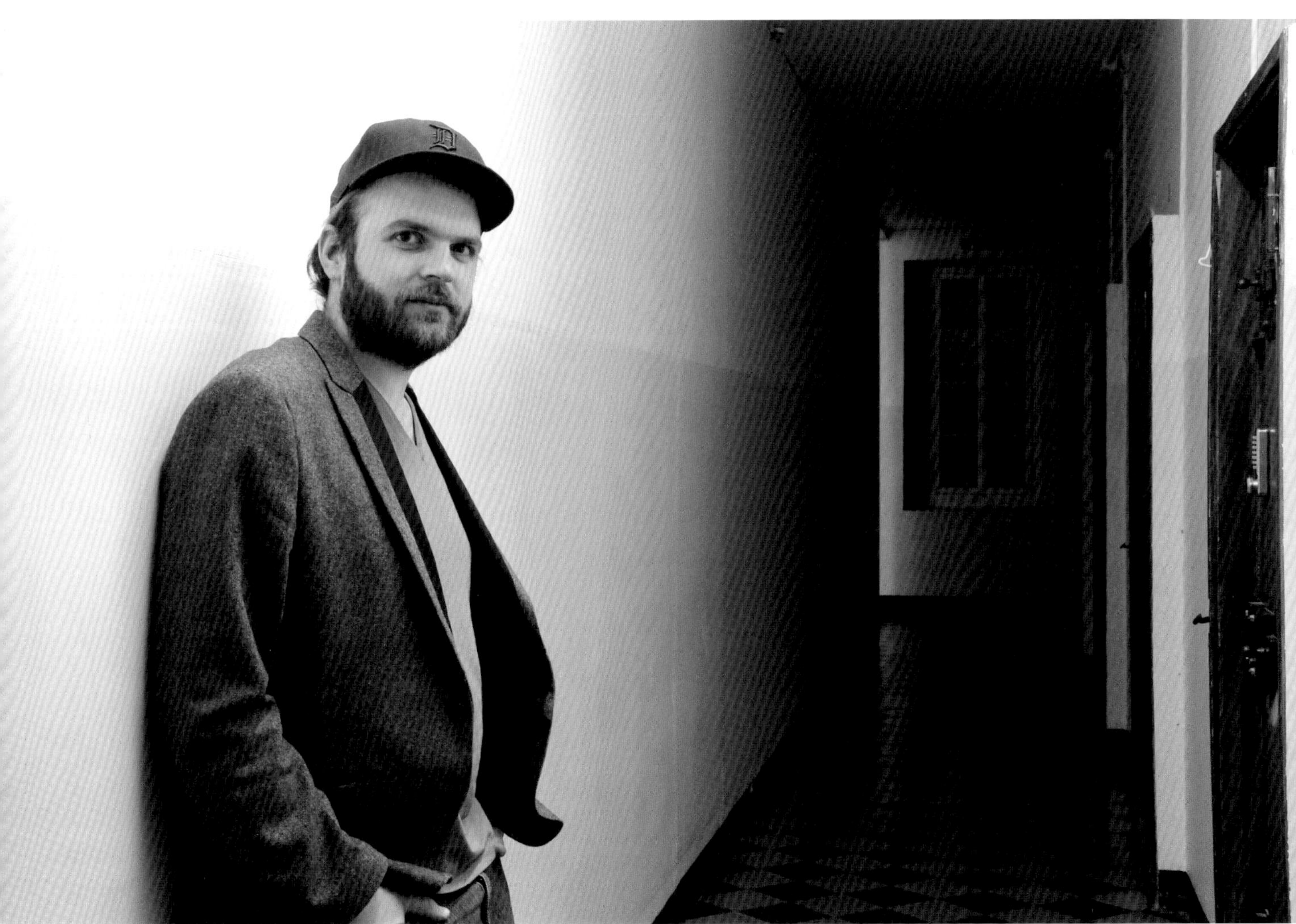

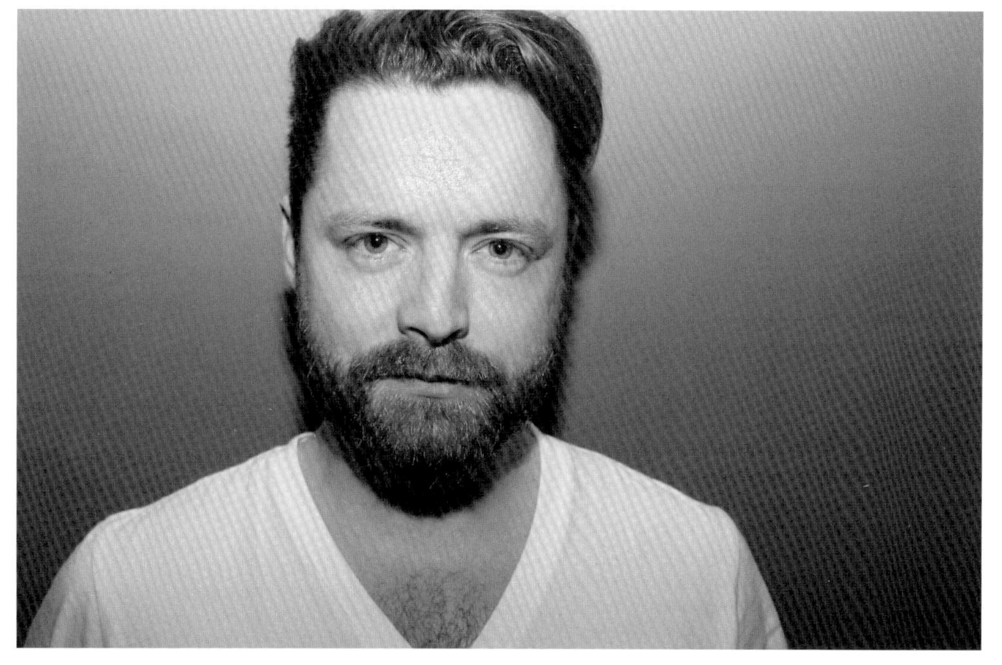

DAPAYK

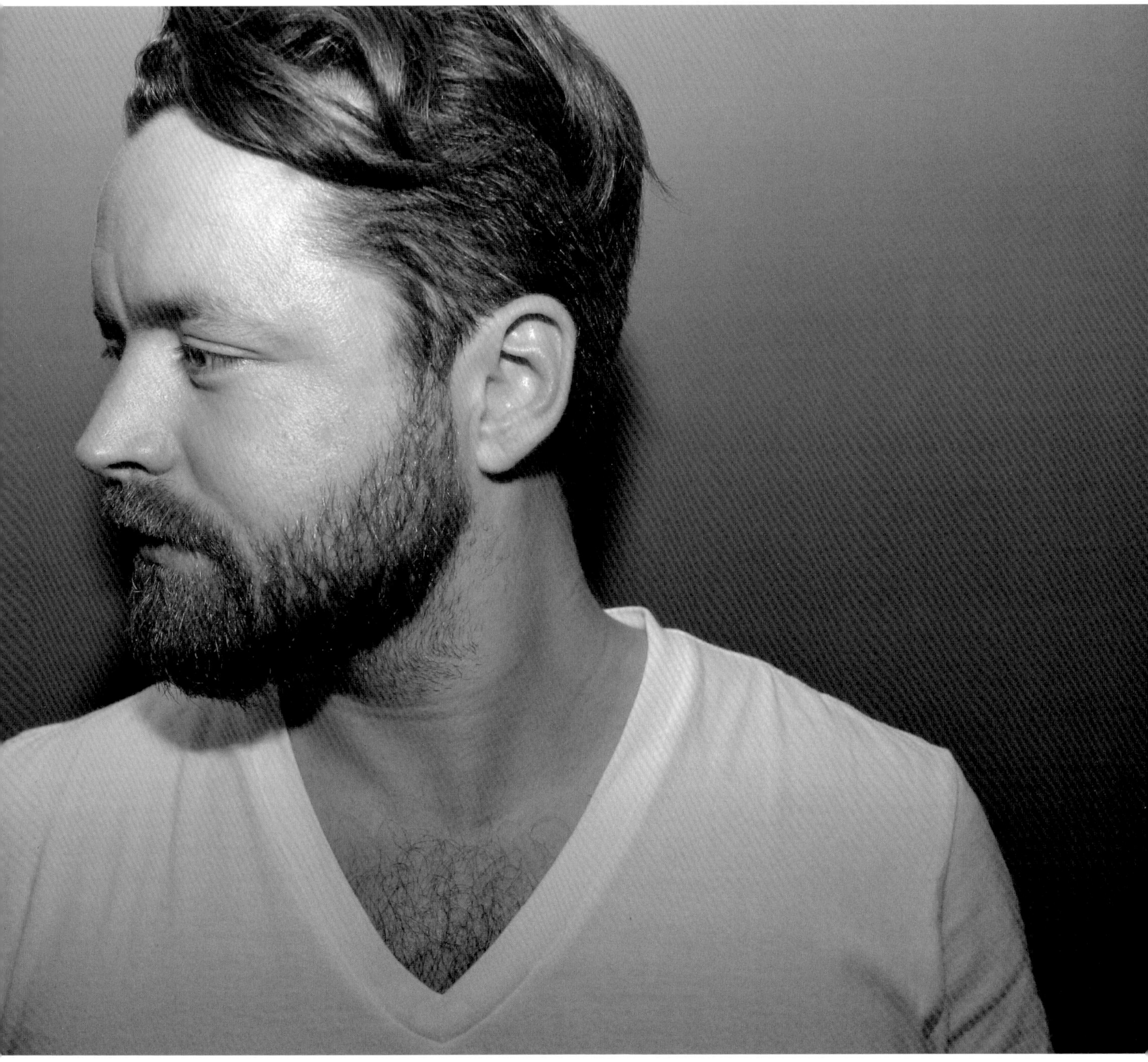

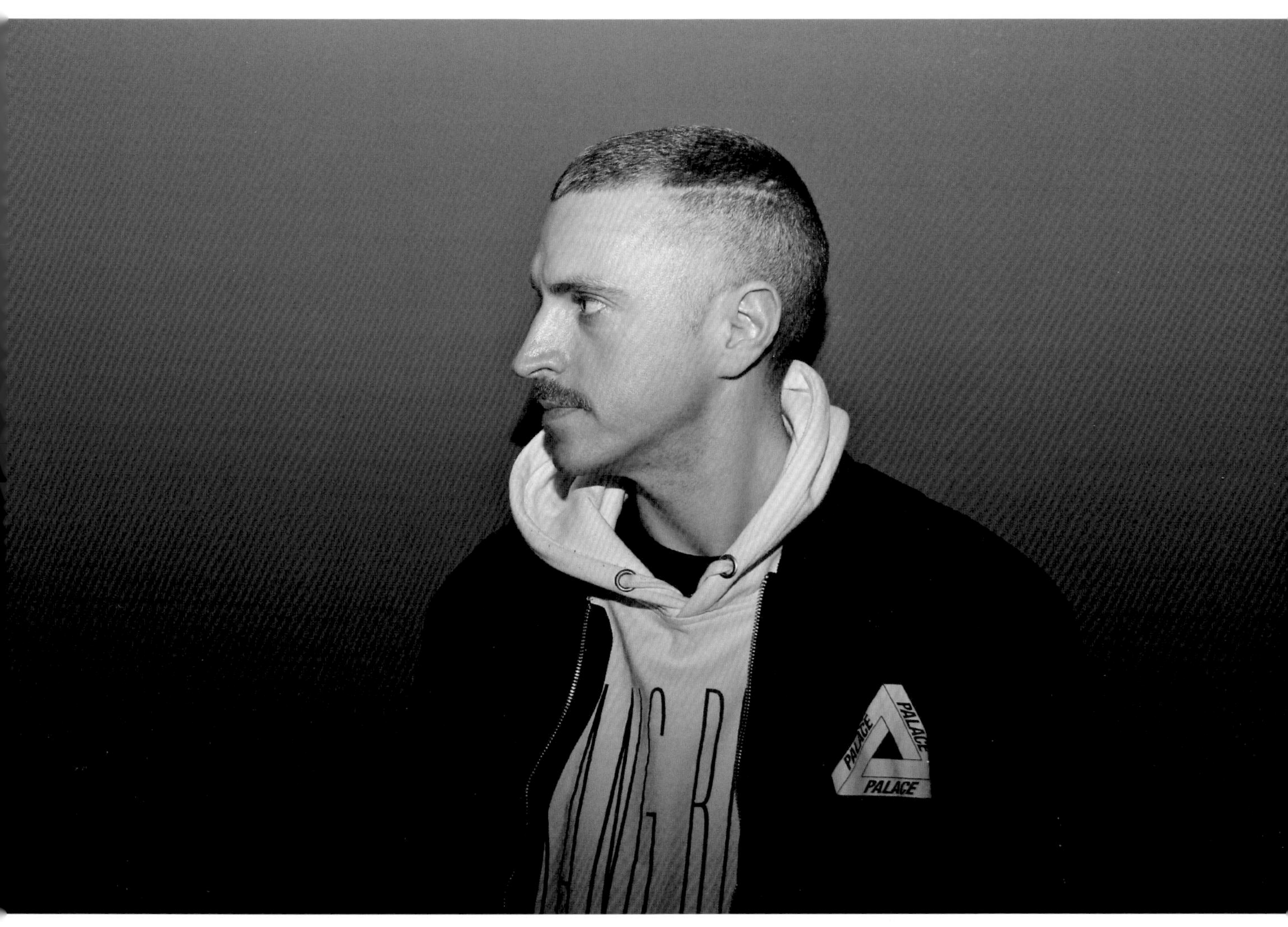
PALACE
PALACE
PALACE

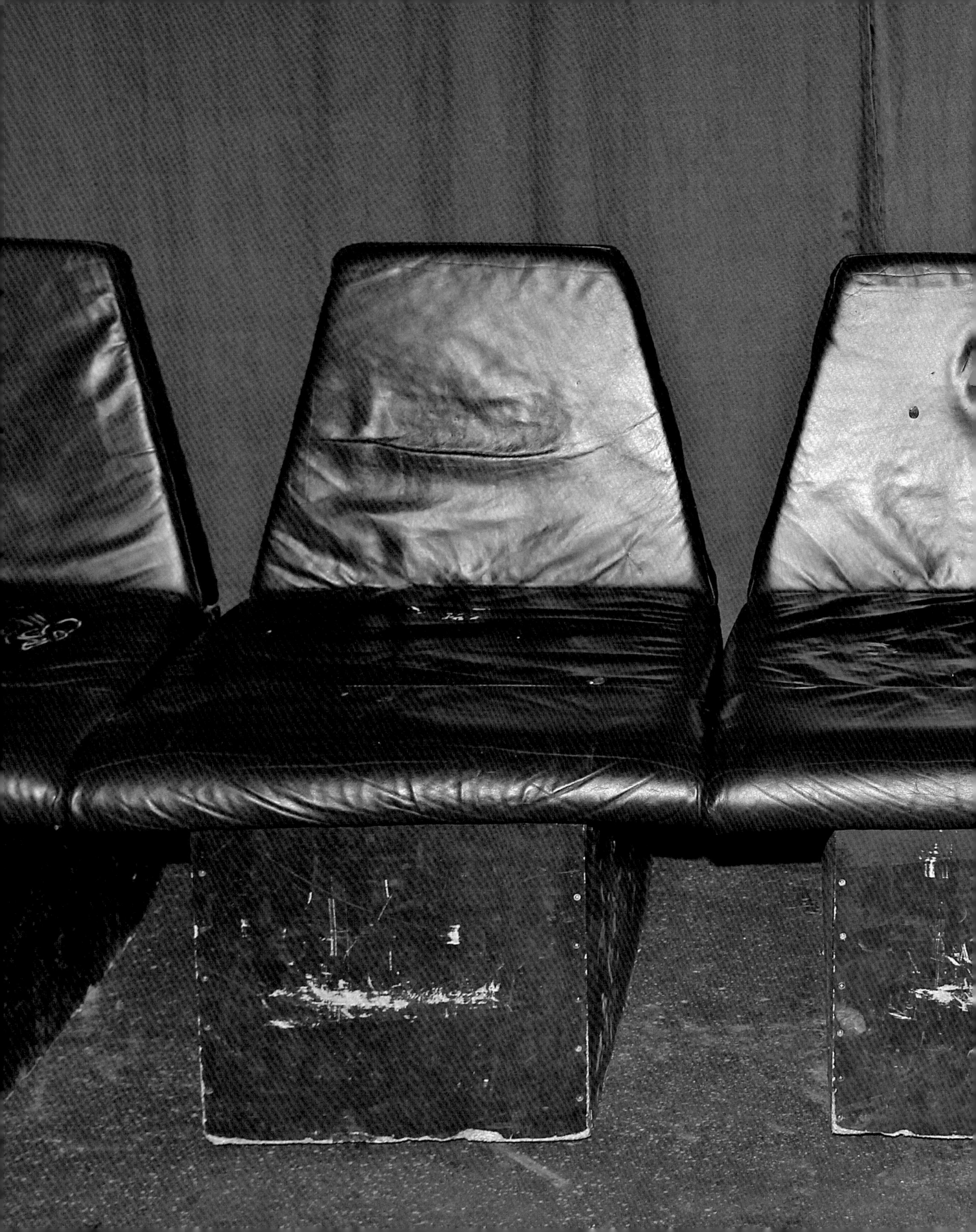

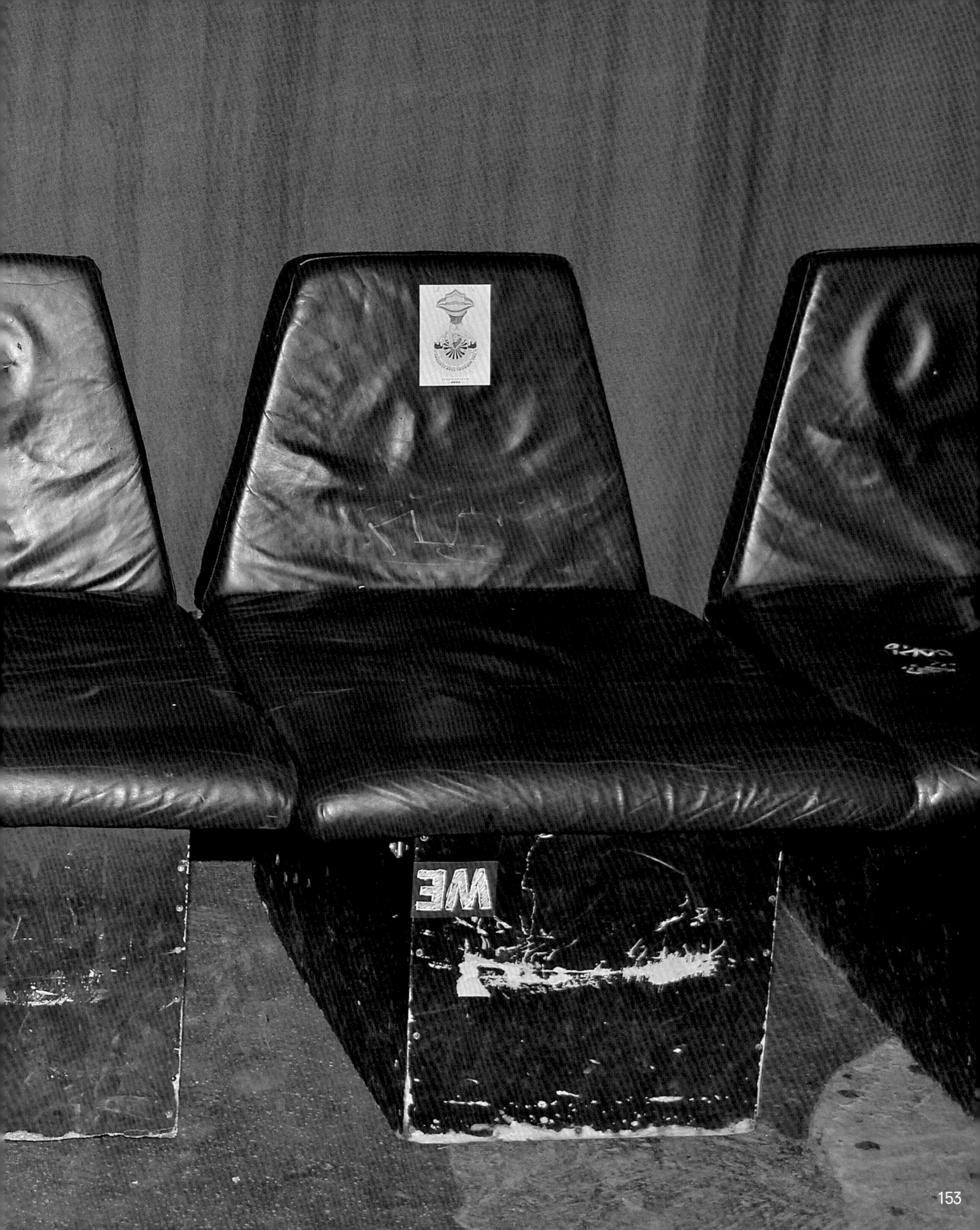

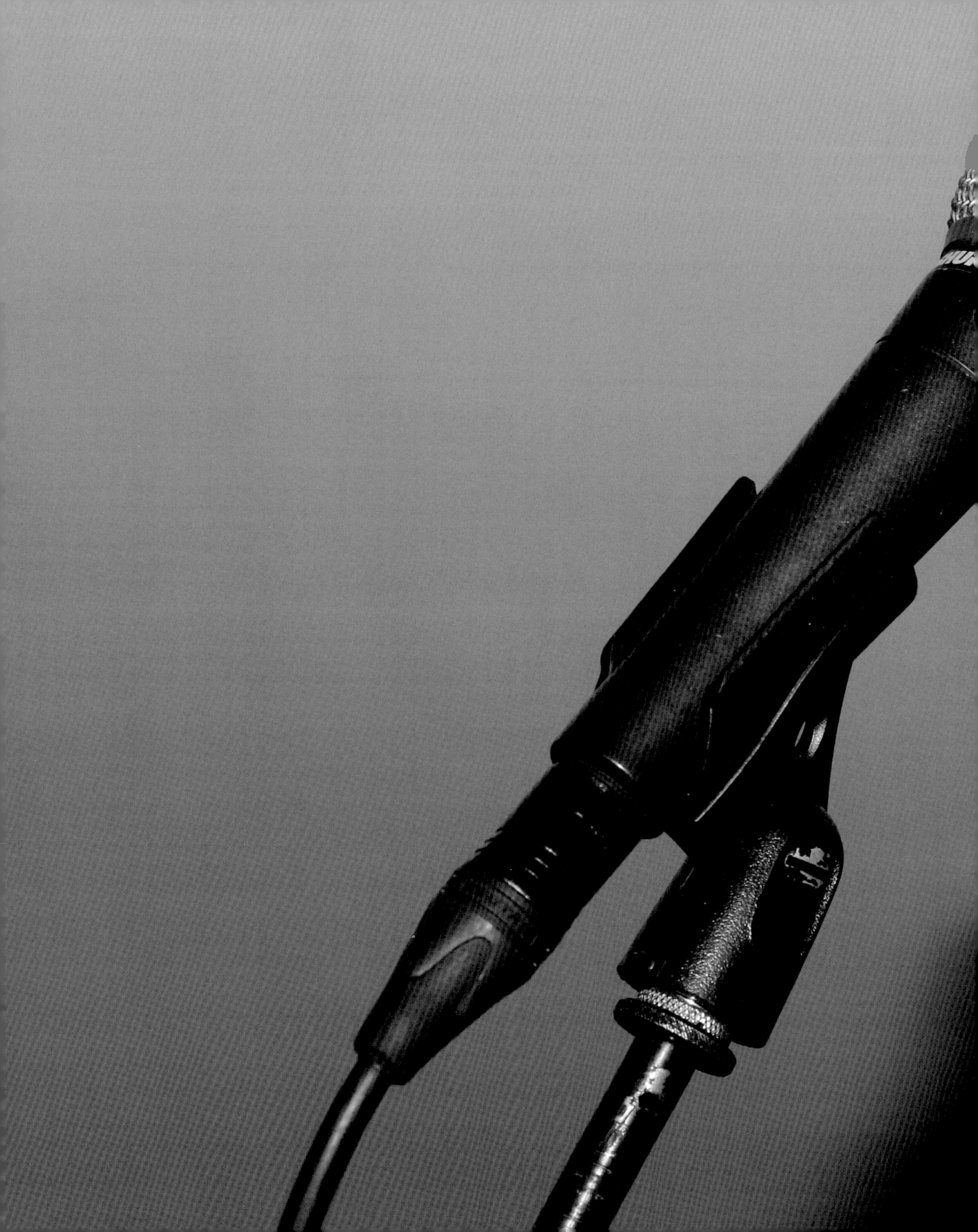

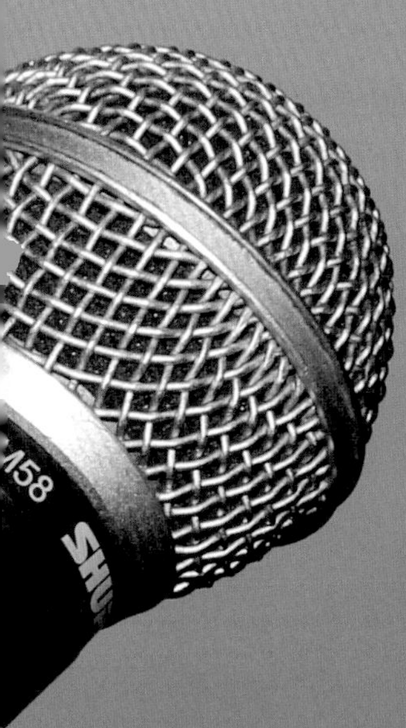

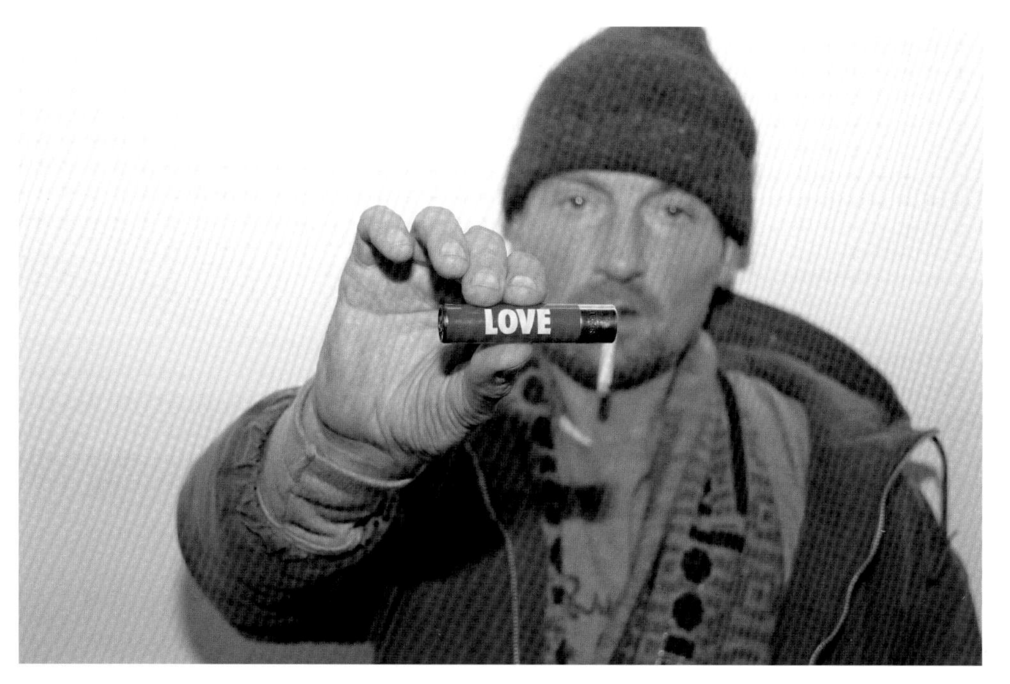

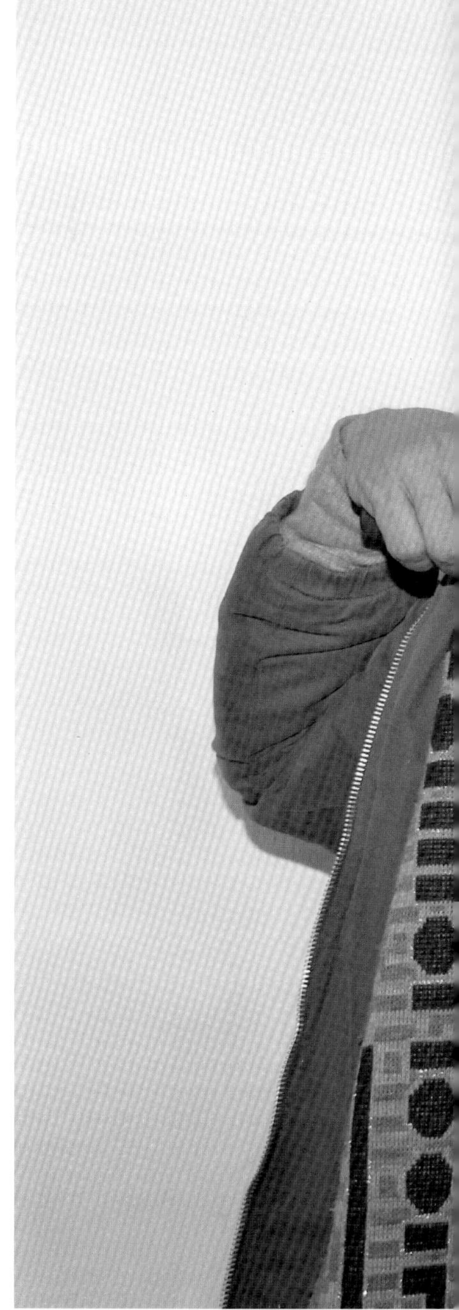

FETISH (TERRANOVA)

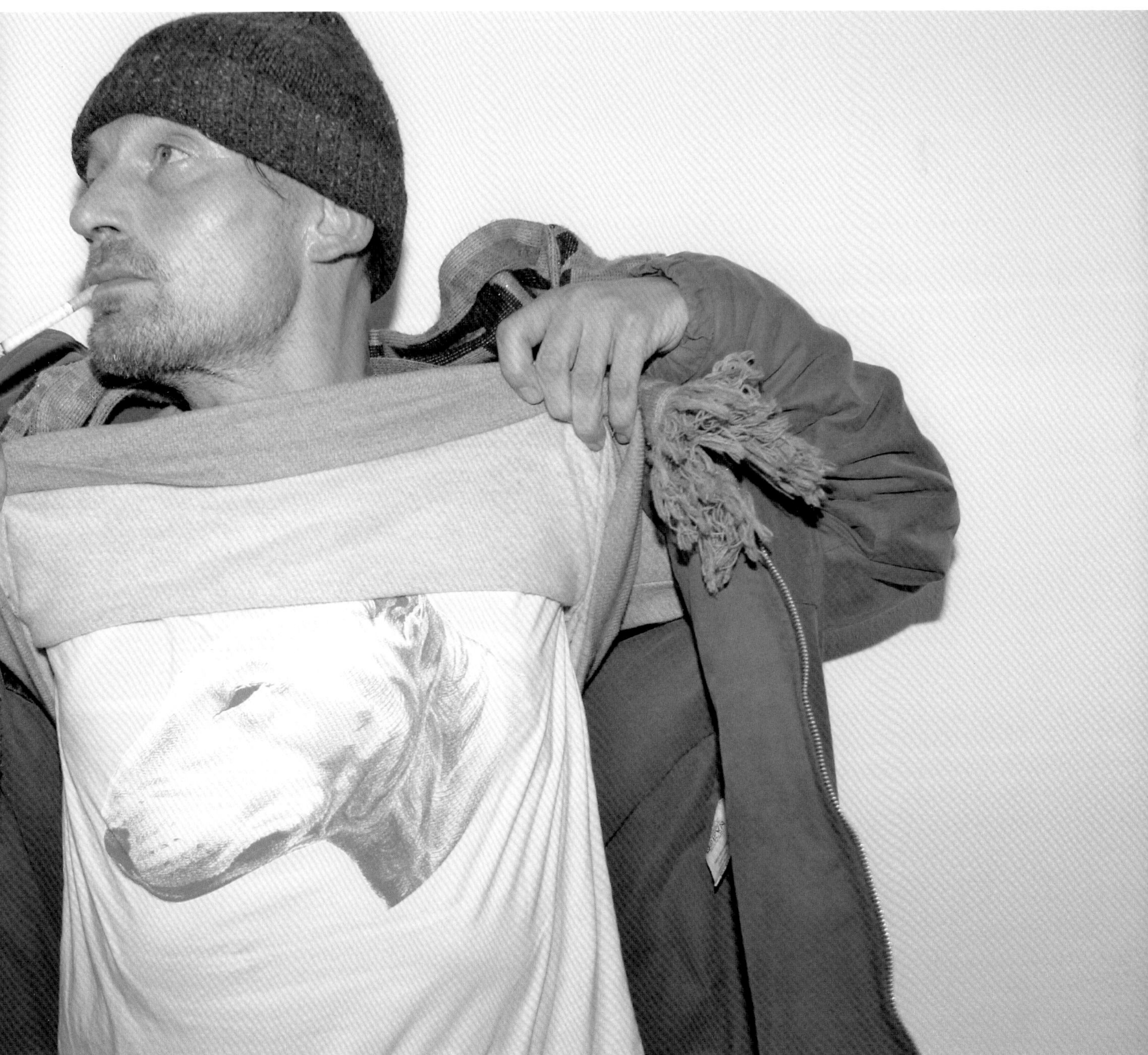

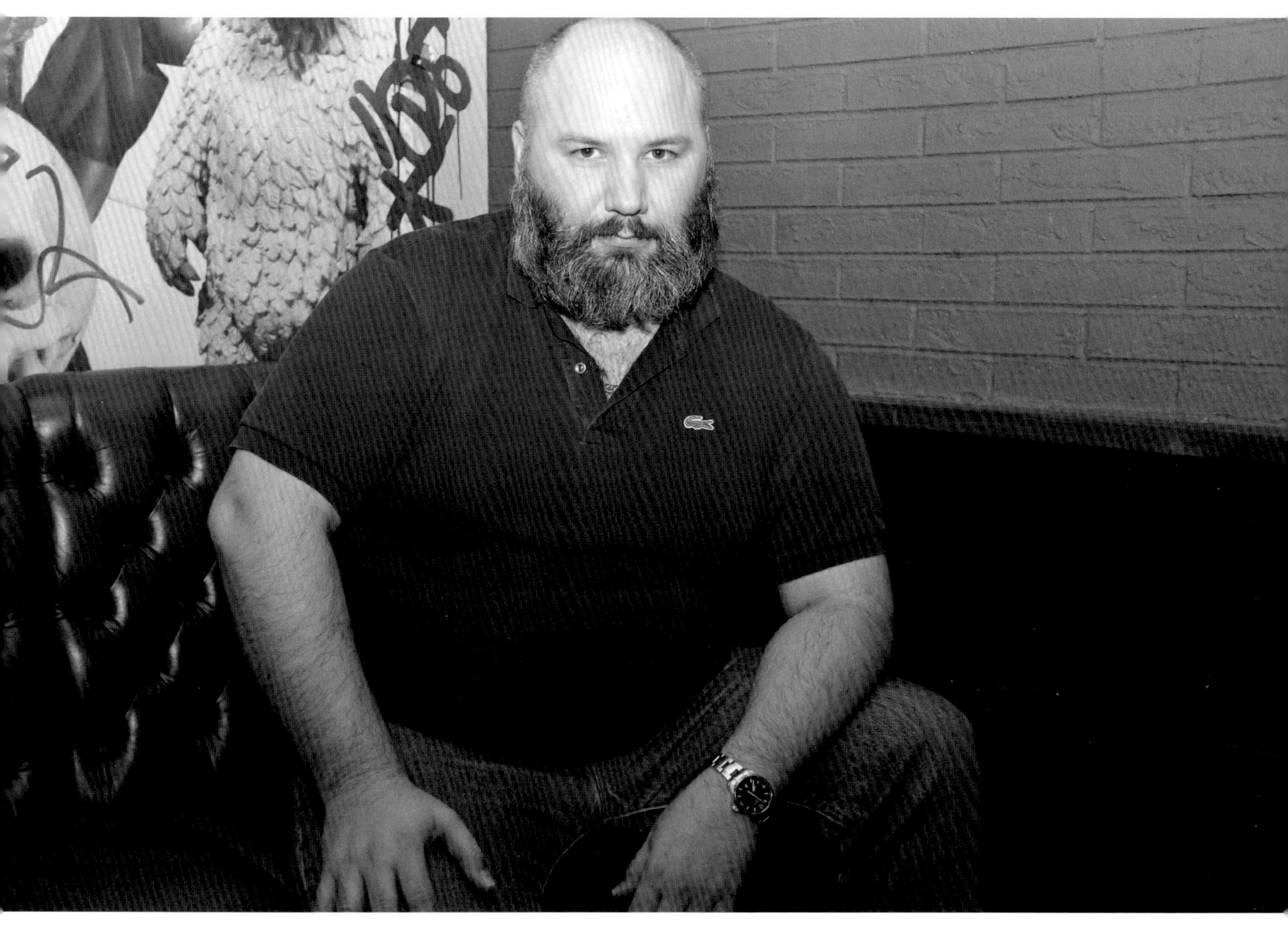

JUSTIN STRAUSS

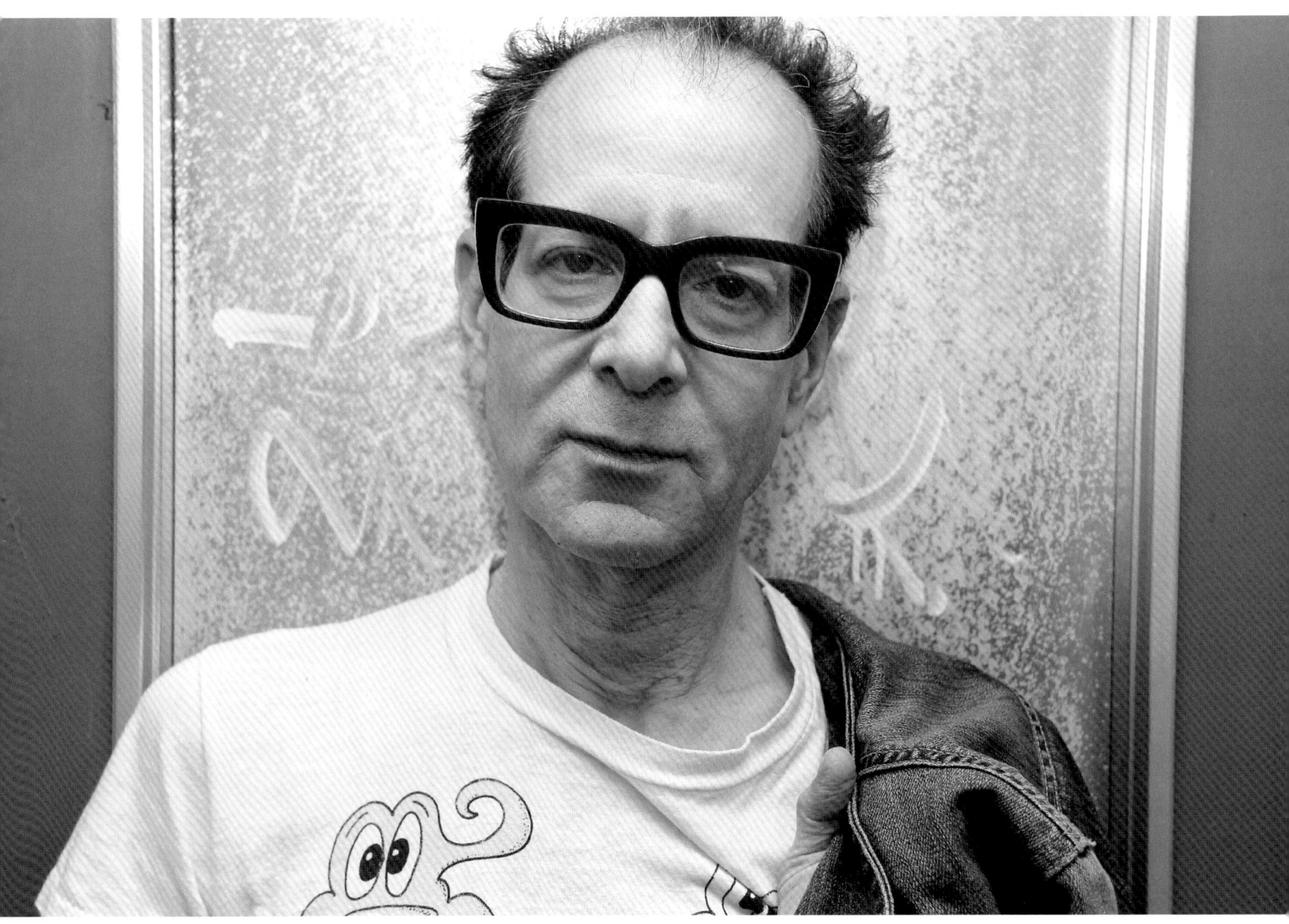

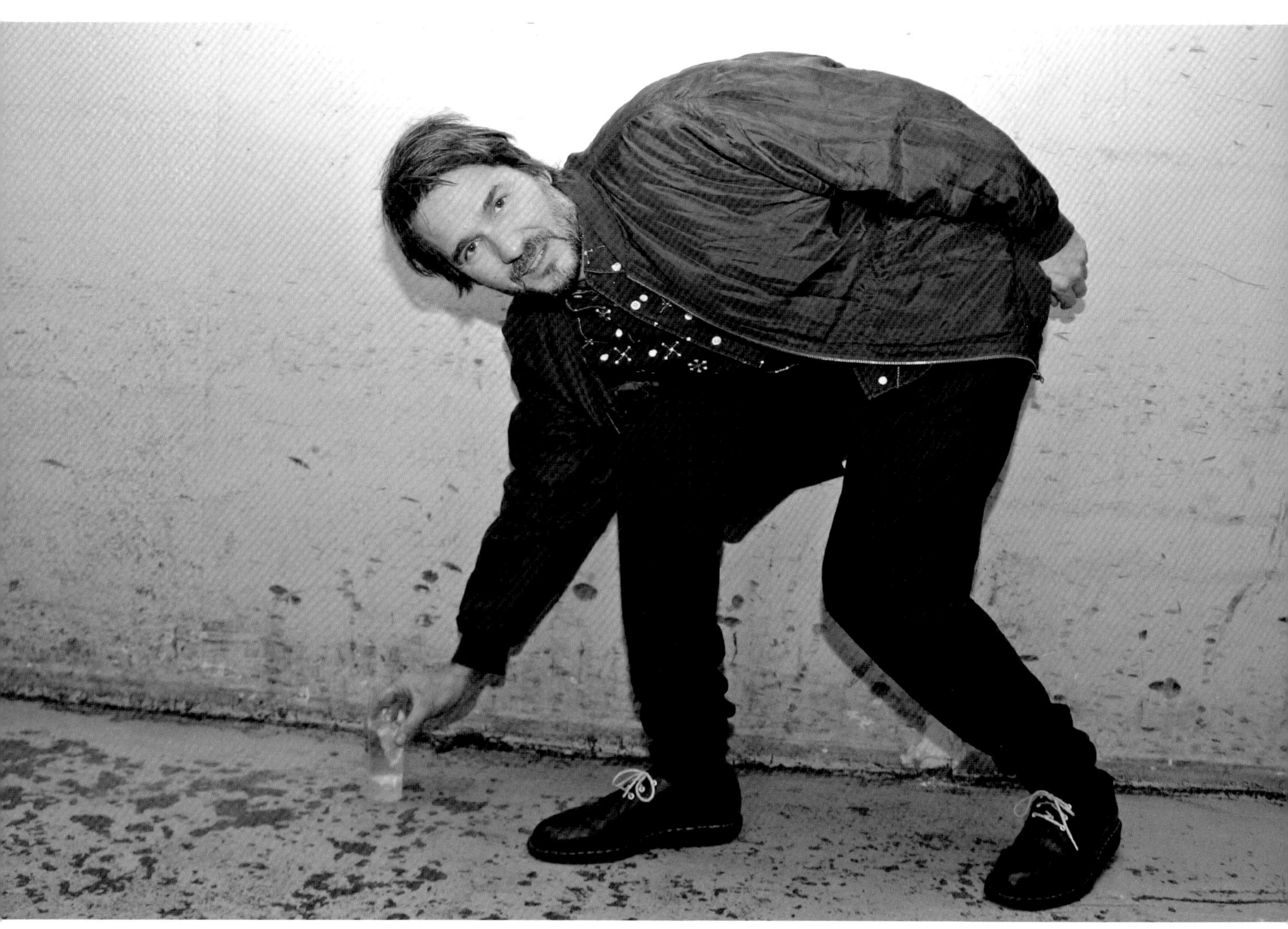

TIEFSCHWARZ

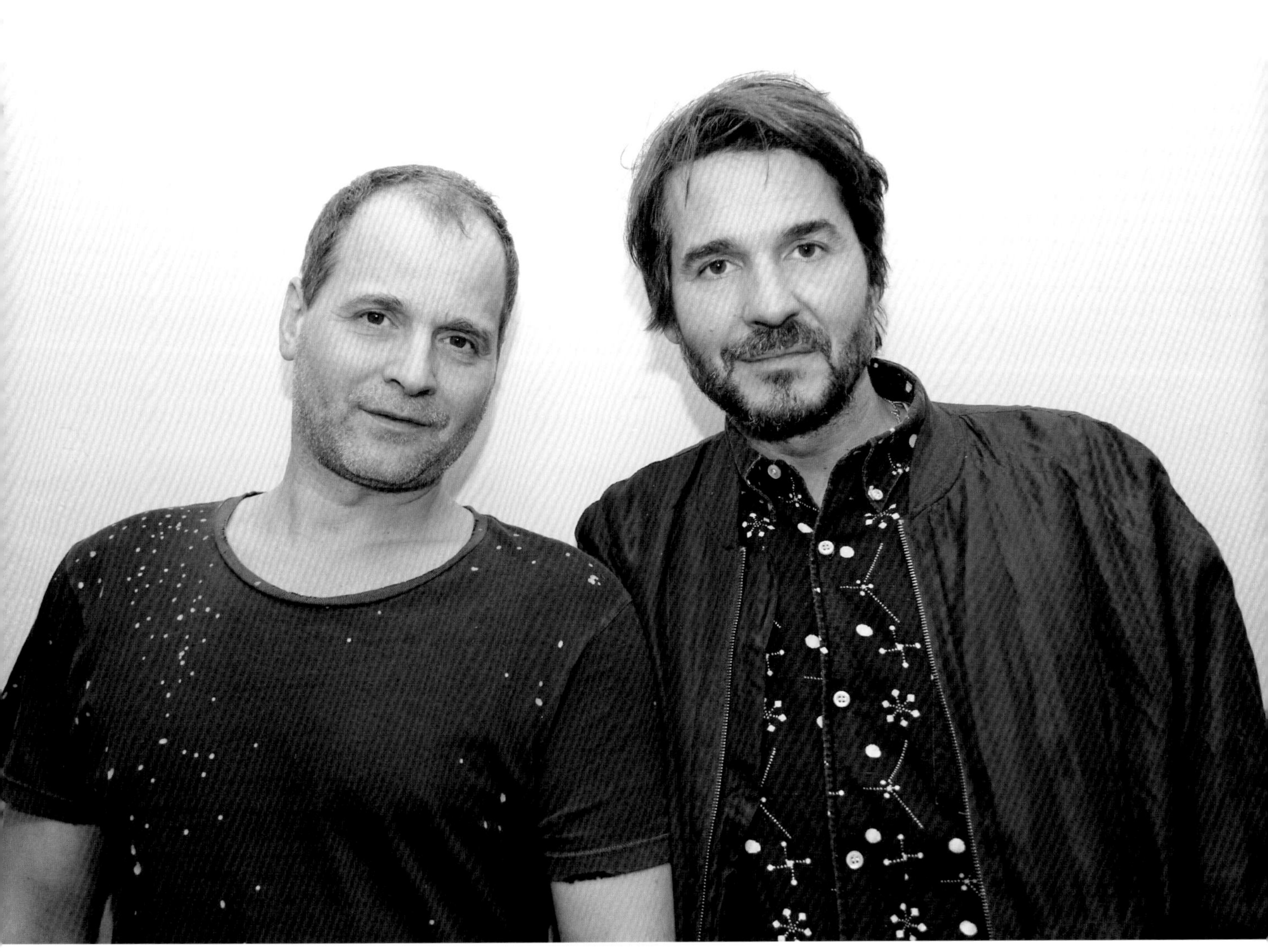

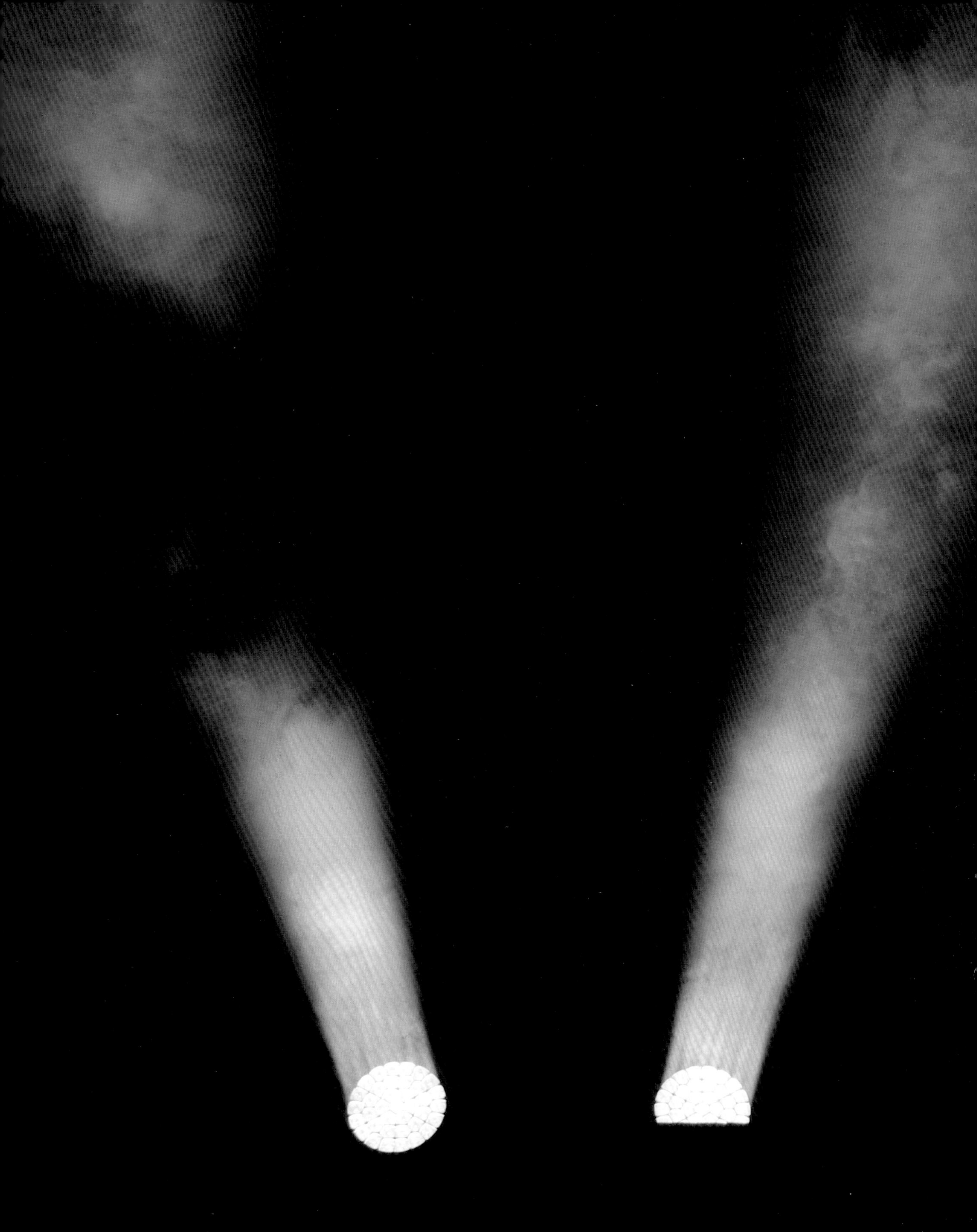

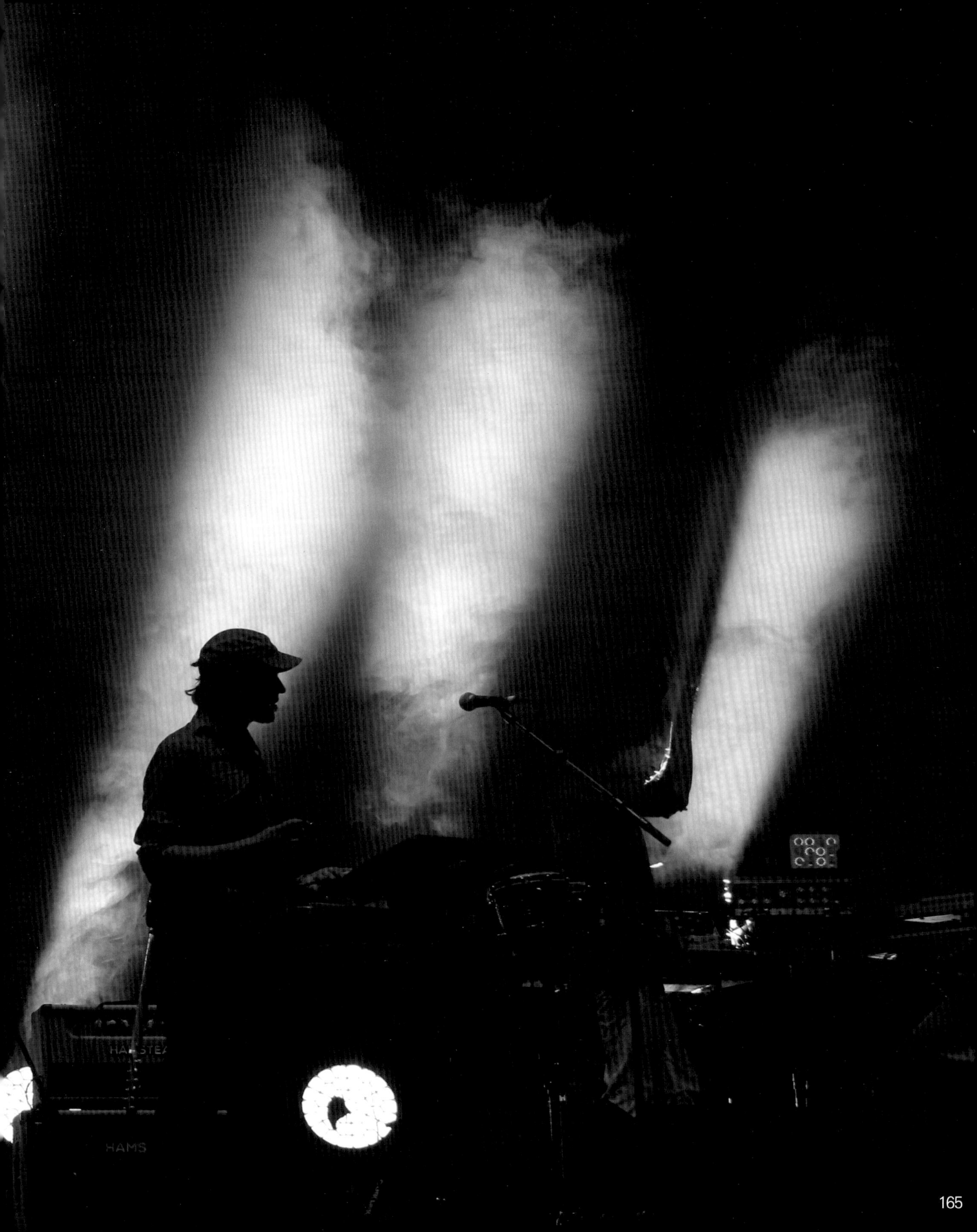

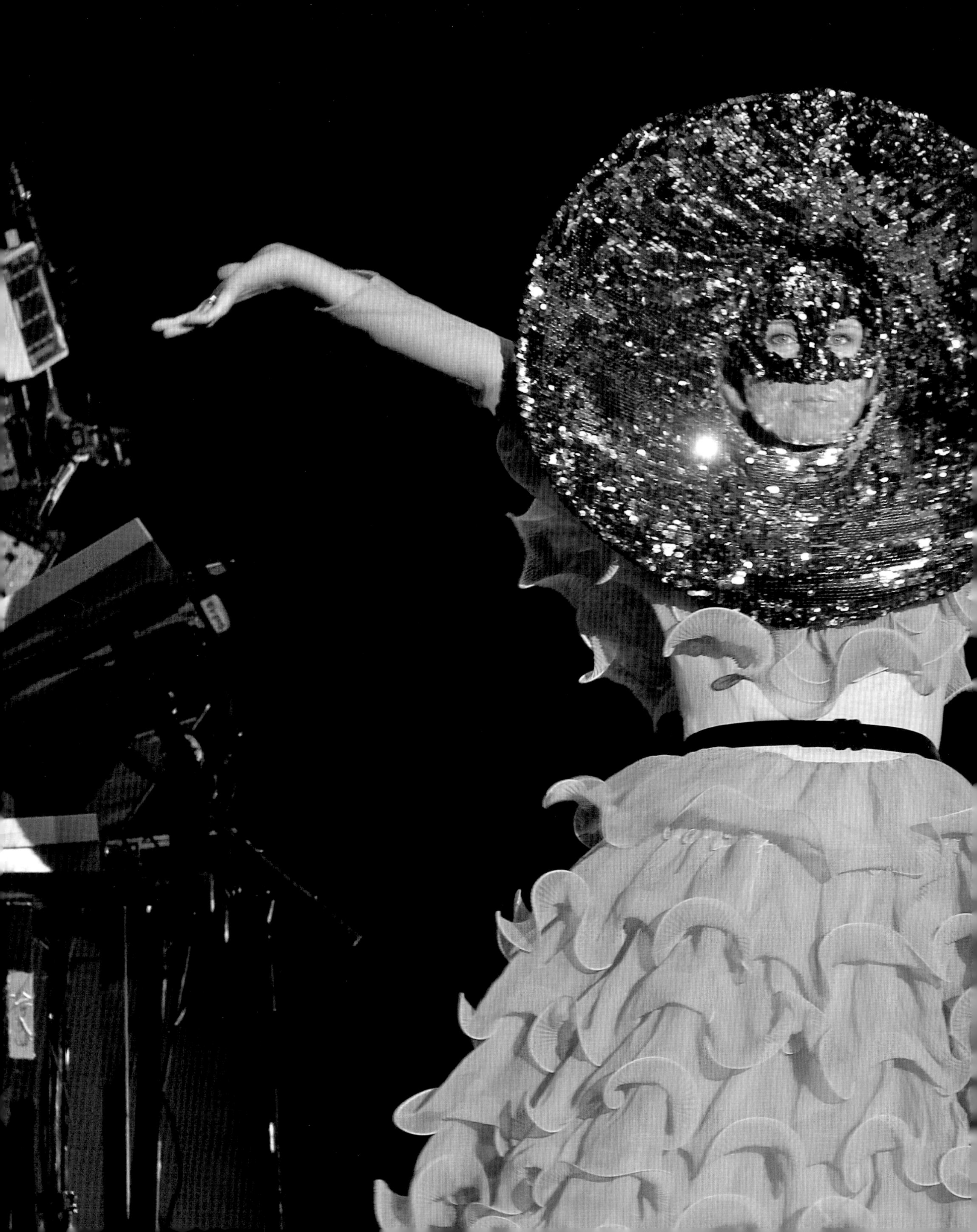

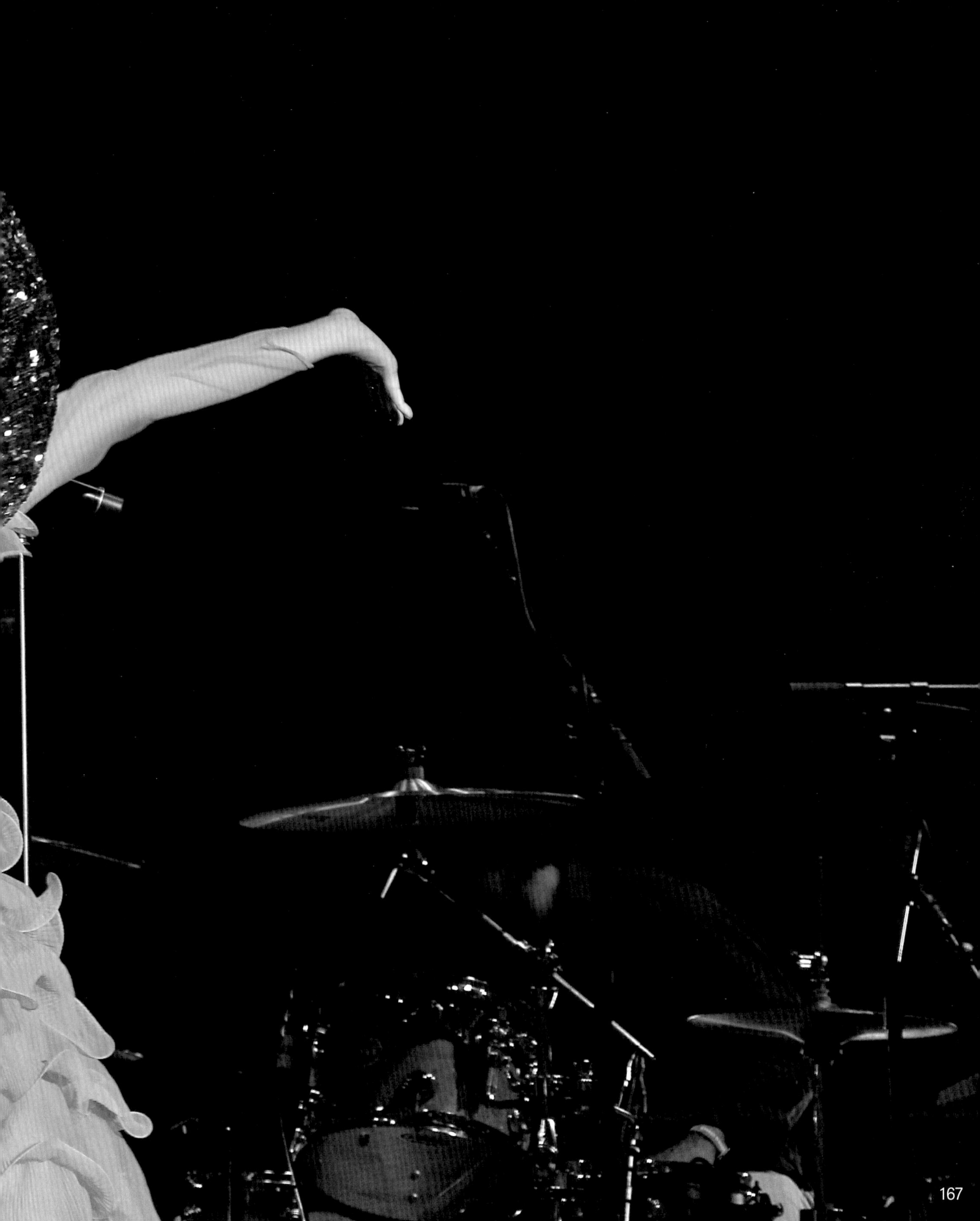

DJ HELL

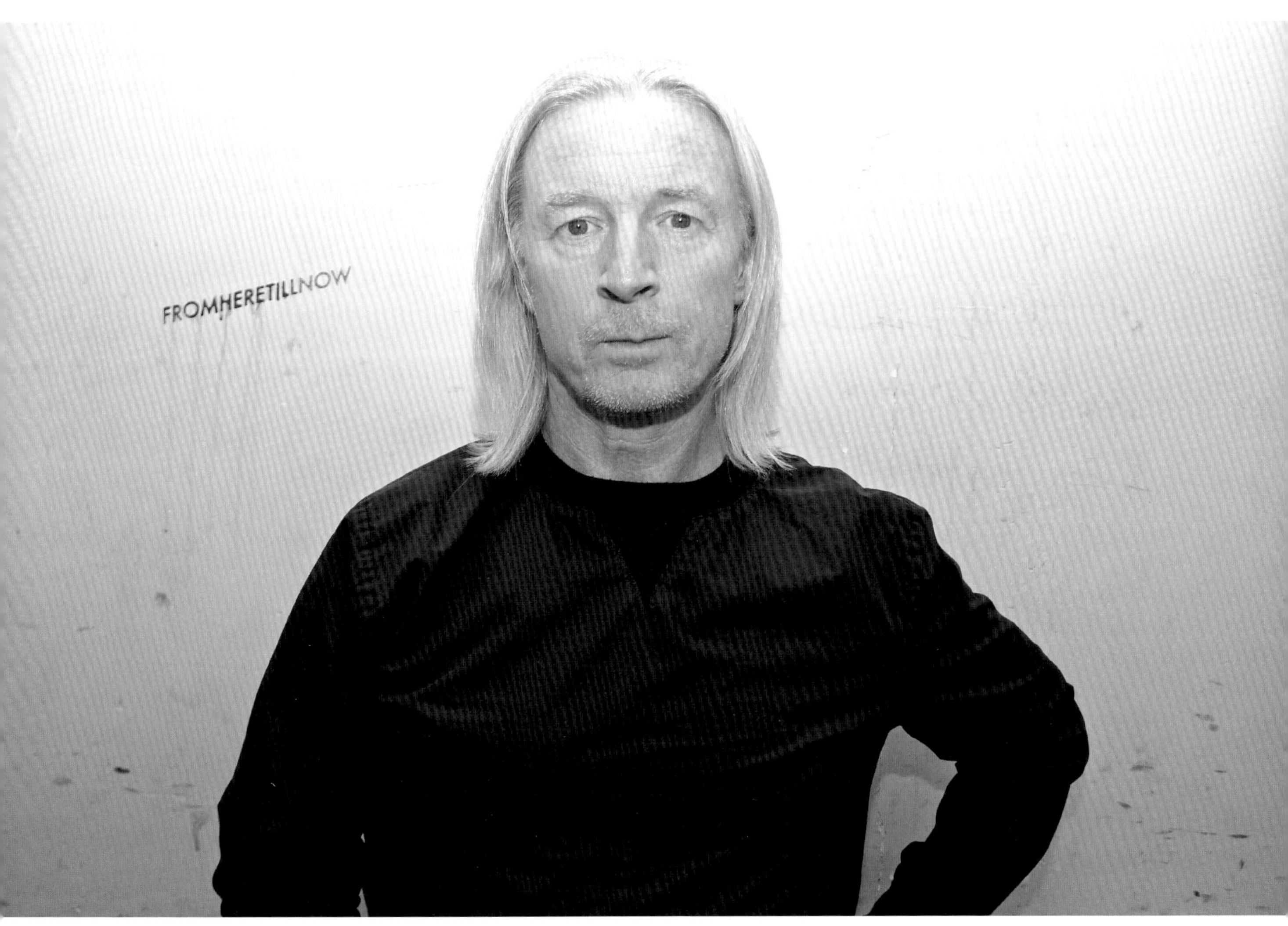
FROMHERETILLNOW

LAUER

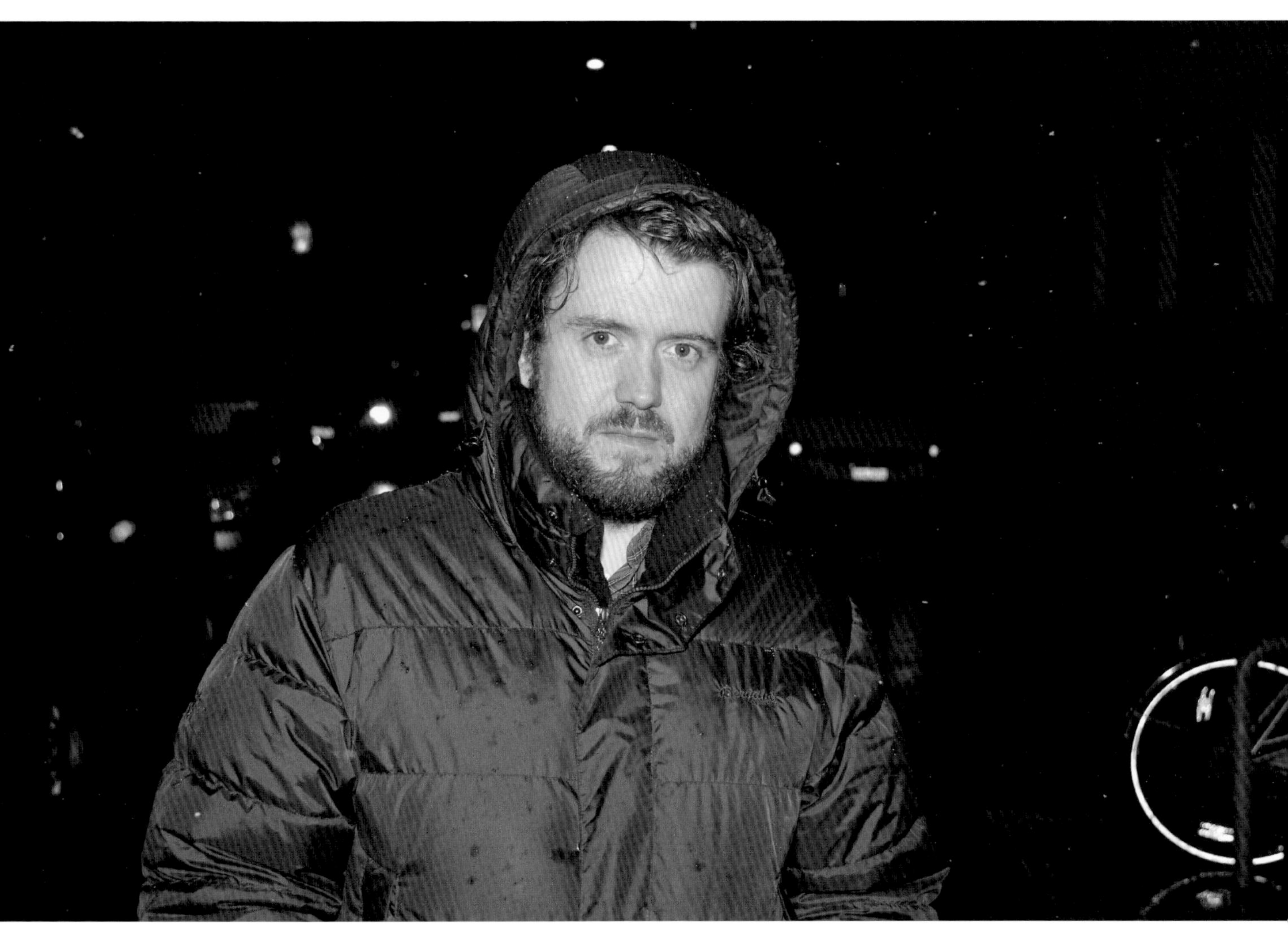

MATTHIAS MEYER

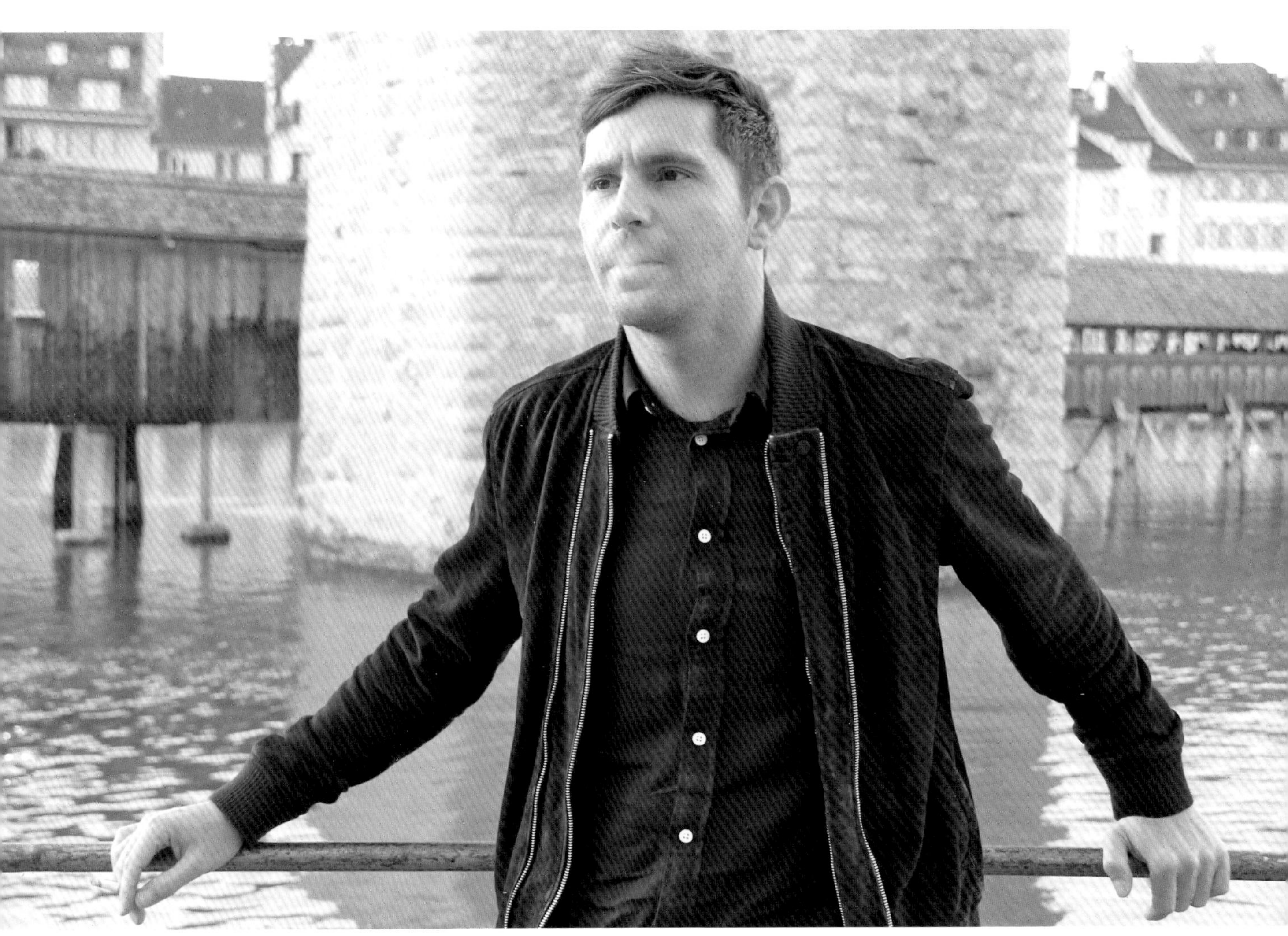

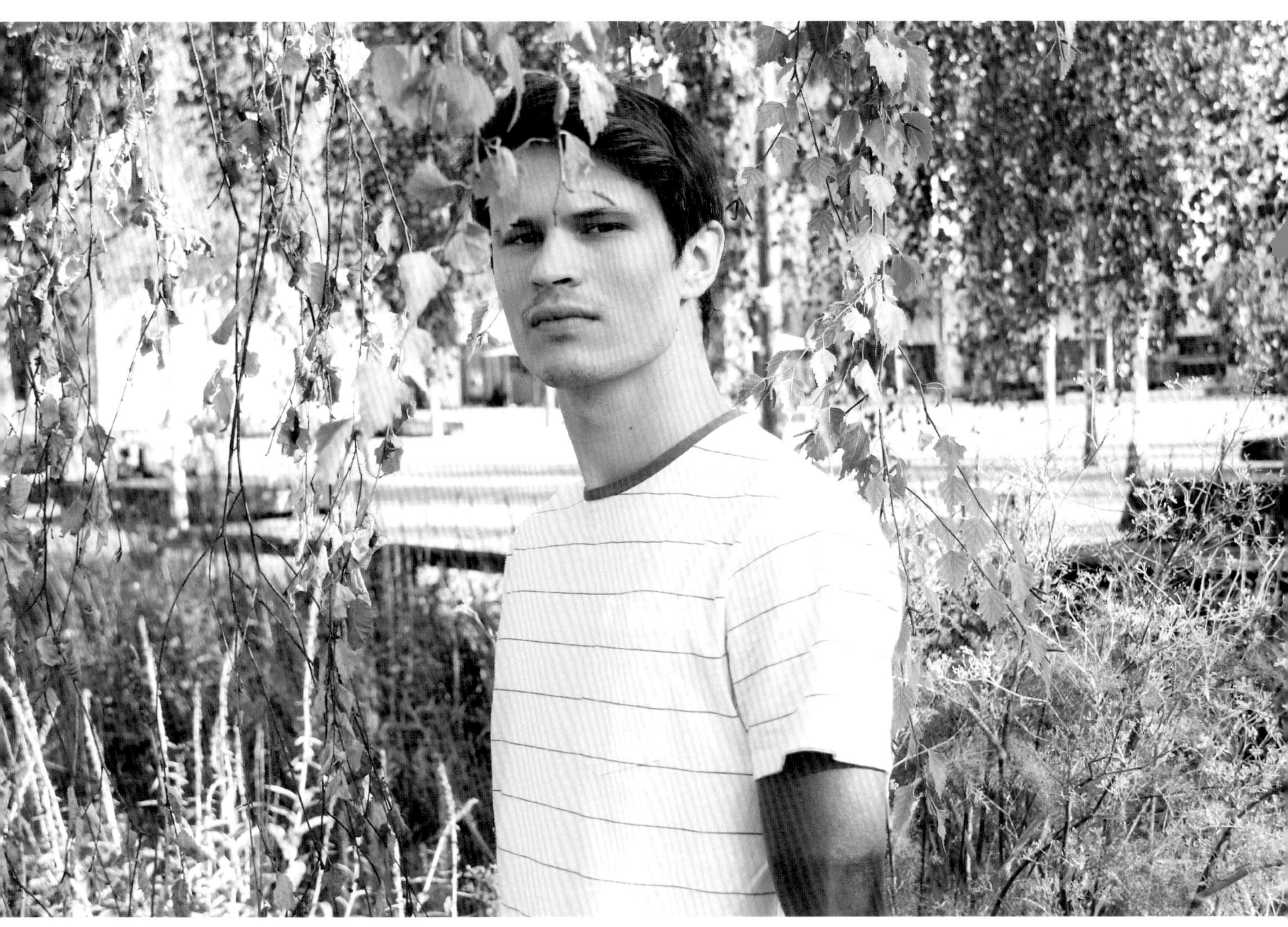

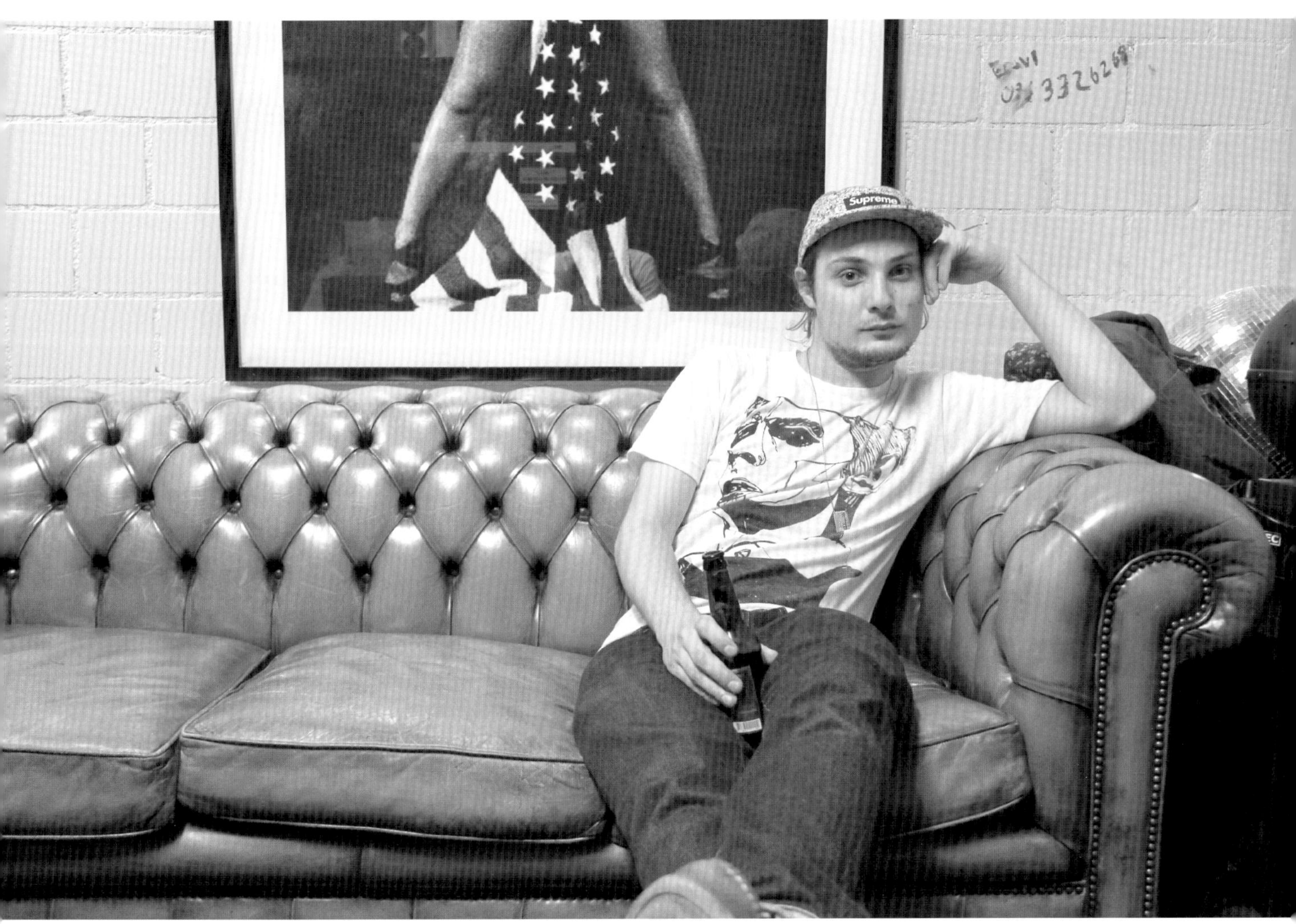
Supreme

IMPRESSUM/COLOPHON

Konzeption/Concept **Maximilian Becker**

Gestaltung/Design **Stefan Joachim**

Text/Text **Matthias Pasdzierny**

Übersetzung/Translation **Alicia Reuter**

Produktion/Production Management **Distanz**

Gesamtherstellung/Printing and Binding
optimal media GmbH, Röbel/Müritz

Vertrieb/Distribution
Gestalten, Berlin
www.gestalten.com
sales@gestalten.com

ISBN 978-3-95476-188-3
Printed in Germany

Erschienen im/Published by
DISTANZ Verlag
www.distanz.de

Doppelseiten/Double pages

Dank/Acknowledgement

Ein großes Dankeschön fürs Mitmachen bei diesem Projekt, Unterstützung und gemeinsam durchgetanzte Nächte an **alle abgebildeten DJs und Musiker, sowie die beteiligten Clubs, die die Räumlichkeiten zur Verfügung gestellt haben.**

Many thanks to **all participating DJs and musicians for your support and for long nights of dancing, as well as the clubs for sharing their spaces.**

Und an/And to

Yumi Kunz, Rino Pelli, Magdalena Zbiec, Lukas Müller, Deddou Burkhard, Remo Bitzi & **Stefan Joachim**

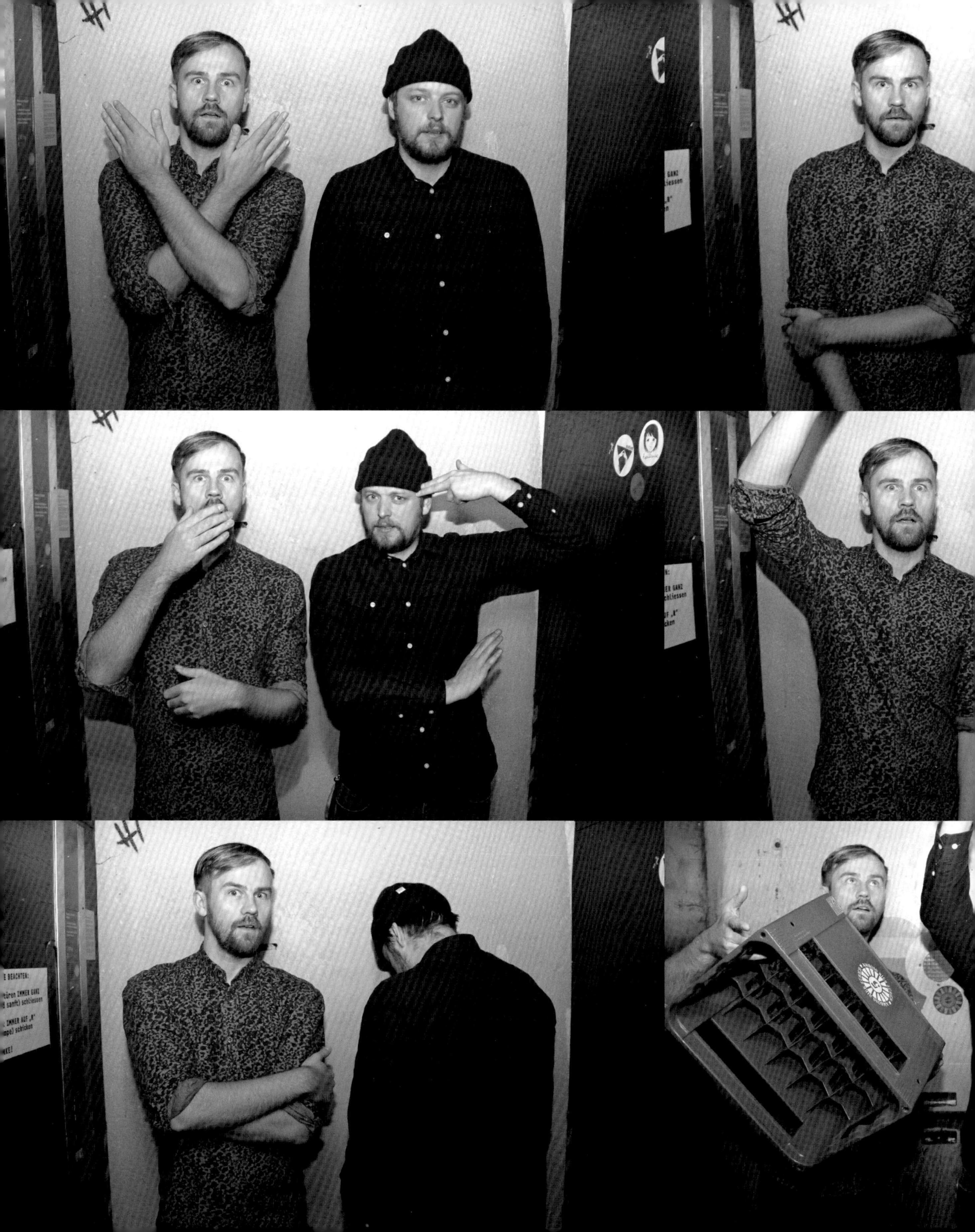
E BEACHTEN:
türen IMMER GANZ
sanft) schliessen
IMMER AUF „R“
mpe) schicken
NKE!

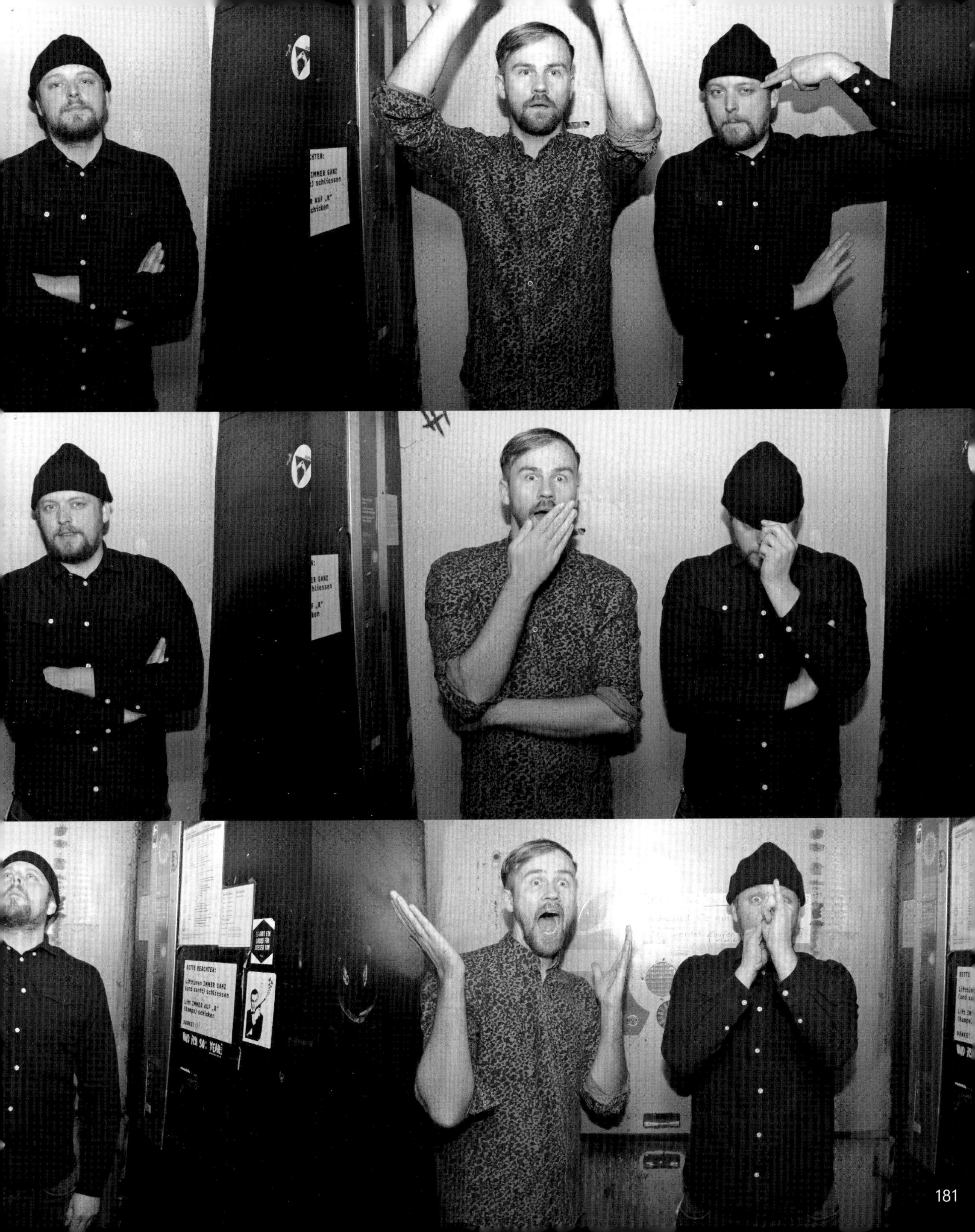
BITTE BEACHTEN:
Lifttüren IMMER GANZ (und sanft) schliessen
Lift IMMER AUF „R" (Rampe) schicken
DANKE!
Und ich so: YEAH

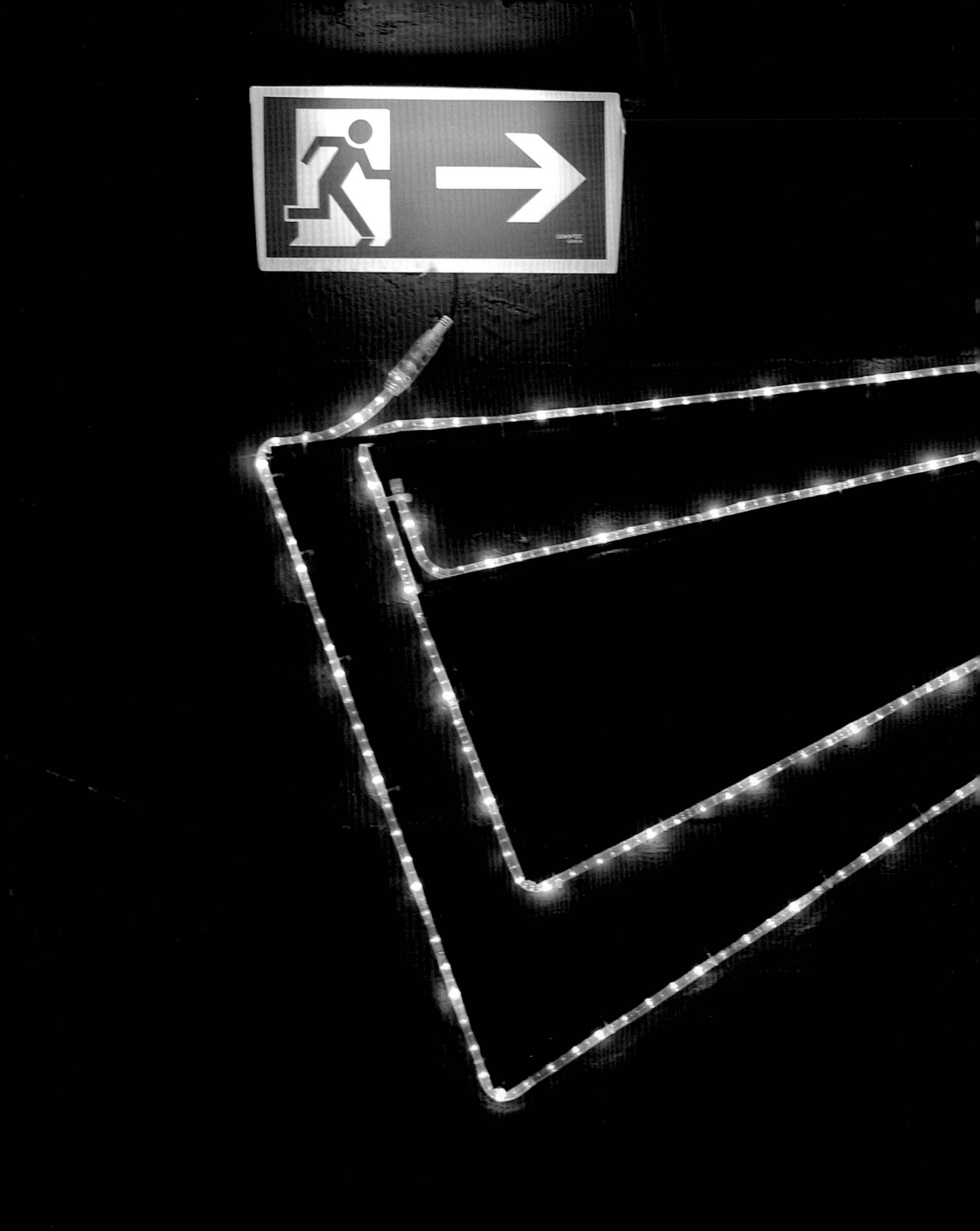

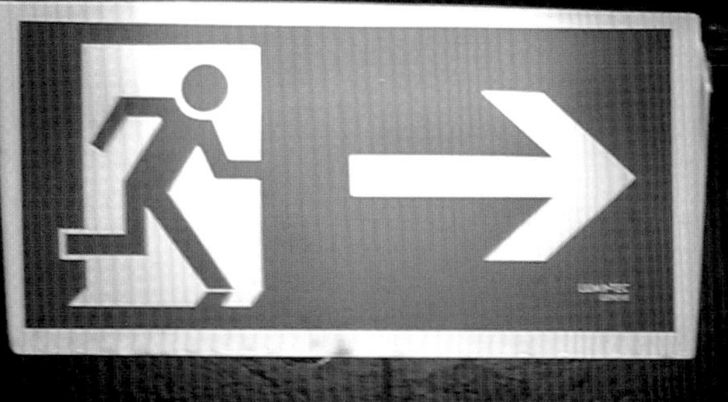

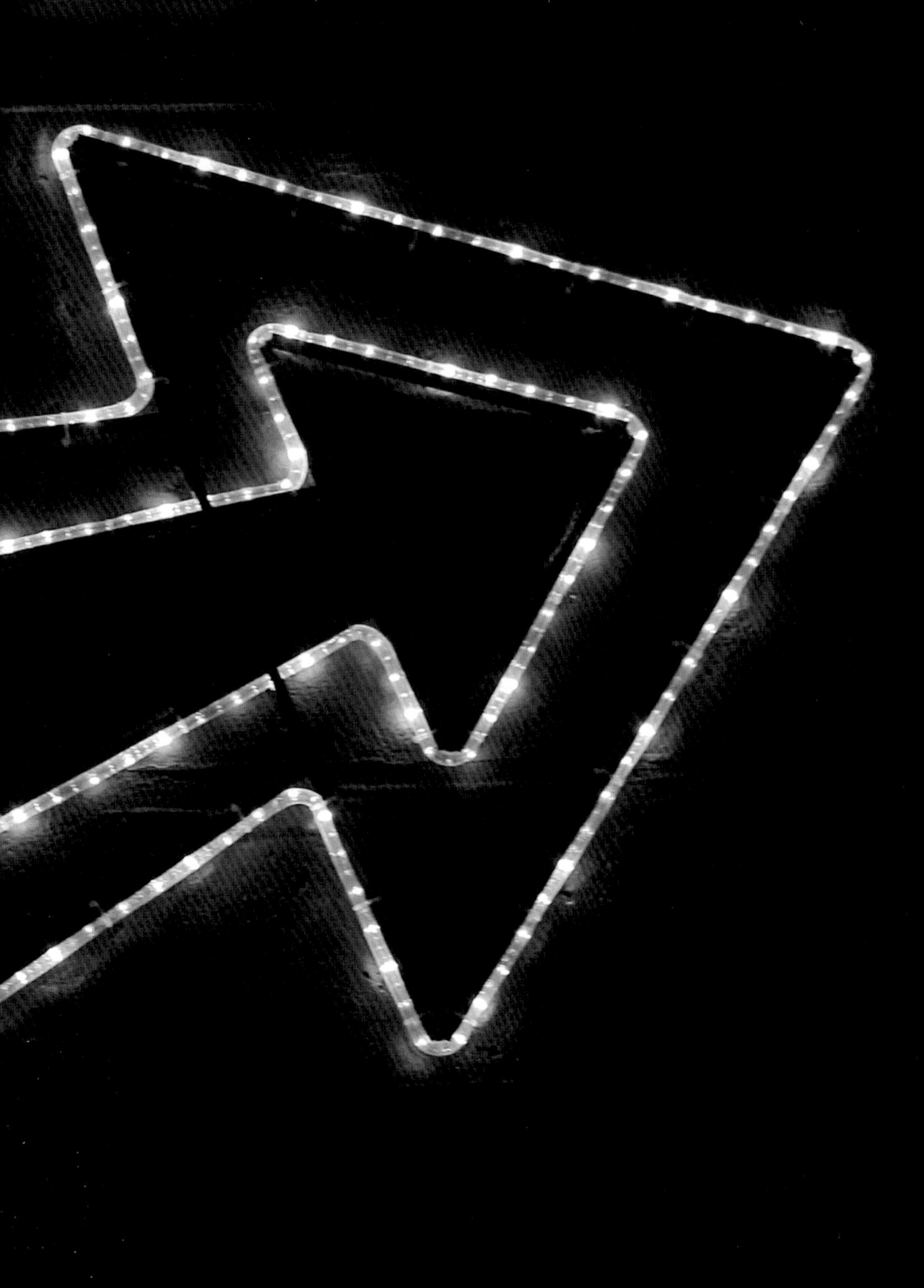